Aunt Nancy —

Thanks for being a friend

David
AKA
Havon Dove

IT'S ONLY CIGARS

By

David Weisenthal

authorHOUSE™

1663 LIBERTY DRIVE, SUITE 200
BLOOMINGTON, INDIANA 47403
(800) 839-8640
WWW.AUTHORHOUSE.COM

First published by AuthorHouse 3/10/2006

ISBN: 1-4184-7142-9 (e)
ISBN: 1-4184-4010-8 (sc)
ISBN: 1-4184-4009-4 (dj)

Library of Congress Control Number: 2003097401

Printed in the United States of America
Bloomington, Indiana

This book is printed on acid-free paper.

Acknowledgements

I want to thank my family... father, mother, both sisters and brother... for their inspiration and support throughout my life. But most of all, I want to thank Gracie... whose support, guidance and inspiration led to my writing. And for her warmth and love that has led me through doors that I never knew existed.

I also want to thank the following for helping make *IT'S ONLY CIGARS* a reality: Toby; Linus; Steven Patrizio; Balthezar; *THE* U.S. Government; and, all my friends and others whose encouragement and kind words kept me writing and editing.

And, finally, a special thanks to David Eckhart! A friend who's help provided me with the ability to bring this book and all that goes with it to you...the reader. I can't thank him enough! But, maybe, being friends... may be all the thanks I need.

Chapter 1
The Story

The Beginning

***

Please allow me to introduce myself. My name is David Fabler… and I'm a son of a Fabler! I much prefer that term to others I've been called over the years. Bastard and *BVD* are two that come to mind! As a child I always thought *BVD*'s were men's underwear, but early in my adult years I discovered that *BVD* had become a nickname some bestowed upon me… *Bad Vibes David*! At the time, I didn't mind it all that much. However, with age comes wisdom. Now, few have probably heard of me. Perhaps, because I'm a man of little wealth and less fame! Through extensive travels in Jamaica's back bushes, Colombia's thick jungles, and Mexico's outer less-populated expanses, I was left with little time to pursue a career chasing the nine-to-five rat-race routine. And although that wasn't the way my life's journey began, that's the way it became. I've heard there are no mistakes!

The Bust

***

April 18, 1997
Philadelphia International Airport

In past lives, there'd been encounters with 'the' man. But, I was over all that. I was starting over. It was a new way in another day. A new life!

No more entanglements! I was free. Free from leashes and other obstacles. My hair was longer than it had ever been before. In a small way, it was a way to show my freedom. Freedom from fear and oppression! Feelings that can happen from encounters with 'the' man!

Containment has a way of changing a person. Especially if they aren't careful to keep what is theirs in the first place! Guarding possessions brings about a certain change in itself. It comes with the territory. Oh, what a tangled web is weaved… when the practice is to deceive! However, I was over all that.

I was on the return leg of a trip from a self-enforced banishment. Somewhere along the way I read something that said I could do what I did. Only, what I did was bring back the old days.

Appearance matters little… although it can aid in bringing about the encounter! My appearance was to blend in, even though my hair had grown. Otherwise, there was little to separate me from others… when standing in line. Unless mental images are visible in a physical manner! Anyway, I was on a trip back to where I'd been before. Only this time, I might've been running away more than striding forward. And that was taking me toward embracing whatever it was I didn't want. But there I was anyway. A new way in another day! A new life!

I've heard the future can't be changed. When denying destiny, it gets closer. Apparently, my destiny was on a collision course with fate. And, maybe, fate would be my undoing. However, that's the way it was.

***

3

I picked my bags up from the conveyor belt and started to head out of the airport. A Customs agent approached and asked to see my declaration card. After examining my card, he instructed me to go over to the secondary checkout counter. The secondary checkout counter resembled a series of long flat tables that looked like a supermarket checkout lane, except the cost for the goods I had was a small piece of my freedom.

The tables were set in parallel groups of two and sat some six feet apart. Each group had two computers… one per table. The computers were placed side by side on stands located at the closest end of the long flat tables, when approached from the baggage claim area. They were positioned in such a manner that no information listed on either screen was visible to anyone… except those who stood between those tables. Two uniformed agents, representing the U.S. government, stood inside each group of those long flat tables.

The flight from Montego Bay was longer than the three hours and ten minutes the pilot said it would be. In fact, it was over seven hours long… counting the time waiting to board and take off. Add the one and a half-hour drive to the airport and I was spent. Exhausted from the trip, I only wanted to lay down and go to sleep. But I had to finish my trek through clearing Customs first. More than half-tired and more than half-excited from the prospect of the cache stashed away inside my attaché case, I walked over to the closest group of those two long flat tables. Customs agent Busta Narco asked for my declaration card and told me to put my bags on the table… in front of me.

Agent Busta Narco was a no-nonsense guy who came from a family of Customs agents. His father, brother, and an uncle all worked for the government. Although born Buster, a slur of his tongue changed the Buster to Busta. And Busta wasn't born with his family's gray cells. They went to his sister, brother, or cousin. However, none of that mattered because Busta was standing in front of me… asking what I had to declare.

I told Busta, "Alcohol and tobacco as well as misc. merchandise." But, he didn't hear a word I said. Instead, agent Busta opened my attaché case and swiftly pulled out the cache of smokes that had been acquired down Havana way. It was as if he knew they were there. And I just wanted to know how he knew.

In other times, I would've expected to have been flagged. Wearing a hippie label brought such examinations. A lack of long hair and facial growth didn't matter. Nor did the clothes I wore. What was in my mind gave me away. Only, that was the past. The here and now came with a new era and a new mindset. And, although my hair was longer than it had been in the past, I was a different person. I thought they knew that. Long enforced vacations from reality bring about change. But when everything was cast aside, I guess I was still the same... after all. In a world of constant change, it was probably nice to know that some things didn't.

I was prepared for this! I was ready... or so I thought! I knew this scene would probably occur were those sticks to be discovered. But I acted bewildered none-the-less. I asked agent Busta what he was doing.

Busta said, "The cigars are contraband and are being confiscated."

I protested! Customs agent Busta Narco was told my passport and a Customs book, **Know Before You Go**, said those stoogies could be brought into the country... legally. But Busta the Customs agent man just looked at me like I was crazy. Little did he know!

I told Busta the Customs agent man that I had a copy of the Customs **Know Before You Go** book and asked if I could get it from my bag. Holding a copy of the **Know Before You Go** book between his fingers, agent Busta questioned, "This book?" And, while it wasn't the same book that was in my bag, it was the same book that said I was allowed to bring those prized Cubanos into the country.

I responded, "Yes... that's the one."

In a disbelieving voice, agent Busta asked me, "Where in dis book does it say ya kin do dis?"

"On page six," I said.

Agent Busta promptly opened the book to page six and read those government words. Quite possibly for the first time too, judging by the expansion of his eye sockets as he pondered the meaning of those words! Busta the Customs agent man looked at me and said in a raised but unsure voice, "Ba... ba... ba... but, these words... DON'T mean this."

My response was simple and cut to the chase. "Ask Rush... words have meaning!"

He was confused and didn't know what to do. It was obviously a first time experience for agent Narco. Off he went in search of a supervisor with the Customs **Know Before You Go** book in hand.

Several minutes later, agent Busta the Customs Narco returned. An average sized slender man, in his late 40's, walked by his side. The man's short neatly combed hair was slightly gray. A trim mustache covered his upper lip. I noticed the gait in his walk. It portrayed a very authoritarian manner and I assumed his stride was intended to intimidate me. And I have to admit the mere implication of oppression, the very thought or concept of tyranny purveys a certain amount of stress and fear. But I never thought I'd go to jail! I mean, this was America... land of the free! Nobody went to prison... for sticks. Besides, I had read their books!

The man introduced himself as Customs supervisor Rudemann. Customs supervisor Rudemann and I had the same conversation, literally, as agent Busta and I had earlier. Finally, supervisor Rudemann said in a very polite and advisory tone that he only represented Customs and Customs only confiscated contraband. He said, "Sir, the merchandise in your possession is contraband. We have to confiscate it." He also said, "The only way you'll be able to get these cigars back is if you went to Cuba and acquired them there." He said he didn't care if I went or not. He was Customs and Customs only seized and confiscated. Those were the rules. Then he asked, "Did you go there?"

Customs agent Busta never asked that question, thus the subject never came up. But now I'd been asked. I said, "Yeah, I went there."

My response wasn't quite finished before more than half the people clearing Customs heard a loud bellow of a roar come out of the mouth of the man I was talking with. His body became rigid and the muscles in his face went taut while his cheeks turned red and flushed with anger. "YOU'RE UNDER ARREST! GIVE ME YOUR PASSPORT!"

Thinking something happened behind me, I immediately looked over my shoulder to see whom the G-man supervisor was directing his pent-up, hostile, raging authority to. First to the left, seeing nothing I turned to the right. There was nothing! Then, I looked back at the G-man supervisor.

I knew I had to have a stupid what-the-hell-is-going-on look on my face and, in fact, I did because I wasn't sure what the hell was going on. Then, the G-man supervisor screamed it again. "GIVE ME YOUR PASS-PORT! YOU'RE UNDER ARREST!"

Suddenly, I realized supervisor Rudemann was yelling at me! I reached into my pocket to retrieve my, well - actually it's the government's, passport. Read the damn thing - it says in small print, 'THIS PASSPORT IS THE PROPERTY OF THE U.S. GOVERNMENT! IT MUST BE SURRENDERED UPON DEMAND!' Reaching into my pocket, I removed the passport and told supervisor Rudemann he needed to count to ten. "Take a look around! Take a deep breath! You're out of control!"

He screamed it a third time. "GIVE ME YOUR PASSPORT!"

I raised my arm and extended my hand. The Rudemann Customs supervisor forcefully yanked the document from my grasp.

I questioned supervisor Rudemann why I was under arrest. "You're **A TRAITOR**."

"A TRAITOR?"

"YOU WENT TO CUBA! That's **IN** *violation* of the law. You're **A TRAITOR** to your country." Several words were enunciated in a loud voice with a distinctive pronunciation.

I told supervisor Rudemann that the trip was a gift as were the cigars, but his cheeks just puffed out a fiery red hue. His anger was felt with every word said and with each body movement made. "It doesn't matter, we're confiscating **EVERYTHING!**"

Supervisor Rudemann left me with Customs agent Busta for several minutes who, by then, was going through every piece of my luggage... with a fine-toothed comb. Every piece of paper was opened and examined, every article of clothing unfolded and turned inside out! A few minutes passed before supervisor Rudemann returned with my passport in his hand. He was hungrily searching through the official government travel book... hunting for wording, anything that stated my actions were in violation of the law.

7

He knew something was there. It had to be! I thought, no postulated, those G-men agents needed to impugn my actions. It was their obligation, no requirement, to do this on behalf of their government. And their country! However, what they didn't seem to comprehend was that it was my country as well. After a moment of intensive reading supervisor Rudemann yelled, "Here it is! It says right here you can't do this."

I questioned supervisor Rudemann about where in my passport it said one couldn't go to Cuba or import cigars... having read and re-read every word at least five hundred times. He held my passport in one hand with a forefinger from his other hand pointing, jabbing, at a specific spot. Reading the words... he said, "A*s of November, 1963, the purchase or importation of Cuban goods... are **generally** prohibited.*"

I looked at supervisor Rudemann with what I knew had to be a dumb, stupid look on my face. And, in fact, there was just such a look on my face... because I knew the G-man supervisor couldn't be serious. He couldn't really mean what he said. Customs supervisor Rudemann couldn't really believe that sentence indicated the total prevention and complete prohibition of importing Cuban cigars. Especially since what supervisor Rudemann said was a sentence was really only half a sentence. Somehow, supervisor Rudemann forgot to include the half of the sentence that included, '*... except for... limited goods imported directly as accompanied baggage.*'

My eyes opened wide. I asked in a slightly higher than normal, but very polite and firm voice, "What does the word **generally** mean?" I was about to ask supervisor Rudemann a second question, even though my first one hadn't been answered, when a tall, thin, older black man with mostly white hair cropped close to his head entered the Customs area. Displaying a calm disposition that underlined a professional demeanor he wore the uniform of an Immigration officer. Walking through the room, he was asking where the Cuban 'national' was.

Supervisor Rudemann left my side and walked over to meet the officer. He was pointing at me with one hand closed into a fist... except for one long straight forefinger. His other hand was extended, clutching the passport between his thumb and closed fingers. He was eagerly awaiting release of the seized document. He said in a raised and very bold voice... **"There's NO Cuban. Just him! HE WENT TO CUBA!"**

The government's passport changed hands. Both government men looked at me before returning their attention to each other. The Immigration officer appeared to have a 'why me' look straight out of <u>Madd Magazine</u>, Alfred E. Neuman style, when he took possession of the passport. He looked at the official document and flipped through the pages… page by page. Then, after a few brief but tense minutes he extended his hand with the passport back to the Customs supervisor and said, "Give him back his passport!"

The startled Customs supervisor screamed, "WHAT? BUT, HE WENT TO CUBA!"

"So what? Give him back his passport! He didn't do anything wrong."

"BUT… HE WENT TO CUBA," supervisor Rudemann protested.

Shaking his head from side to side, the Immigration officer turned to leave. As he did, he said once more to the dumbfounded Rudemann Customs supervisor man, "I don't care! He didn't do anything wrong! Give him back HIS passport!" It was more a demand than a statement. And, when he finished talking, he walked out the door without turning his head around for another look.

The Customs supervisor was stunned and confused. Hadn't he just busted, arrested public enemy *numero uno*? A traitor to his country… and his government! A menace who traveled to Cuba! Obviously a revolutionary who conspired with Castro to overthrow American democratic principles of freedom!

There was only one small, tiny problem. It wasn't supervisor Rudemann's responsibility or in his department's jurisdiction. All he could do was seize and confiscate. He couldn't do anything, except turn the violator(s) over to those whose department was responsible… and to those who did have the jurisdiction. But to those whose department did have the responsibility and to those who did have the jurisdiction, they didn't want nor were they interested… and they differently had no intention in arresting me. What the hell was going on?

Rotating his body, the Rudemann Customs supervisor turned his attention back to me. The G-man supervisor had a blank look of astonishment etched on his face. His lowered head showed the clear sign of embarrassment. He wore the face of a child who'd just been scolded for getting his hand caught in a cookie jar. Our eyes locked and thoughts touched for only the briefest of seconds. Then, he broke off the contact. A bell rang. H-E-L-L-O! *IT'S ONLY CIGARS*!

Slowly and methodically he walked back toward me with the passport in his hand. Each step taken was carefully plodded and he didn't look at me, in the eyes again, until after I took my passport back from his grasp. When the passport was back in my possession, he became the aggressive, assertive Customs supervisor he'd been trained to be once again. "Why did you go to Cuba? What was it like? How long were you there? Where did you stay? Those questions were followed by more questions. And every question required an answer.

The G-man Rudemann supervisor demanded to know what I'd been doing in Havana in 1968. He questioned me in disbelief. He knew in 1968 America was *at war* with its neighbor to the south! Vietnam was killing, destroying, Americans. China backed Vietnam and Russia was an ally of China. Russia was also a protectorate of Cuba which meant (either directly or indirectly) Cuba was killing, destroying, Americans too. Politics make strange bedfellows. Unless I'd been in the Navy back then, he wanted to know how I'd been in Cuba in 1968!

"No! I was never in the navy."

Meanwhile, my German friend, Andreas Dueling, had come to visit America for the first time. Like me, he was instructed to go to the checkout counter where opposite the one I chose he had his bags opened and searched... his Cuban cigars seized and confiscated. The other Customs agent between those two long flat tables found and took his smokes as well.

A question was asked, "Are you two traveling together?"

We both responded, "No!" We actually, technically, weren't.

Supervisor Rudemann's head was spinning back and forth between Andreas and myself with each word said... "You two know each other?"

We both looked at each other and said, "Well... yes!"

"Where do you know each other from?"

We both responded, "Jamaica."

"How do you know each other?"

Andreas said, "Playing chess?"

I asked, "What do you mean by how?"

Supervisor Rudemann asked Andreas, "Where are you staying?"

"Holiday Inn."

"How long will you be staying in MY country?"

"Two weeks," Andreas answered.

"Who do you know in America?"

Looking at the Rudemann Customs supervisor man, Andreas pointed toward me.

"Who'll you be visiting here with?" Supervisor Rudemann followed that with, "What is your purpose here?" Those questions were followed by answers that were followed by more questions... and more answers.

For me, besides being asked questions while those government agent men dissected my property, it was just more stuff for them to add to their file(s)! The one(s) they created beginning with my first and, until then, only trip to that far off and distant island. Then again, maybe they just wanted to create a new file. But I had some questions of my own. "Tomorrow is my mother's thirty-ninth twenty-ninth birthday. Will I be spending it with her?"

The Customs agent Busta man who had the bust of a lifetime couldn't nor would he even bother to look up when he spoke. Customs agent Narco simply, merely nodded his head... ever so slightly. Blink and it would've been missed! And everyone just wants to know why our country treats its common citizen as if we're the enemy! But to them, in their government - we are!

Shortly thereafter, Andreas was introduced to the free world's concept of democratic enforcement of justice. To Andreas, it was an enforcement of justice that somehow seemed the equivalent of having entered East Germany during the height of the Cold War. His every paper was opened and examined! Every article of his clothing unfolded and turned inside out... then left on the counter.

Andreas was taken to a rear room where he was stripped searched. Their hands traveled all over his body. When finished, and disappointed with not finding a narco-terrorist skinhead, he was taken back to the checkout counter. There, he was told to pack his bags and to get out. He was handed a receipt for his cigars and told they, the cigars, would be given back to him when he left OUR country. But he'd have to let them, the government, know twenty-four hours prior to his leaving the country. And those Cubans would be delivered to him, Andreas, on the plane, at the time of his flight. I know the arrangements that were made because I heard those instructions.

I wanted to give my smokes back to Andreas... the ones Customs seized. It seemed no sense in losing them. Andreas could smoke them abroad. He was a German! Cigars weren't illegal for him anywhere in the world. Anywhere, that is, other than America. The American government has no control over a non-American outside U.S. territory and their jurisdiction. Especially, if the non-American didn't violate any law... American or foreign! I asked the agents to give those seized Cubans back to Andreas.

Agent Busta asked back, "Why?" He seemed taken back that I'd even think of such a thing.

The agent men were told, "They're a birthday present... from him, Andreas... the German. If he's allowed to leave with his, then he should also be able to leave with these! They were given to me by him and I want to return them back to him."

Supervisor Rudemann said, "It doesn't matter! They're yours!"

Finally finished with their investigation, Andreas stuffed his clothes into his bags and disappeared through the double doors with his suitcases somewhat repacked. The receipt for his confiscated cigars was tucked somewhere inside one of his bags… along with his other papers. In his haste to remove himself from that area and those people he threw everything he had into his luggage with little to no concern for what went where or how it got there.

Andreas' first experience with America and its gigantic police force had been quite an experience. He was almost arrested for possession of foreign smokes that he was legally allowed to have. It was probably just as well because had he been locked up, more than likely, he would've been the laughing stock of every jailed American. But he would've been treated, none-the-less, like the criminal he was because he legally had those Cubano sticks. And everyone, except Customs, just wants to know... what's the big deal?

Watching the doors close behind him, I saw Andreas disappear into America… and I never felt so very alone. Agent Narco picked up my eyeglass case and opened it up. The glasses were removed and a drug-sniffing dog was brought over to smell the case. However, the pooch showed less than no interest in the container what-so-ever. Contrary to the dog's non-reaction, Customs agent Narco knew there had to be something in that eyeglass case. Agent Busta said to the dog's handler, "Check it out!"

The canine cop disappeared with the eyeglass case in one hand and the end of the dog's leash in the other. All the while the mysterious substance was being checked out I was being asked questions that demanded answers. The answers given to their questions prompted more questions that never seemed to stop. "Do you smoke?"

"Not cigarettes."

Agent Busta asked, "What do you smoke?"

I asked, "Why? Why are you asking me these questions?"

There were more answers to more questions that were followed by more questions. "Do you smoke marijuana?"

Several minutes later, the bulldog looking agent with his bullish looking dog returned. He placed the eyeglass case down on the counter and proceeded to walk away without saying one word. Customs agent Narco caught sight of them only steps before disappearing into the crowd. He quickly asked, "Well, what did it show?"

The bulldog agent man turned and replied, "A beautiful bright pink" as he walked away. He took the look-a-like hound with him. And he never missed a step!

I looked at the G-man agent who was searching my bags and asked, "What does beautiful bright pink mean?"

Without looking up agent Narco said, "POSITIVE... DRUGS!"

"BULL SHIT!" Then in a slightly softer tone, but very loud voice, I repeated my statement! **"This is bull shit! No G-d-dam way in hell!"** Then, I thought very carefully about what I was saying. "You better have more because I'm going to make you produce it!" I was livid. I was saying *'my lawyer'* this and *'my lawyer'* that. "Drugs... NO way! *IT'S ONLY CIGARS*!" And just how many times do you think they've heard the *'my lawyer'* routine?

I was asked to follow agent Busta and another agent to a more secured area of Customs. It was an area where a more detailed inspection could be, and would be, performed. I was told to remove my clothing, piece by piece... as instructed. Finally with only my pants on, I was told to place my hands on a wall... like cops and robbers. It was just like the movies, but no camera filmed the scene. With my legs spread, my manhood was firmly held in one hand of Customs agent Narco... who stood directly behind me. His other hand slid up and down my body to see if I had any hidden packages or weapons. He wore a plastic glove... the kind doctors use to stick their fingers where the sun doesn't shine. When nothing was found, they left me alone in that room for what seemed like forever. It was probably just half-an-hour, but it could've been more or less time.

I sat down on one of four chairs. Other than the table and those four chairs, there wasn't anything in the room except the one two-way mirror on the wall. I felt every move was being observed, but I knew they couldn't see into my mind. In my mind's eye, I was traveling down the road less-traveled that took me to the seat I was sitting on in that room. And, oh, what a trip it had been!

Flashing Backward

***

A leash is a leash! It doesn't matter if it's real or not! In another life or three, I'd been on a leash! Surprising for someone who prided himself on not living a life restricted in any way. None-the-less, that leash had to go.

In a previous life, I apparently wished for the bondage of love to be re-placed with the chains of legality. I got my wish, but the price was greater than the cost I wanted to pay. However, a wish is a wish! Now I know to beware of what I wish.

When I was twenty, my father died. His death altered my world! How my life changed doesn't matter because it turned out to be what it is. I've heard there are no mistakes! However, in a blink of an eye, I changed.

The nice Jewish boy who was expected to take over the family business became a colitis-smoking dropout who, some say, went astray somewhere along the line. And if anyone had bothered to look, they would've seen the road I turned off on. Some claim it was some smoke filled cloud that fueled the error of my ways. But, if the truth were known, it was really just my life that took me where I went. Such is life! Besides, it was my own damn fault!

Over the years I met many people who claimed to be my friend. But when the need arose, they disappeared without a trace. I always thought friends went through thick and thin. What did I know! I knew they weren't my friend(s). Only I didn't know what a friend was. Thieves, liars, con artists, old or young, men and woman... it mattered not. Sex and age weren't factors in my search for candor and loyalty. Truth was an equal gender fact finder that figured into the equation somehow!

There was a time when those I knew wanted to know why my attitude reflected a nickname for men's underwear. All they had to do was look into their soul to see their evil ways. I already did that and saw the depravity corrupting their baseness. It was easy for me to see my path wasn't theirs and their route was a road I didn't want to traverse. Instead, I chose to roam a road less-traveled. Somehow, it seemed safer!

In a life before this tale began, I found myself stuck in a vacillation mode. Lost between a struggle to succeed and living in the rues of love gone astray, decisions had to be made. However, I wasn't in love. Far from it! Maybe it was unfortunate, but that was the core of my troubles! Mired in an affinity no one would want, I saw no way out except the way I chose. I always heard it said *never act in haste*. But, in the heat of the moment, decisions had to be made.

Monday morning everyone is a quarterback... especially the quarterback. Regardless, I wanted my quarter back... despite the fact that it was way past too late. By the time the time had run its course, I discovered I'd lost it all... including the girl. Even though what I wanted when I got what I had wasn't what I wanted to have, I knew I didn't want the girl back. Far from it!

I knew better to avoid what I did, but did it anyhow. One day, I found myself stuck in some far off locale with no one to call friend. Down and out for longer than could be counted, I turned inward for solace. There was nothing but turnkeys to count on and I knew that wasn't an option! So I locked down the hatches and secured the fort... closing all the doors and windows to my being. Switches were shut off and feelings got left behind somewhere out in space. Somehow, I knew it was the only way for me to survive.

In a later day, there would be consequences for those actions, but that day would be another day. And, that day wouldn't be for another day... or one thousand five hundred and fifty-five! I'd worry about it then.

Finally, the clock ticked all its tocks. When the gate opened, I returned back though a door to sanity. Repelling in the real world had me feeling like a fish out of water because the tides of life had changed. I looked around for a new life only to find another leash slung around my neck. Although longer than some, it was shorter than others! And, in the end, I knew that leash had to go too. But not with another!

I decided a move to another country would help find a path to reality. Only that road led back to dementia instead! In charge of the roost were many heartless wannabe kings. I heard someone say 'words didn't mean what they meant,' and felt no one should believe anything anyone spoke. Not believing wasn't a problem... I was a non-believer! At the time, I needed a place to be grounded and had boarded a flying boat. But, before the sunset, I found myself sailing through troubled waters. My mind was racing at supersonic speed. Suddenly, I was **Back at *THE* Beginning**.

Back at *THE* Beginning

***

When I began writing the yarn of this tale, the story seemed like it happened a lifetime ago. In reality, it actually was only twenty short months earlier. Time goes so fast when it's enjoyed! Everyone has a definition of enjoyment and a threshhold level for pain. But somehow those two things can get intertwined and confused or intermingled between the strands of life... like hair after being washed. At the time, it was a time in my life to take stock of my life. And in order to do that I needed to reflect on what had transpired over the past two years. It had been quite a story and an interesting adventure.

I could see Danny DeVito in the movie... were there to be one. There would be one too... were the story to be written. It all started on a trip back into America. I was curious! Even though I've heard it said that *curiosity killed the cat.* Although I've also heard it said that *satisfaction brings it back.* And, there's nothing like *satisfaction.*

January 1, 1959 - the early morning hours - Havana, Cuba
***

The music played a salsa beat while people enjoyed dancing the night away. They seemed oblivious to the events taking place outside the Hotel Nacional's ballroom doors. Up in the hills and out in the streets, the resonance of explosions could be heard. Whether guns or firecrackers, the intermingled sounds formed a collective mixture that illustrated the celebrations a New Year and revolution had brought. Suddenly, the doors opened and men dressed in camouflaged jungle gear entered the ballroom. Armed with rifles and stern faces, they approached the stage where the band played. One of the men grabbed the mike off the podium while some of the others motioned for the band to cease their music. The rest of the men stood with their guns ready while they watched the people in the room. "¡Hola, señors, señoras y señoritas! ¡La revolution es aqui! ¡Viva la revolution! ¡Ahora... ondale con la musica!" Finished with his announcement, the mike was turned off and the music started again. The people who stopped dancing to hear the announcement started dancing once more when the band began playing again. To them, it seemed a footnote in history. Hardly the kind of information necessary to interrupt so joyous an occasion!

David Weisenthal

Villanova, Pennsylvania, USA
***

The Times Square celebration reached its climax when a ball dropped and a diapered child lit up. At the time, I was sixty-six days short of eleven. But, that mattered not. Earlier in the year, I turned ten and with the coming of that age, I had reached double figures. The teenage years with which I'd be when my twelfth birthday arrived had little importance. To me, the big day had been ten. And that day already came and went.

The next important day would be sixteen... the *legal* driving age. Then it'd be twenty-one... the *legal* drinking age. Except in New York, the drinking age was eighteen! However, those times were well off in the future. On that cold snowy night, the most important thing to me wasn't that that was the last New Year celebration of the 1950's. It was the football games that were to take place later in the day on that first day of the last year of the decade.

In the morning papers, stories were written about the freedom Cuba had won. It was likened to the American Revolution fought almost two hundred years earlier. No doubt American leaders were, if not overtly then quietly, celebrating freedom's victory because America had been directly or, in the very least, indirectly involved with the success of the conquest. We were poised for the rewards that came with the spoils. Rewards that Fidel would surely filter to the north as payment to the debt incurred for our support. But as an almost eleven-year-old Jewish boy growing up in an almost all WASP Villanova community, Fidel was just a name that meant less than nothing to me. However, Castro's Cuba would have a vast impact on my life in the coming years. So much so it would eventually cause me to look at my own country's definition of freedom with questionable eyes. And relate to the word freedom as just another word... for nothing left.

On that first morning in 1959, while I was getting ready to go to bed, Fidel Castro proudly rode into Havana. He had just chased the bad man Batista off Cuba and ascended to the top of the power tower. All this mattered not to me. I didn't know who Castro was. Nor did I care! I'd never been to Cuba and had no interest in going. To me, Fidel was just a footnote in history. History I hadn't been taught. Years later though, Castro and Cuba would have a role to play in my life! Some say, the lives of those around me as well. Whether that's good or bad is insignificant. The determination of that decision has to be up to the viewer. However, one has to consider their sources. For this is my story!

Know Before You Go

***

"Good luck," the lady fed said when she handed me the pamphlet, **Know Before You Go,** written by the U.S. Treasury Department, revised April, 1994. She said, "Call the number in the book and whoever answers will discuss the rules." She was talking about bringing an ivory chess-set into the States that I'd purchased in America before taking it to Jamaica… when I moved there the previous year. On that cold winter night in January 1997, little was known how that pamphlet would cause quite a stir from deep within the bowels of a political branch of the bureaucratic wing of the federal judicial system, known as OFAC, over the next couple of years. And OFAC is the Office of Foreign Assets Control!

Prior to leaving America on my next trip, I contacted an old friend who said, "You live in Jamaica. Next time you go, bring back some Cubans. Come through Miami!" After advising me of his insight with the illegality of anything Cuban, my lawyer drooled, and numerous friends voiced approval… at the prospect of smoking a good stoogie. A short time later I returned to Jamaica.

I looked at my passport to see what rules there were about going to Cuba. My previous passport, issued during the Reagan regime, said no one could go. However, my current passport was issued during the Clinton administration. Under Reagan's leadership, America was mired in the depths of a bitter Cold War with Russia, China, and other dreaded communistic political systems. During the early 1980's, it was *Star Wars*! But that was another decade in another era.

By 1996, dust was collecting where the Berlin Wall had fallen… a few years earlier. The Russian people had ordained their totalitarian leadership to utilize capitalistic principles of order in a bloodless revolution that ended the Bolshevist revolution. America was moving ever so close to extending most favored trade nation status to its still present communistic enemy China… a license that would be granted the following year. And democracy had savored the sweet taste of a victory cigar from their decade's long battle with communism. Even luminaries like President Clinton and Newt Grinch declared it so. "The Cold War is over," they said.

How my new passport reflected the *current* global political environment was what I wanted to know. Where was I allowed to go, or not... as it were! In the Treasury section of my passport I read, '*As of November 1963, the purchase or importation of Cuban... goods... are **generally** prohibited, except for... limited goods imported directly as accompanied baggage.*' Later the only other reference, '*Transactions related to travel in or to Cuba... are **generally** prohibited.*'

My eyes stared at those two words in those two sentences. Well, it was really one word, the same word, in those two sentences. I kept thinking how the inclusion, or not, of that one word, and that one word only, in either let alone both sentences completely changed the message sent. *Usually, more often than not,* even *most of the time*, but it didn't mean - all the time. Besides, I had less than little interest in the **generally** prohibited times of 'THE embargo.' It was the *non-**generally** non*-prohibited aspects of importing Cuban cigars that had ignited my interest.

I was curious. I knew words had meaning. They had to! Through countless different courses studied in university, I took more tests than could be counted and read more books than Carter had pills. In every book, and with each class and test taken, words were read, written, and interpreted. Every word had a meaning and each word meant what it had been taught to mean. But somehow over the years, and granted those university studies occurred many years ago, words don't seem to have the same meanings they used to have. Then again, maybe, I just don't remember what the meanings of the words I had been taught were. For recreational drugs probably corrupted my short-term memory somewhat. However, it's long-term memory I'm talking about. My first puff on anything considered cannabis was long after my university studies began, so that outside influence had less than zero effect on my memory perception of the meaning of words. And *specifically* the word **generally**! Because the meaning of that word was learned no later than in high school! No! Nothing means what it did anymore!

Maybe that's good. Although confusion reigns because I still think liberals are liberal and not conservative. I don't remember when or how the political change came about. In truth, I have to admit the smell from all those smoke clouds that rose up into the air may've clouded my memory somewhat. I've always thought William Buckley a conservative, but lately I've discovered his liberal politics. And Al Sharpton is the most conservative liberal in politics. It's difficult to grasp how the left and right flip-flopped while middle of the roaders became settled on either side of their street… regardless of where that road leads. But through a veil of the burning fumes of disenchantment I've watched a lifetime of systematic elimination of the middle class be carried out in the name of democratic righteousness while the seeds of malcontent grew from a spouting bud into a full grown tree.

Anyhow, I was curious and being curious… a <u>Webster's Dictionary</u> was sought. Looking in the 'G' section *more often then not* and *usually* was found. *Always and under every circumstance* wasn't listed. With a perception of that word's meaning verified, vindicating an advanced education, I returned back to my *current* passport and re-read every word. On page two in the Customs Service was the following; *'The pamphlet* **Know Before You Go** *gives you* **current** *information about Customs' requirements and how they apply to articles acquired abroad. Obtain a copy from your nearest Customs office…'*

Having already obtained a copy from a Customs agent recently, I opened it up. On page six, I read under Cigars and Cigarettes: *'Not more than one hundred cigars… may be included in your exemption.'* The next sentence, however, really stopped me dead in my tracks. *'Products of Cuban tobacco may be included in your exemption if purchased in Cuba, see page 20.'* Whoa! Cuban cigars were allowed?! Page twenty had to be their disclaimer list. The exceptions… to the exceptions, I reasoned!

I turned to page twenty and read. Nothing! I continued reading. There had to be something… somewhere. On page twenty-one… again nothing! Page twenty-two had more of nothing. On page twenty-three, in blocked print was the word MERCHANDISE. A plethora of somewhat useless information was assigned to it. The first paragraph rehashed the same information already read. *'The importation of goods from the following countries is* **generally** *prohibited… Cuba.'*

I turned the page and continued reading. The third paragraph, second sentence read, *'Spending money on travel related transactions involving Cuba… is… closely controlled and monitored.'* It continued with, *'Because of… strict enforcement of prohibitions, anyone considering travel to any of the countries listed above should contact the Office of Foreign Assets Control.'*

Had I missed something? Was the meaning(s) of those words digested correctly? I re-read every word in, both, my *current* passport and the **Know Before You Go** pamphlet. I re-read them again... and again and again! Numerous people were approached. Some were strangers and others were who I'd call friend. Showing them all of that information, they were all asked their opinion about what they read. And it was unanimous.

From the middle-aged, pony-tailed, American manager of a busy local bar / restaurant to an older Canadian women with a very thick eastern European accent! She was an owner of a very small sea front guesthouse. And it was unanimous.

From the many tourists who came and went and engaged in meaningless conversation when nothing else was left to discuss to the proprietor of the classiest small hotel! The owneress came to Jamaica twenty-five years ago... a quarter century. She proved it true that one can take a girl out of THE big city, but not take a bite out of her big apple life. The same about her religion... Jewish! And what a yenta!

"Yes," she said. "But what do you hope to gain? The government is very big and very powerful! You're stupid to fight them. Forget it! You know they won't let you do this! They'll make you spend a lot of money." Her best Jewish mother impersonation imitation wasn't lost after so many years down in the fun of the sun. Some things just seem to be ingrained! And it was unanimous.

From the Danny DeVito character type owner of a local scuba shop... husky, scratchy voice and all. "I just want Danny DeVito to play me... in the movie when the movie is made." To a Marlon Brando type motorcle gang member character impersonator as was portrayed in The Wild Ones. And it was unanimous!

Everyone who read all that information came to the same conclusion. And it was unanimous!

Were one not to spend money on travel-related transactions, airline fares and hotel bills, they were allowed to or, in the minimum, not pro-hibited from traveling to Cuba. Since no money would be spent on those transactions, prohibitions and restrictions wouldn't be violated... and the Office of Foreign Assets Control only controlled and monitored the spending of money. The public was only advised (should), not ordered

23

(must), to contact the government were they considering travel to Cuba... meaning travelers didn't require permission (per se) to go there. Once there, a limited number of cigars (100) as stated in the **<u>Know Before You Go</u>** pamphlet could be acquired and imported into America... provided they were '*imported directly as accompanied baggage.*'

The Road To Havana

***

March came and my 49th birthday arrived. Some non-American friends were going to Cuba. They asked me to go along.

"I can't," I said. "Not allowed to spend money."

Andreas, a young 26-year-old German, his blond hair cut in a crewcut style, offered to pay the airfare and hotel bill for my birthday so I would accompany them. "What is it with your country? 'THE embargo' stuff is crazy. There is no more war!" It didn't take a fat apple second to make a decision.

In Cuba, minor trinkets and souvenirs as well as Cuban tobacco was acquired; and, most interesting, one carton of American produced and grown Marlboro cigarettes! This last particular purchase was beyond bizarre because my friends and I thought there was an American embargo against Cuba. Obviously... everyone must've been mistaken.

Cuba was awesome - though. It was like going back in time and visiting a lost island... which I, in particular, had done. Twenty-eight years earlier, Havana, a brief unscheduled layover. The plane some 165 other passengers plus crew and I were on was escorted into Jose Marti Airport by two Russian Migs... one off each wing tip.

The plane was barely on the ground when the pilot's voice filled the air... resonating through the speakers in the ceiling, "Ladies and gentle-men, please do NOT be alarmed. Please remain in your seats. We've just landed at Jose Marti Airport, Havana, Cuba. This plane has been hijacked to Cuba. Again - Please do NOT get up from your seats. Please do NOT panic... "

Silence! Total unbelievable silence! Then... laughter! Out of control laughter! And I couldn't stop! I thought it was the greatest thing to happen. To experience being on a plane hijacked to Cuba was awesome! Over three decades later... mention it, and it's an instant conversation. People still want to know what it was like.

I only got to see a very limited view of Havana. It was the view the Cuban government wanted us to see. It was the inside of two airports, the inside of a bus on a trip from one airport to another, and what could be seen at two or three in the morning... while traveling from one airport to the other.

This time a promise was made that I'd see Havana from a visitor's viewpoint, and not as the prisoner I was when last I stood on that island. I wanted to go out and meet the people and see the culture. I wasn't to be disappointed!

The antiquated cars, dilapidated architecture, and mentality of the people... it wasn't what I was told to expect. Maybe 'THE embargo' really had a good effect on Cuba, after all. It could justify why the Cuban people hadn't been corrupted by capitalism. And that was the city of Havana. I knew were there to be another time, I'd have to venture out into the interior or try the beach.

The moment I stepped on the plane it seemed like <u>Fantasy Island</u>. It began with the vaporized release of condensed gas coolant through the cabin air supply so strong one couldn't see their lap from a sitting position, and it didn't disappear until only minutes prior to landing! It was straight out of <u>The Twilight Zone</u>... or <u>Outer Limits</u>. I remember seeing episodes when I was a child. The misty fog followed by a change in place, time, and reality. Poof... and magically we were back in another time! It was around the 1960's. It was as if we'd stepped into a movie! And, maybe, it was the sequel!

Leaving the airport, we immediately saw old vintage cars. There were automobiles not seen for decades... tens of them, hundreds of them, thousands of them. Edsels, fifty-seven Fords, fifty-six Chevys, round-bodied Benz's, Cords and, of course, Ladas! Lots of Ladas! What did it matter their guts, drive shafts, engines and transmissions, everything that made them run, ran on Russian components. What did it matter? It was a vintage antique car lovers' heaven. And the historic ruin of their architecture was beyond words.

Old stone structures dilapidated from neglect and decay were in much need of painting... that was the least required. They lined every street and filled the skyline! Arched entryways emitted an air of historic ambiance that told a story those buildings had seen their share of history. And every building seemed to have a story to tell! Air conditioning was unheard of. However, entry to any of the antiquated buildings brought much needed relief from the oppressive heat and humidity that filled the thick city air.

Western society would do well to study and understand how Cuba's suppressive lifestyle can be obtained free from the necessities inherent with modern conveniences seemed not to be able to be done without. Air conditioning units whether central or placed in a window, fans, computers, telephone answering machines... let alone telephones or faxes... photo copiers, TV's, and the like are only a few of the items the Cuban people have done without. If only the same could be said of those in the States and other Western world civilizations. Then again, maybe, there is a price to be paid... for such innocence!

The streets were filled with people hawking their sexuality and vending their wares. With the sunset, the markets open and every street becomes a place to market something. Yes, buy this and buy that, but what did it matter if you bought or not. "Señor no salida... hablamos. ¿Que lingua habla usted? ¿English? ¡Bueno! What country you from? America? OK, let's talk about America!" The people desired to communicate, to talk, to learn... and to teach. Other countries... it's buy, buy and buy. But, if you don't buy, leave... because you're no good. However, in Cuba, the people wanted to exchange ideas and thoughts. And language wasn't a barrier. They made sure there was communication.

The Cubans were very warm and friendly... and most gracious. There was something nice and pleasant about the Cubans we met. Maybe it was their innocence or maybe their friendliness, but I think, maybe, it was their passion! Their passion for life, their passion for music... and their passion for love!

We checked into our hotel and decided to walk around Havana before the sunset. Not ten steps off the hotel property we were besieged by an onslaught of Cubans. Buy this and buy that, but mostly they wanted to sell cigars! "¡No salida! ¡Hablamos!" We waded through the deluge and found it never quite ended, but was just thinner in some areas more than it was in others. And everyone was dressed to kill!

The guys, in ties or not, wore nice freshly pressed pants or trousers. Their shoes were newly polished... the shine glistening. The smell of cologne filled the air, announcing the men's presence well in advance of their arrival. The women were... well, women! Everyone was a belle of the ball... and sexy. They oozed sex! They reeked of sex. Every woman looked you in the eye and held your contact as long as you kept hers. Within a block of the hotel I was grabbed, pinched, and gawked-at by more women than ever, previously, in my entire life. It was wild! In Havana, the women made it clear and in no uncertain terms they wanted men and they wanted sex... especially if the men were foreign. Even more so... if they were American!

The official Havanatur tour of Havana was taken... tour guide and all. And why not!? It was included in the package. One couldn't help but feel like they were in Disneyland! Actually, it was more like Hollywood. On your left and on your right, but this was Havana. The tour operator even spoke English. Yes... ENGLISH! The tour that was only to last four hours somehow wasn't finished until we returned back to our hotel over seven hours later... and for the entire seven-hour trip he stood and spoke English.

He discussed the history of the Cuban people as well as the history of their island. We were told all about the people's revolution and about all the great artists who lived in Havana. Not to be forgotten was how Havana had been built or how the Cuban currency, the basis of their monetary exchange policy, was based on the U.S. dollar. Not on the Cuban peso! In fact, not on any peso! But *ONLY* on the U.S. dollar! It was hard to believe their money *WAS* the U.S. dollar! And, we were told not to accept any Cuban currency... when change was owed.

Being tourists, pictures were taken. Lots of pictures! Pictures were taken at the Plaza of Independence, the square Castro marched into, rode into, on the eve of the revolution. Pictures were taken on the street where Hemmingway hung out. On it, supposedly, was a bar where, rumor had it, he wrote about his <u>Old Man And The Sea</u>. Pictures were taken at El Moro, the old fort, the bastion enclave built over four hundred years ago that still is a marvel today. Pictures were taken at the Partigas Cigar Factory. Only it was closed! Pictures were taken everywhere... getting on and off the bus. There were pictures of everything... ourselves, others and of nothing. Everyone, including the other tourists, thought we were from Japan. Or, in the very least, had Asian roots running through our veins. No one believed it when they were told some of us were American. But our accent and the dialect and, most importantly, the language gave us away.

Every seat in the mini tour bus was occupied with a hodgepodge collection of languages. People from all different walks of life filled the bus. There were two French girls who were ever so French and a German couple that seemed so much in love. The girls always walked arm in arm while the love bugs never stopped holding hands. There were the three Aussie men who were so stuck up every person swore they were British and there was one Spanish family who reminded me of my family when I was young and used to travel with them during the summer. The balance of about ten or eleven seats were filled with a mixture of North Americans. Mostly AMERICANS, citizens of the United States, who wanted to see this fabled land.

Lots of people, whose curiosity about Cuba is greater than their fear of oppression, aren't intimidated by an imaginary war of words instigated by any government... let alone their government. For example, there were the two elder black men and their two lady friends... also African American. The men indicated they were from Washington, D.C. The women resided in Virginia. Both were named William, although one went by Bill. William was a retired postal worker, a government employee, who was very open and very talkative. Bill never quite revealed his true profession. At least, not to me! He could've been a *Mafia* hit man or a secret U.S. operative. Then again, maybe, he was a high-level drug courier. But, what did it matter, we were all in Havana... 40 years away.

There were two college guys and a very pretty tall coed with long blond hair who traveled with the guys. They all went to the same southern university and were on spring break. Susan was an art major who wanted to transfer to Miami so she could study marine biology. One of the two guys was tall and thin with tattoos on his upper arm and lower leg... a cobra that showed its fangs when he flexed and the face of a sorceress. His name was Carlos, but he could've been the Jackel. His friend Samuel was slightly shorter... and much heavier. Both were business majors and all three were in the second year of their studies. They all had wanted to go to Cuba for years. They thought '*so what if their government hassled them for going!*' They hadn't done anything... illegal, that is!

Americans are flocking to Cuba by the tens, hundreds, thousands, and tens of thousands. The flights are filled with spring-breakers, vacationers to Jamaica and other islands, and with those who just want to go for the adventure. It includes business people! They jump over from the Bahamas, Jamaica and other countries... for a short weekend or more.

One such person was Philip. He was loquacious, middle-aged, heavy set, of medium height, with salt and pepper hair. He could pass for anything, Spanish, Jewish, Arab or Italian... any nationality or other ethnic group. Philip was U.S. born and talked about his dealings with Cuba. His partner was a Saudi who actually dealt with Cuba... not he! "It's a loophole," he said.

When Philip was last seen, he was getting off the plane and meeting some people. One who he introduced as his partner, the Saudi! Then everyone went the way of Immigration and Customs checkpoints, while he went another way. And that way didn't include the proper normal admittance entrance procedures everyone else was required to take.

The weekend came to an end oh-too-quickly. Then, it was time to go back to Jamaica and back through the travel tunnel of time. Back through the vaporized condensation of gas coolant... and back to the present. Having too many cigars (100) per Jamaican Customs allowance rules, one box of twenty-five Romeo & Juliet Churchill's had to be checked into Jamaican Customs. The alternative was confiscation. When April 18th arrived, I returned to America... after collecting those twenty-five Cubanos left at Jamaican Customs. April 18th! One day before my mother's thirty-ninth twenty-ninth birthday!

The Bust - Part II

***

My mind was racing. It'd been back and forth and around again...
several times. I had just returned from a **Back at *THE* Beginning** sojourn
when I realized where I was. Suddenly, the door swung open and I saw
agent Narco standing in the doorway for a long moment without saying
anything. Seeing the door open snapped me back to reality. Agent Narco
asked what I had to eat... on the plane.

"Chicken," I responded.

He asked, "What else?"

"Rice."

"WHat else?"

"A roll."

"WHAt else?"

"Nothing!"

"WHAT else?"

I thought for a moment... "Gingerale?!"

"WHAT ELSE?"

"Water!"

"AH HA," he yelled.

I questioned, "Ah ha?"

"What did you have with the water?"

I thought for another moment. Then I said, "Ice?!"

"WHAT ELSE?"

"Nothing!"

There was silence! Finally, he spoke. "What drugs did you take?"

"I don't do drugs."

"You don't have to do drugs to take them."

I held out my arms to show him my veins and repeated myself. "I don't do drugs."

He said it again. "You don't have to do drugs to take them." Then, it dawned on me. He thought I was a mule. As in a donkey or a courier... and an ass!

"Excuse me!" I said in protest. "This is getting out of hand."

He asked, "Will you agree to be X-rayed?"

I asked, "Will that get me out of here sooner?" He nodded and I said, "Then, let's get it done. I'm over this."

"It's not that easy," he replied. "We need to find us a doctor... first."

I told him we didn't need to find us any doctor! I'd just lie down in the X-ray machine and he could turn it on. But that wasn't acceptable.

Then, he said it again. "We need to find us a doctor... first." And I knew that meant another how many more hours to play out this game of theirs.

First, I'd have to sign the paper that was their release form. No! First, they'd have to find the paper that was their release form. How many more hours? Then, it would be off to the hospital to find us a doctor. But it couldn't be just any doctor. It had to be *THE* doctor! And the hospital would be the farthest one from the airport. Of course, the X-ray machine would have to be warmed up first. How many more hours?

He just stared at me for what seemed like forever. Not knowing what I should be doing, I stared back. He finally said, "Come with me."

We walked back to the checkout counter in silence. The silence broke when, in disbelief, he asked me again, "You sure you will agree to sign the waiver?"

"Yes!" I said. "Let's just do it... already!"

He told me to repack all my things that were spread out all over the checkout counter. And there were three full bags of things spread out all over the checkout counter. While I was re-packing all my bags, Customs supervisor Rudemann returned. Agent Narco was filling out a form I assumed had to be their release form I had to sign. I thought, '*Great! At least, they found it! Now how many more hours of this shit?*'

I was almost finished packing all my things into all my bags when agent Narco stopped writing. He put his pen down, picked up my eyeglass case and walked over to a trashcan. Then, he opened the case up over the container. And with a doing-you-a-favor look, agent Busta placed his thumb over the glasses inside the case while he made a sweeping motion... as if he was cleaning it out with his other hand. I was probably supposed to be grateful he didn't arrest me for something that had never been in there. Sometimes, I just don't comprehend their mentality!

Finally, he reached over to hand me the glass case and told me to put all my bags on one of the nearby carts. I complied! He handed me a form I thought was their release form that I had to sign. Only, it really wasn't the release form, but my receipt for the things they confiscated. Then, agent Busta asked me to sign their forfeiture receipt. I refused. He seemed taken back I wouldn't sign their forfeiture form. I told him I wasn't agreeing to forfeit anything. But, he couldn't understand why I wouldn't agree to sign their form.

Supervisor Rudemann asked, "Want to know why this stuff is being confiscated?"

I said, "Yes!"

He told me, "They're contraband."

"The literature says I can have them!"

"They weren't declared"

"I verbally declared them."

"They aren't allowed!"

"They fall within the Customs allowance of allowable items."

"They weren't licensed."

I told him, "Nothing says a license is needed."

Holding the **Know Before You Go** pamphlet in his hand that he held at eye level he said, *"THIS*... **ISN'T 'THE Bible!"**

I asked, "Then why do you print books that tell people to read what you print and to rely on what they read if what they rely on when they read what you print isn't what they should've relied on when they read what you printed?" No answer! Nor any response! Then I said, "And then you penalize them for it. As well as hassle them for doing that which you told them to do!"

Agent Narco just said, "Don't let the door hit your butt on the way out."

Not knowing what to do, I just stared at him. Then, he reached down and picked up the carton of Marlboro cigarettes purchased in Havana that was still on the countertop... and placed them on my cart. I couldn't believe it. So I asked, "Why aren't you taking those?"

Customs agent Narco answered with a dumbfounded question, "Why would I?" And he said, "They're American." His statement belied the stupidity of his questioned answer.

I said, "But they were purchased in CUBA... from the Cuban government! The Cuban government sold them."

Agent Narco raised his eyebrows slightly and shrugged his shoulders as he repeated his statement, "But... they're American."

I questioned what 'THE embargo' with Cuba was all about because American products like Marlboro cigarettes and Coke were being sold in Havana. Then, I questioned how those products got into Cuba in such mass in the first place as to be able to be sold by the Cuban government. They didn't know. Nor was it their problem. They ONLY seize and confiscate!

I told them, "'THE embargo' is being violated." I said, "Marlboro cigarettes and Coke are being sold all over Havana and probably Cuba for that matter." They didn't know. Nor did they care! But I was telling them. They were being informed our laws, the laws they swore to serve and protect, were being violated at that very minute. However, it wasn't their problem. They ONLY seize and confiscate!

The Shark

***

One week later, an official looking letter arrived from the government. There was a U.S. Dept. of Treasury seal on the envelope. It came in the mail - certified! Inside were six pages. All were type-formed and stapled. A cover letter was also enclosed. The cover letter said the six pages were the right that gave me the right to exercise my right to smoke those cigars.

I had two choices! If I were to do nothing, they'd be gone. History! Up in smoke! However, if I were to contest, to fight, argue or sue... then, first, I'd have to fill out all their forms. And I'd have to make sure that I answered everything... every question. Especially the unanswerable ones! Any mistake meant *tilt... you lose*! This was our game! If you wanted to play... you played by our rules.

My lawyer laughed at my story when I told him what happened. He said, "I told you Cubans were illegal, didn't I? I have a good friend in Customs I can call. Let's see how far the government is going to go with this. He will tell me what kind of trouble you're in."

I said, "But *IT'S ONLY CIGARS*!" And I showed him my passport.

"Yeah, OK, what else you got? I see where you're going, but..." Then, I showed him the **Know Before You Go** pamphlet, opened to page six. He read it. "WHAT!?" He looked at me and asked, "Why would the government print this? What's on page twenty?" And he quickly turned to page twenty to see what was printed there.

I said, "Been there, done that... and I've got several T-shirts to show for my troubles."

He questioned what I was talking about as he turned the pages. I told him I did the same thing he was doing... that I had already looked at page twenty, more than several times, to see what it said about disclaimers, exemptions... and the like. I said, "You'll find nothing... nothing on page twenty, page twenty-one or even page twenty-two." By that time, he passed page twenty and had turned to page twenty-one... and he'd found nothing as I said he would. He kept reading and turned to page twenty-two as I spoke. He knew there had to be something, somewhere. So I told him to look at the bottom of page twenty-three.

The shark asked, "What?"

I said it again. "Turn to page twenty-three."

He looked at the bottom of page twenty-three... and read the information! Then, he turned the page and read some more! Finally, he looked up and asked, "Is this all?" Very slowly, I nodded my head. He said, "I'm going to re-read everything... every word in both these books."

I told him, "I already did that... approximately five hundred times, more or less. And, not satisfied with my own eyes, I had other people... a lot of other people... do the same thing."

But all I heard him say was, "There must be something here we aren't seeing... have overlooked."

I told him, "I thought that too."

The shark reached for the petition and said, "There must be!"

I said, "I thought that also. But, there wasn't! And, there isn't!"

He picked up his phone and dialed the number the cover letter gave to call if there were any questions. "Hi! Can I speak with...?" The shark was told the woman he asked for wasn't in, but a lady named Beth who answered the phone said he could speak with her. He said, "My name is Stephen Shark. I have a client who thinks he's a lawyer. Last week he entered the country and had some property confiscated."

He was asked what property. I heard him answer, "Some cigars!" Then he said, "Yes, they were Cuban." What seemed like a long Southern hour passed before he asked, "Does this happen often?"

The conversation lasted for the better part of twenty minutes. I heard him say that I read the literature, the government literature that said I was to rely on the literature I read. He said, "It indicated allowance of the activity done." He also said that he read the literature and came to a similar conclusion as I had. Finally, he said, "Considering what was written, it wasn't unreasonable to think what had been written was allowed."

At some point the shark in my lawyer leaned back in his stuffed leather high-back chair and swiveled it back and forth. One hand cradled the phone nestled between his cheek and shoulder while his other hand was on top of his balding head. His eyes were rotating in their sockets as he said, "Let me see if I have this correctly? The government literature doesn't mean anything because what it says it means it really doesn't mean!" I heard him say, "Well, I'm certainly going to advise my client he's entitled to have his day in court." The shark hung up the phone. **"YOU BITCH,"** he yelled into the phone as he set it down on his desk.

I asked him what they said and he said, "I mention cigars... they ask Cuban? I say yes... they mention your name. What happened last week at Customs?"

I told the shark the whole gruesome story. He just shook his head from side to side. The shark in my lawyer couldn't believe it. I told him I wouldn't have either had I not been there, done it myself. The kicker, I told him, was Andreas left America four days later... one and a half weeks sooner than he'd planned. He left because, as he said, if he hadn't he would either have been arrested or shot. He'd only been in America for five short days, but he'd been hassled, stopped, and questioned on three separate and totally different occasions.

I finished telling my lawyer the story with Andreas being hassled for sightseeing in Fairmount Park! Andreas had never seen anything like it. Being from Germany, he'd spent time in the East before THE Wall came tumbling down... and he'd never seen that much police control. Andreas said he felt he had to flee, leave for his life... and escape with his freedom. But what would Andreas know about such things?

I continued with Andreas' story about leaving to go back to Jamaica. I told the shark that before Andreas left he went to Customs and told them he was leaving. He asked for the return of his cigars. A Customs woman left him to get the papers he needed to sign. While he waited, he read the Customs **Know Before You Go** book for foreigners. It told him he could have Cuban cigars. When the female agent returned with the forms Andreas had to sign and lots of forms that he had to fill in all the blanks,

Andreas asked why his cigars had been confiscated. She told him they're contraband.

He told her the book said he could have them. Then, he showed her the book. She looked at the book. She said it was in German… and she couldn't read German.

"Not a problem," Andreas said. He turned the page. It was in English.

She read their words. Then she looked at him and said, "This is an old book. The law has changed."

Andreas asked when the law had changed.

She answered, "1994!"

Andreas said, "But this is 1997!" He asked, "Why do you have this book if it is no good for three years?" Under the circumstances, he thought he was asking a reasonable question.

She responded, "We haven't had time to change it yet."

Andreas was speechless. He didn't know what to say. All that came out of his mouth was, "The East German government collapsed ONLY three years ago. I don't understand how it got here so quickly?"

David Weisenthal

IT'S ONLY CIGARS

***

The shark and I talked for an hour or three... more or less. Papers were copied and notes made. A file created and a price negotiated! "I think you have a really good case," the lawyer in him said. "But what are one hundred cigars worth to you? I still can't believe they printed that stuff. And I wouldn't have believed it either if you didn't show it to me. But remember... it's THEIR judges. This will go before THEIR judges. Who knows what they will say or do! What a case though! This will be fun! *IT'S ONLY CIGARS*! Boy, this will be fun!" Those were the words I kept hearing him say. Especially the 'this will be fun' part! Of course, there was the usual disclaimer... who knows what they'll do or say.

Before I left his office, I told my lawyer I'd get a copy of **'THE bible.'** Naturally that meant reading it also. He agreed it'd be a good idea. Which for warnings fell way below, and was substantially less than, necessary! I only wanted to be in America for three or four weeks. My desire to return to Negril intensified with each passing moment. Within the following couple of weeks I made it a priority to visit the public library... first floor, Government Publications.

Not only was every legal book misplaced, but pages were also missing! Eventually, through persistence, I found the book I was looking for. The one with the citing, 31 CFR Chapter V, 7-1-96 edition! It was **'THE bible.'** I began reading it... and I fell asleep. I woke up and started reading more of it... and I fell back to sleep. When I woke up again, I read some more... and I fell back to sleep and slept some more. My cure for insomnia! Read 31 CFR Chapter V - any edition! For that matter... any CFR!

I photocopied the official federal citing. At the rate it took, I almost had to camp out at the public library for several weeks before I was finished copying the government statute. Two rolls of quarters later and, having to borrow the last twenty cents, at fifteen cents a page, the entire statute wasn't even Xeroxed. However, I was finished copying the basis of the government's justification behind the enforcement of 'The (Cuban) embargo' – legislation enacted almost four decades earlier. I replaced the Code of Federal Register back into its proper place and walked out the library a much poorer man monetarily, but a much richer man... knowledge-wise.

Finished with everything I came to America for, I was preparing to head back to my newly adopted island home. Prior to leaving, I stopped by my diamond-studded, pierced-earring, shark of a lawyer's office once more. I left him a complete copy of my incomplete copy of '**THE bible.**' It was complete with all my handwritten notes all over the pages where I placed a circle here and a circle there, and a star here and a star there! And I wrote a word here and a word there, as well as a sentence here and a sentence there! Two days later I headed back south once again.

The day before dropping off the statute, '**THE bible,**' to my lawyer I called Customs at the phone number listed on the cover letter. I wanted a man to man or man to woman, but in any event a person to person, heart-felt chat with the government communiqué signatory. I didn't know what I hoped to gain. Maybe, it was verbal confirmation. But I called anyway!

The lady who answered the phone told me the woman who I asked for wasn't in. However, she said I could talk with her. We spoke for a brief minute or two joking and laughing as we did. Then, I informed the female voice with whom she was talking. She immediately said, "Ahhh yes... Cuban cigars." Her pleasant attitude changed into ice-cold drone mentality. Thereafter, our conversation was very difficult. I had to remind her of a previous conversation we had. One where we had acted like friends! She said, "We never spoke before."

I told her, "The conversation I was referring to was the conversation we had just prior to me identifying myself." I felt her warm ever-so-slightly. But warm she did! And in my mind, I could see the faint crescent shaped form her lips made as she smiled. I asked what she thought about my petition. After a brief moment, she replied. "The right to petition the government for the return of those cigars is your right."

I asked her to forget that she worked for the government. "What do YOU really think?"

Beth thought for a brief minute before saying, "Well, it's not like this is... drugs, OK! *IT'S ONLY CIGARS*... right? But you need to get past two things first. First, you must prove you went to Cuba. Then, there's the statute! "

David Weisenthal

Without hesitation, I responded. "Went to Cuba?! Hey, I admit I went there. From the beginning, I told Customs I was there. That isn't a problem."

"You went to Cuba? What was it like?"

The Cohiba Bandito

***

The Memorial Day holiday marks the beginning of every summer in America. By the beginning of the 1997 summer, I was basking in the Jamaican sun, lying in the sand, and swimming in the Caribbean. When the July 4th holiday celebration arrived, it landed with a loud bang and set the midpoint mark for the summer. Yet... it was just another day in Margarita-villa for me. There was still nary a word from across the sea. During the prior seven weeks abroad, I had forwarded the necessary deposit to my straightforward hippie lawyer so he would initiate '*the games afoot'* game. It was *sir-lock* Holmes humor and all... and it was my legal fight to liberate all those poor defenseless imprisoned Cubanos. And, humor... why not?

Some of my friends, and some say I *specifically*, decided then decreed that since the Chinese have years of the dog, cat, rat, horse, and several other various critters, Negril should have it's own list of years as well. It was decided that year would be called the year of humor. So it was said... and so it was written!

The summer passed. I continued waiting for word, any word, about the government's response. I waited... and I waited! From the time the petition was filed, the government legally had thirty days to respond... and to file their answer. Thirty days!

By the time the July 4th weekend bash came to a close, thirty days were way long gone. In fact, it was beyond gone. At summer's end, ninety-five days would pass before my eyes. Yet, there still wouldn't be any word from the government... or my lawyer. Once before, I had to wait for the government to decide something it didn't want to decide. It took them in excess of nineteen months to make their decision. Since I had already been there and done that, I thought *'not this time!'* I knew I'd have to fly back to America sooner than I would've liked. Meanwhile, I was spending most of my time with friends... one in particular!

"Danny DeVito! That's who I think should play me in the movie... when the movie's made." The Cohiba Bandito said it on more than several occasions. Then he'd asked, "Yeah... and why not?" The Bandito is short with long dark hair... and is a spitting image of a short Hollywood actor. He's also a Canadian of Jewish decent who spends his winters in the warmth of the tropics. And for him, warmth means between the 'A' months... August thru April!

The reason he leaves Jamaica in the spring is to return to the land of his birth so the forms required to be filled out every year in order to avoid penalties associated with not paying one's blood money will be filed timely. In another life, he's a pencil-pushing bean-counting accountant who goes by the moniker of the name ToBe. But like many other ex-pats, displaced and unsettled in that exotic out-of-the-way distant far-off place, *'once a junkie... always a junkie!'*

The Bandito first came to Negril back in the 1980's. He was in search of some solace from a nether world north of where he wanted to be... when he fell to Earth and landed in Negril. Hell, the living there was easy, the women loose, and the drugs... oh, those drugs! He finally fixated on Negril soil during the beginning of the 1990's, while I was off on a long enforced *vacation*... courtesy of the government. And any enforced *vacation* is a long time... no matter the length of time.

Cohiba is a name he was given partly because he liked it, and he did like the smokes that sold under that monogram, and partly because he looked like a Bandito. The only things missing were the two ammo belts that should've been draped around his neck, hanging across his chest. But instead of bullets in the leather slots, pellets filled with helium, opium or ganja would've been encased in the shells. And instead of inserting those tiny missiles into weapons of death, he'd simply amuse himself by opening the cartridges up to ingest the contents of euphoric bliss. Somewhere in a different life I saw similar signs of addiction, but on him the *junkie* label didn't carry the same tone of ruination of the soul. However, I've heard it said on more than many occasions, *'once a junkie... always a junkie.'*

After my *vacation* had run its course, and freed from another lease slung around my neck, we were introduced when I was back in Negril for only a few short days. Within a very short time we became the *best* of *best* friends. I spent the summer of 1997 walking the beach, hanging out on the sand, swimming in the water, and taking in the sun. Upon the Bandito's return, at the beginning of August, we spent our time looking at women walking the beach in their less than nothing bikini's. We also talked about a lot of stuff. But mostly, we surfed the Net for anything associated with cigars... Cubanos... Cohibas! We found an incredible amount of info was out there to be found. All one had to do was look.

We found Ari Smokin... a leader of some previously unknown revolution who has a following. A loyal army of *aficionados*! We discovered there were over 700,000 hardcore smoking members. They represented a silent, and maybe not so silent, but vigil proponent of the people's struggle to overcome oppression. All they wanted to was to smoke some Cubans. And, maybe, kill some too! We found those liberation riders willing to go to great lengths for their cause. In the previous year alone, over 3,700 freedom fighters had their puffs confiscated at U.S. borders. But how many had made it through? It's akin to smuggling drugs. Only one doesn't go to jail! Or do they? After all, *IT'S ONLY CIGARS*!

They weren't the only freedom fighters fighting *the good fight* for the right cause either. Everyday a smorgasbord of people, tired of tyranny, tired of oppression, and tired of their rights being subterfuge, ban together to voice their opinions. More and more, liberation seekers are pursuing the expression of their displeasure with what they perceive to be decay. Sometimes, their frustration mounts into anger of the past that was, the present that is, and the future that will be theirs to bear. The reality of their life really isn't a pleasant realization. For the most part, their anger remains pent-up and repressed. But, while it's usually controlled and always suppressed, they're looking for avenues to escape, to release... and to vent.

Many people believe government settlements with cigarette companies, regardless of the little to no public benefit, will foretell a harbinger of future crisis... unheard of by today's standards. Some will be frustrated over a duality standard. A relentless regression of individual control coupled with unequaled prosecution of those caught up in the hyperbole could make Tiananmen Square pale in comparison. Add the effects of everyday stress experienced in a quest to enjoy life's finer riches. The sum total of this may provide a clue to the atmosphere that has created an almost G-d-like quality for such a non-life thing as a cigar! But, not just any cigar! For, it **must** be a CUBAN. And, only a CUBAN can it be.

Non-*aficionados* want to know what all the hoopla is about! They'll say, 'Ask a hundred people. One hundred knowledgeable people! Then again, maybe, not so knowledgeable! But one hundred people who think they know something, anything, about cigars. There will be one hundred different answers from this consortium of *in-the-know intelligencia.*' For what would they know anyhow? Some will say bouquet, while others will boast the aroma. Still others will insist it's only in the taste. And the only thing they will agree on is to disagree.

What would any of them know? Well, they all know it's *vogue* to smoke a good cigar. They know smoking a good stoogie is a sign of wealth and success by anyone who's heading somewhere... anywhere. They know smoking a good stoogie is a signal one isn't stuck in a nothing town living a nothing life. Or working a nothing job! In the least, they know it gives an appearance of that opulence. And Cubanos are the *best*! In fact, they're the *best* of the *best*. Embargo or not!

For a few dollars, anyone can taste the beautiful bouquet of delirious delight or sample the essence of the splendid aroma from the smoke that only a *rock-or-fella* would partake. Even if it's only for a few short puffs! Simply put, we're in the age of a new millennium. Reality is out... fantasy in! It isn't what you are, but who you are! It isn't really who you are, but who you appear to be. It's the image... and the mirage. And the whole world's nothing, but a stage.

However, to give such homage to a lifeless thing like a Cuban, thanks can be given, in no small part, to the U.S. Government. Because to remove 'THE embargo' is to remove the illegality, and that would remove the mystique. After that, it's only a cigar. A good cigar notwithstanding! A very good stoogie indeed, but only a smoke none-the-less! America is solely responsible for taking a one-dollar stick in Havana and turning it into a hundred-buck butt in New York City. ONLY in America! It's capitalism... at its best. That's what America has to give the world. Earth's greatest gift!

Only in America can importation and distribution of (Cuban) cigars be more profitable than importation and distribution of drugs. Maybe that can explain how the drug war has finally begun to show signs of victory. With importation and demand down. Or so it's said. But, if I had to believe something, I'd think it wasn't that demand for drugs is down as much as the profitability for Cuban stoogies is up. As is the demand!

The Cohiba Bandito and I discussed the cigar thing constantly. Twenty-four / seven! We talked about where I should go to gather help with the good fight. We talked about who I should talk to that could, and would, give assistance to the cause. We sat in his office shack on the beach and between selling scuba lessons and girl watching we talked cigars this and cigars that. One time I asked my DeVito cloned friend, "Am I crazy? Am I the only one who sees this as it is? Am I alone?" I was neurotic! And my anxiety was visually manifesting itself.

He told me, then he tried to reassure me that I wasn't alone on this. I didn't really believe him! But, at the time, it seemed to sound good. Besides, I liked the reaffirmation. He said, "You're the football!" I could only hope this wouldn't be like in high school during football practice… when it seemed as if I was the football.

To calm my racing nerves, he suggested a movie called The Raffle. He said it was on tape and could be found in any video store… except the video shop located in Negril didn't have it. What else was new? Although it was 1997 and there were payphones in Negril, a milestone that just recently occurred, the talk boxes were few and far apart. And getting connected was another matter entirely. Getting connected off the island was still almost next to impossible.

I told him my thoughts with getting the cigars back. "I want to have a dinner party with the *best* food and wine accompanying the very *best* cigars. It'd be the ultimate cigar dinner event of all time." I said, "Think about it… the *best* food, great wine and fabulous cigars no one has." Then I told him, "Maybe, I'll establish a legal offense fund much like the legal defense funds set up by just about every President America ever had. The only difference being that I'd admit my guilt, which would allow me to do it again. I'd admit it, I did it… and I'll probably do it again. Everyone likes the truth. And, maybe, if Nixon had said that he'd still be President today!" Finally, I told him that I'd promise to be very offensive to get those cigars back. And I told him, "I can see it all! The fund, dinner, T-shirts, TV and the radio! Not to mention a book and a movie… or two."

The Bandito said he had a copy of Cigar *Aficionado* somewhere and went off to find it. Later, he returned with his crumpled copy. I saw the cover with a picture of his double. He said he felt I needed to get to the man on the cover or to some others like the physical fitness man Arnold or that bad man Jack. But the *best* would be the man himself, Ari Smokin, who was responsible for maintaining those stoogie ratings and stoking the fires of dissent.

He told me his theory when he said, "The *best* way to win is to lose. It doesn't matter if you get the cigars back. The man wants to play. What he does is a spoof! What you're doing is one too! If he's contacted and given a piece, he'll play the game. Think raffle!"

I had to admit The Raffle seemed good and, in the least, humorous. The Bandito's idea was to just sell tickets for a chance to eat a dinner... with fantastic cigars, fine wines, and the company of some interesting and, maybe, not so interesting people. Of course, the usual invitees would have to attend. The Bandito, my shark, maybe the cigar man himself, some writers, photo-takers, and myself! Along the way, other ringers like Danny, Arnold, and Demi or any celeb that could be lured with a hook of humor from within the humor door wouldn't hurt the cause either. It'd be a small price to pay.

Anyone and everyone was a potential ally. The idea was to place an ad in the *aficionado* of cigar mags and, maybe, an article would be written. The ad would sell chances to a dinner for a hundred bucks, U.S. currency. The revolution's media man would be given a piece of the take from The Raffle rake. He'd also get to pocket every buck from a sale of an ad. I couldn't get the dinner out of my head while the Bandito just kept reminding me to ONLY think raffle. "Think Raffle!"

We were all over the Net. We went from articles written about articles, to articles written about events, to articles written about people. One sight led to another that led to others. We spoke to the local island Net nerd, a kind of comic Doonesbury type character come to life. Netman went nuts on the cigar thing. "This will be on everyone's lips... over coffee, dessert, cocktails and their dinner conversation. This is all everyone will talk about... for one week. Then, it'll all be forgotten. But, hey, I can use the Net! This'll be great. I love it."

When the end of August came, there was still nothing happening in America. Still no word from the government! Nor any sound from my hippie mouthpiece! I knew the silence from the government could be expected, but from my lawyer it was another matter entirely. While I was more than a bit unnerved from the deafness of communication, I knew it wasn't because the shark had gotten his fill as is usually the case with cases like this. He hadn't been paid! Except for the one thousand five hundred big ones I had to pay for him to initially take the case. Wanting the remainder of his blood, I knew he'd call.

My course was clear, but I continued to wait. Why should I expect anything different? The government never wants something decided that it doesn't want contested. Down in Jamaica, I was doing absolutely nothing. In fact, I was getting more than bored. I read and re-read the statute, **'THE bible,'** 31 CFR, Chapter V, more than many times over. I went over and over the language and the wording of the law. I knew there wasn't anyway those words couldn't mean what they didn't mean. The words had to mean what everyone thought they meant... based on the words that were written.

When Labor Day came I decided to go see a friend who lived in or by a Windy City. I thought I could accomplish a thing or five with a trip to the Midwest. I had a back-end portion of a free trip anywhere Air Jamaica flew. They flew to Chi-town... from Jah-land. It didn't cost anything to change the city I flew to. So into the Windy City I flew.

I thought it'd be interesting to see how my last trip into America would affect any future trip back into my country. Especially into a city I didn't normally travel to and had never traveled to before... nor had any apparent reason to go there. I knew those government pencil-pushers would've had to have been at their computers for the better part of several days... with all the information they had to add to the file(s) created when last I entered America with those Cuban cigars. It was going to be interesting. It would be fun! At least, that was what everyone said it would be... including myself.

Shortly after the summer ended with the festivities of the Labor Day celebration, I made plans to re-enter the country of my birth. By then, more than ninety-five days had come and gone since the petition was filed and an answer expected from the government.

At the airport prior to boarding the plane, I entered a duty-free lounge and purchased two boxes of Jamaican cigars. Both boxes had an unbroken seal on them. The seals were proof that no one had entered either box since the factory sealed both boxes closed with those seals. In addition, a clear cellophane wrapper was heat-sealed around each box. It enclosed them in a tightly shut wrapping within the airtight covering. And was further proof that neither box had been entered since the factory heat-sealed both boxes closed with those wrappers.

With my purchase of those two boxes of Jamaican cigars, I received a computer receipt showing the purchase price I paid. The receipt also indicated the date, time, and location for when and where those two boxes of Jamaican cigars had been bought!

The Theory
***

Arrival through Immigration in Chi-town was pretty easy. However, as I departed the gate after having my passport stamped, I was called back. False start!

The computer that wasn't working suddenly sprang to life. It took longer than usual for the big brother data machine to produce all the results it was asked to seek, due to all the information placed in my file(s). More than several days worth of imputed information had to take time for those results to come up on the screen. The Customs declaration card was taken away and the officer wrote something on it. He was smiling when he gave it back and told me to have a nice day. But I thought it odd. Then, I looked at the card and saw in very large print across the top of the front, the letters 'P.A.T.!' I knew it had to be some sort of secret code... or something!

'P.A.T.!' I wondered how many secret agents it took to think that up. They probably had to stay up the whole night too. NO! That would have been giving their intellect too much credit. And what did 'P.A.T.' mean? Maybe, 'Pay Attention To.' What was the first clue? Could it have been I was called back. Flagged! Anyhow, with the card returned and back in my hand, off I went... to meet my destiny.

I entered Chi-town's Customs area. A Customs agent asked for my declaration card. He wrote, in a larger more **bolder** and darker stroke, the letter 'T' in the upper left-hand corner. A drug-sniffing canine and his look-a-like companion approached me. They walked away. Both had better things to do. I thought it another stupid secret code. The letter 'T!' And only those who actually worked for their government really knew what it honestly meant. I wondered if it had anything to do with the dog cop and his twin coadjutor. Maybe the letter 'T' stood for test. As in 'Drug Test!' But then, that would've been the letters 'D. T.' Who knew? I knew they did!

I thought it so trite and childish! They looked at it as if it was a matter of life or death. I picked up my bag that I checked on the plane. My carry-on bag had the Jamaican cigars. With my bags in hand, I proceeded over to where one leaves the area. An agent walked across the entire length of the floor to stop me and asked to see my declaration card. He examined the card for less than several seconds. Then he told me to go over to the checkout counter. Like I didn't know that was coming! What was the first clue?

"Let me see your pass-a-porte!" A very thick Latino accent cut every word said. I asked where he was from. He asked back, "What you mean?" I told him he didn't sound like he was born in America. He said, "I ask the questions here." And the questions he asked. "Why you here?"

"I'm an American! I didn't know I need a reason to enter *MY* own country."

"Who you see here? Why you see them? Where you see them? When you see them?"

"I don't understand what who I see and when or where I go is of any concern to you. But since you asked, I'm meeting friends and family."

"What friends? What families?" And the questions continued. I gave him answers to his questions. Only with every answer came more questions. "How long you out of the country? How many times you leave the country? Where you go? Who you know? Where you know them? Why you know them? How you know them? Where you work? Where they work?" However, he didn't seem to understand half of what I said because English wasn't his native language. What was the first clue?

Maybe, he had a bad English teacher as a child. Or, maybe, he was from Cuba! Who knew? I knew there was no way he was born in America! Maybe, Puerto Rico! But not America! However, my government hired him to represent our country on behalf of my fellow American citizens. And this foreign Latino type thinks I'm an enemy of my country? How would he know who my country's enemies are! How bizarre! Hell, this isn't even his mother's country. What am I missing?

I couldn't help wonder if there weren't enough unemployed Americans, Americans born and bred, REAL Americans, TRUE Americans... AMERICANS... who'd like to work for their government and their country! And he's the one they hired to defend our borders! How frightening! I wondered how many cousins or friends he let into the country... my country? People who shouldn't be here, but are! He's probably still doing it. Getting them in somehow! Then, I wondered how many drugs and other prohibited stuff entered the country because of agents like him.

People who are in the position of trust they're in. Oh, I guess it's true as someone once said it was. I'm just a skeptic!

The Hispanic Customs agent finally tired of asking questions while doing nothing else. He turned his attention toward my bags on the check-out counter where he directed they be placed. However, he never got tired of asking questions. The bags were opened and those two boxes of Jamaican cigars were removed. While he was examining the exterior of each box, I told him I had the receipt... date and time stamped... that proved the purchase. He didn't care. Nor did he want to see it!

I was asked to open one of the cellophane wrapped heat-sealed boxes and break the seal that sealed the box closed. It was more than obvious he was looking for someone. Maybe, a smuggler! Someone who had a disposable heat-sealer! Someone who could, and would, change two boxes of Cuban for two boxes of Jamaican! Bands and all! All while flying at thirty thousand feet in front of an audience of one hundred and fifty, more or less, witnesses.

I couldn't help wonder what had happened to the Jamaican cigars or the two Cuban boxes. And, all the bands! I could only wonder why one would have a Cuban cigar, let alone fifty of them, if they couldn't tell everyone or at least someone without having to utter a single word that they smoked the very *best* of the *best*. I know it was pompous. But that was the name of this game! It was the nature of the beast.

He said, "I know in Mexico they put Jamaican bands on Cuban cigars."

I asked, "So what?"

He repeated himself. He said he knew they did that there. Instead of repeating myself, I told him I didn't go to Mexico. But he said, "Well... I know they do that there." When I told him I hadn't been to Mexico in over a year, he looked at me with a more-stupid-than-stupid look on his face. Then, he asked me why I went to Mexico.

I answered, "My sister lives there."

"Why she live there? What she do there? How long she live there? Where she live? Who she live with?" His questions continued! Each question required an answer. Each answer led to another question... that required another answer. His attention returned to the cigar box that he had me open. He picked up a stick and removed it from the box. Then, he walked over to a civilian dressed man who sat on a counter some fifty feet away. Leaning near the man, he had a private chat with the unknown soul who continued shaking his head in a negative manner.

The Hispanic agent returned and gave my cigars back after he placed the one he took out back in the box and closed the lid. He said, "Next time you bring cigars into the country, I'll confiscate them and say they're Cuban." I told him he couldn't do that. He said he could. Once again I told him he couldn't do that. But he said in a very arrogant tone, "I can do anything I want. I work for Customs." And this is the country freedom lives in today!

Next, he ordered me to empty all my pockets of everything I had. I was told to dump every item out on the checkout counter in front of him. He looked at all the things placed there. A lighter; some silver coins, Jamaican as well as U.S.; misc. papers; a few business cards... and all my paper currency, Jamaican as well as U.S.! He counted the U.S. money. "How much you have here?"

I told him the exact amount. "Approximately two-thousand five-hundred dollars!"

He yelled out a huge sigh when he finished counting the currency a second time. "You have two-thousand five-hundred and twenty-seven dal-lers?!" It was as much a question as it was the statement he wanted it to be. "That is a lot of moo-ney! How come you have so much moo-ney?"

I always thought one had to pass a civil service intelligence test prior to working for the government. What did I know! And I thought the prede-termined threshold number was ten thousand dollars before a government agent was alerted to inquire why someone, anyone, would have so much moo-ney. But, then... who was counting? I think he had it down to the penny.

After he finished asking his questions, checking my bags and counting my moo-ney, I was told to go. Instead of walking out the doors that exited the area to enter my country, I walked over to the other Customs agent. Although in plain clothes, he appeared to be a supervisor because all the uniformed agents went to him with their questions. He seemed to be an American. A REAL American! And he had a pleasant personality. But, maybe, that's because he was in his civvies... street clothes. I wondered if putting on HIS uniform, the uniform of the U.S. Customs service, somehow magically transformed his personality into a drone-like mentality!

We discussed the cigar thing. He agreed it wasn't against the law to travel to Cuba. He also expressed an opinion that he didn't care if I had cigars... Cuban or otherwise! Then, he said the laws in America were very vague... and that vagueness worked in the government's favor. I told him there were laws... in America. I finally said, "NO ONE IS ABOVE THE LAW! NO ONE! NOT EVEN, AND MOST ESPECIALLY, THE GOVERNMENT... OR THE PEOPLE WHO WORK FOR THE GOVERNMENT!"

When I returned to Philadelphia, I called my hippie lawyer Stephen. I asked what was happening and he said, "Still no answer." Then, I told him what had happened. He said, "We should make an appointment to meet."

The following day, I sat in his office while he phoned Customs. After dialing the number, he waited a minute or two before speaking into the mouthpiece. "Beth... this is Stephen. I'm calling about David's cigars. When can he expect them back?"

After he hung up the phone I asked my lawyer, "Do you know what this means?"

Stephen wore an inquisital look on his face. A brief minute passed before he reflected on my question. He said, "David, we can file anytime you want. We're only giving them an opportunity to rule on your petition. However, if we don't get an answer... let alone a favorable one... we can file anytime you want. If you want, we can bypass the process and file whenever you want."

I responded, "No Stephen! That's not what I meant. When the government doesn't know what to do, they don't do anything. Nothing at all! I've already been there and done that! They hope you go away! Kind of like - don't go away mad... just go away. They think, maybe, possibly, and more than likely, if they just delay, delay, and delay... it'll run up the clock. Cha ching! Cha ching! Shark fees can get out of hand! And they usually do! But, hey, you know about that. A shark is a shark… regardless the sea! All they're doing is hoping we give up and go away."

Stephen questioned, "What do they know?" He answered his own question. "I guess they don't know you very well!

I answered, "It's not like this road hasn't been traveled before. But now, I'm over it. Or thought I was. Anyhow, they don't give a rat's ass. One would think they would. But they don't."

We sat in my legal beagle's office for a couple of hours discussing how to proceed. Stephen talked about how he thought the case should be handled. I asked if he'd ever handled a government agency administrative procedure issue before. He said, "I've handled cases for people who were in prison."

I told him that wasn't what I meant. I said, "People can't be denied their day in court by making it impossible to get the necessary administrative ruling(s) to file suit." He didn't understand what I was talking about. So I explained it further. "We'll need to get an answer from Customs on the petition prior to proceeding. And if we don't do that first, it'll be a way for them to delay… further. A lot further! Cha ching! Cha ching!"

Stephen was slightly confused. I continued. "The judge could and more than likely will say we'll have to answer the government petition that was filed with Customs prior to coming into court. The judge will say we have to follow those administrative procedures first. He'll say failing to follow those administrative procedures didn't afford the government an opportunity to settle the dispute prior to bringing an action in federal court."

My lawyer was told the real problem was that the government didn't really want to follow their administrative procedures first. Or they would've… by then. I said, "I mean they had, what, thirty days to answer the petition?! What is it now? Over a hundred and counting! But the judge will have none of that. All he'll be concerned with is those administrative procedures will not have been followed prior to coming into court. I can see it all! I can hear it all now!"

I told him, "We'll be told we must give the government the *courtesy* of allowing them to proceed through the administrative process before we can come into court for justice... or in any case for a ruling on the issue in this case. It really comes down to cha ching! Cha ching! That's what it's all about. Don't go away mad... just go away! But what they're really doing is denying the citizen their day in court by making it impossible to get the necessary administrative ruling(s) to file suit. Besides, it's not like this is a matter of life and death. Right? *IT'S ONLY CIGARS*!" And, somewhere along the way, the fun it was going to be took a dog's leg turn to the right and turned serious.

I asked Stephen if he'd ever read the statute. He shook his head indicating his lack of knowledge on the subject. I told him, "There's some really good stuff there." My lawyer was told my thoughts on 'THE embargo.' I told him I didn't think it was written for Americans, REAL Americans. American born and bred! I also told him the *real* theme throughout was Cuban 'national' this... and Cuban 'national' that. Then I said, "In fact... it's very consistent with the Cuban 'national' thing." He was asked if he knew the basis of the statute. Stephen shrugged his shoulders. I voiced my theory. "Mariel Boat Lift, Cuban Missile Crisis, Bay of Pigs... Kennedy's assassination!"

I was on a roll. "'THE embargo' was drafted during the early 1960's. 1963 to be exact! The same year Kennedy was killed. Oswald spent time in Cuba and Russia... so we were told. We were at war, albeit a cold one, with Russia. Cuba was Russia's puppet regime in the West... so the thinking went."

I couldn't stop! "After the Cuban revolution, Fidel got rid of those deemed undesirable, criminal, and misfit. All those who didn't believe in nor wanted the revolution! And people who may've opposed the change. Not to mention, all those who fought against the revolution! Quite possibly, he even got 'rid of' those few who did believe in the cause and who fought for the revolution. Or who fought on Castro's side. Maybe, Castro had agents in America. Maybe, he placed some of his people in the States! It wasn't unreasonable to think... so the thinking went. But, in any event, when 31 CFR Chapter V was enacted, the American Congress wasn't afraid our own people would betray their country. No! There was a bigger fear!"

I could tell I had Stephen's interest and that he wanted to hear my thoughts. I continued! "Cuba was the *true* enemy! There were Cubans in America, regardless the side on! They were the enemy. The *REAL* enemy!

It was kind of like the Japanese, Germans, and Italians during the first two World Wars. How could it be explained our politics of pursuing political freedom denied that which was the objective to be achieved? Vietnam was another place in another time. It was a place that was a long way from home. On the other hand, Cuba is just around the corner!"

My theory wasn't quite finished, "'THE embargo' was more a method to control Cubans flooding into America than it was a means to enforce a confiscation policy on the natural born populace. Back then, Americans didn't have any interest in going to Cuba. I know! I was hijacked to Cuba in 1968. And everyone, all the people on the flight I was on, was more than scared to death the Cubans were going to kill us." Next, he was told about the man I overheard saying to his little 5-year-old son, while in the bathroom, that he shouldn't eat or drink anything... because it was poison.

Finally, I told my attorney, "Today, the government interprets the statute the way they want! And the way they want to interpret it is the way they're interpreting it. But how they interpret it wasn't the way it was written. Maybe, the government interpretation is what Congress intended. But that isn't what they wrote. Now... it's all politics!"

"How many Cubans reside in America today? How many Cubans became American citizens? How many Cubans vote for a Governor, Congressman, Senator... or, maybe, even a President?" How many? A State's worth... maybe."

Stephen listened while I ranted on and on. "We can give most favored trade nation status to a country that's our eternal enemy. One who's sworn an oath to put us in our grave. But we continue with a systematic method of suppression and oppression to another who's just a spot in the sea. Do you know why? I mean, what the hell is the difference? It'd seem to me that if any country should have an embargo against it, it'd be China!" Stephen raised his eyebrows slightly and shrugged his shoulders as my storm continued. "Money! The almighty dollar! Cha ching! Cha ching! That's why?"

Stephen continued looking at me with little to no expression. I didn't stop. "How many people live in China?" Stephen didn't know. I told him, "A couple of billion, maybe... or, maybe, more! That's a lot of people! None have the things America wants to sell. I think its called Balance of

Payments, Trade Deficit or whatever else you want to name it. But in the end, the reality is, it's really all about money. The almighty dollar! Cha ching! Cha ching!"

Then, I asked the shark if he knew how many people lived in Cuba. He didn't know. So I said, "ONLY twenty-some million. Big difference! Two billion vs. twenty million! Not as much money to be made in Cuba." The look in his eyes told me he thought I was crazy. Little did he know!

I knew he needed to be brought back down to reality because the plane Stephen was on was a different flight than I was flying. I started talking about lawsuits, litigation and such. Things the shark could identify with! "No one's ever done this before. I'm the first to ever challenge the government on this stuff. You're going to make history! You're going to become the foremost knowledgeable source on 'THE (Cuban) embargo.'"

I asked Stephen if he knew anything about the 3,700 and some souls who, like me, had been hassled by U.S. Customs. The ones who had their cigars confiscated within the past year! Stephen shook his head! I wasn't surprised. It wasn't like the government wanted to promote or advertise such deviate activity by the people. Out of sight meant out of mind!

I told him about the stuff the Bandito and I found when we surfed the Net. I said, "Everyone's going to call you to sue the government to get back their cigars or whatever... after we win!" I said, "Stephen, think of it. Magazines, newspapers, radio, and TV news including CNN! There'll be spots on talk radio and interviews on TV with Rosie, Oprah... even Geraldo. Not to mention are some segments on 60 minutes, Good Morning America, 20/20, and Nightline. This could make the Sunday morning political talk shows like Meet The Press or venues like Politically Incorrect. Everyone will be consumed with dialogue on this. Jay or David surely will have some mention of us. And I can see a Saturday Night Live comedy skit." However, I didn't mention... The Raffle.

Stephen's eyes lit up. "You think so?" I could see smoke rising from his brain. He didn't know what to do or say. So he said, "Let's look it up." Stephen turned on his computer and said, "I can get WestLaw on line." With a push of a button, poof... we were in! That's computer talk for we were on line. Which is more computer talk for we had communication and access to information we were seeking! In an instant, we were connected to the *information highway*. Although we had to wade through a traffic jam of people jamming their phone lines to gain access to the information they sought first. Of course, it took more than a few minutes for his computer to connect and I wondered why that highway should be any different from any other road. A traffic jam is a traffic jam. The direction the traffic flows matters not.

After the passwords were entered and finally approved, we actually got to speak to a real live operator person who talked back to us. While waiting for the connection Stephen asked, "You were hijacked to Cuba in 1968? What was it like?

Freedom Is Just Another Word For... Nothing Left

***

In the midst of a brief explanation about my short sojourn down to that sunny tropical paradise, we suddenly heard the sound of a voice through the air. "Hello!" The voice came through a speaker box that was connected through the telephone. It arrived via the shark's computer. The voice from beyond the cosmos introduced itself. "<u>WestLaw</u>"

Stephen the shark spoke into his computer speakerphone voice box. He told the voice from beyond that we were looking for any case citing(s) from, 'THE embargo.' Stephen cited the reference for 'THE embargo.' A few short minutes passed before the voice from beyond the computer speakerphone voice box told us that there were twenty-seven total cases... with a reference to 'THE embargo.'

Stephen defined it a little more. Then the voice from beyond said, "Nineteen cases." Stephen defined it some more. That's when the voice from beyond said, "Eleven cases."

Stephen and I went through each and every one of those eleven cases. And none had anything to do with confiscation... let alone cigars! We reasoned there was probably a very logical reason. But what would we know? We reasoned that, maybe... just maybe... prior to the recent cigar explosion, not one person, at least not any red, white, and blue-blooded American, was interested in anything from Cuba or of Cuban origin. No Cuban products!

In times before this time, Cuban cigars were *ONLY* for the few select... because of the then political situation in America! After Kennedy died, the majority of those few select weren't American-born nor raised. Besides, Americans that were into Cuban cigars didn't advertise their fetish. That would've seemed to the many to somehow have been anti-American.

However, recent changes in Russian and East German political systems have given an appearance to have made it possible to want or have what was here-to-fore unheard of... or, in the very least, desirable. In the past, what was impossible to think has today become very plausible and more than very realistic! 'The Cold War is over,' it was said. 'There is NO more enemy!' But what did we know?

I told Stephen in order to change the sphere of consciousness prevalent in the West today there were two significant, yet paltry, petty and petite problems standing in the way. And in order to achieve global unification they'd have to be overcome first. For, it was those two minuscule obstacles that lay at the core of the prevention of peaceful harmony between these two vastly alternative, but not so different systems. Cuban 'nationals' and the *Mafia*! Because both want what they believe is their property... and all their property. Their lands, their casinos, their factories, mills, hotels, and their houses! They want it all back. Everything... they believe Fidel took from them way back when!

If anyone believes those two groups will ever forget... forget their homeland or property, their lands, casinos, hotels, mills, factories, houses or any other little item of materialistic ownership... then there's some very valuable swampland for sell out there somewhere! Probably for sale by those same Cuban 'nationals' or *Mafia* types! Who knows? Maybe, they went into business together!

Can anyone seriously believe Cuban 'nationals' wouldn't move back to their homeland in a fat-apple second... if given the chance? In disbelief? Simply look at how Cuban Americans handled that little boy, Elian. Under a guise of the freedom word, they were willing to strip the liberty our fore-fathers fought for, including a sovereign right of the family unit over State control. In the end, all that was proved was their revolution is still being fought. Only now, the battleground is in America. Their true colors flew with all those little handheld flags that flew all over little Havana. The ones that weren't American red, white and blue!

Maybe I'm off in another sphere, but it seems they aren't over their displacement and still care about the homeland... even after so long a time. And why do Cuban Americans live in *Little* Havana? Whatever happened to Miami? No! All those 'nationals' are still Cuban! Although, they became American citizens years ago!

Another and possibly better case in point is The Middle East. Did the PLO forget their homeland? Why would one think Cuban 'nationals' to be any different? If they were they wouldn't be 'nationals' anymore. Nor would they care after so many years off the island!

Cuban 'nationals' represent how many votes? How many million Cuban 'nationals' are in America? Even if it's only half the number thought, it represents a lot of voters! And politics is really about vote-litics!

Although Cuban anything-ism is moving into a space known as the *in* thing... as in food, music, artistic endeavors, and political activism... it's a political disaster for any candidate on a national level. It's a political bombshell... waiting to explode! It'd be politically incorrect to open Cuba up in this day and age. But what would I know?

Issues involving global economics and political (in)stability spit out from the mouths of those who claim to be 'voices of reason!' They reinforce their voice of reason with the use of a term once used to define and explain an undeclared war fought many miles from American shores that finally came to an end almost four decades ago. *The Domino Theory* clarifies the basis and offers support for the rationale of American foreign intelligence operations regarding imposed sanctions involving the economic blockade of Cuba!

For instance, one might ask, 'what would happen if Cuba is opened up by America?' The reasoning might be how many people, how many tourists, would have a desire to travel to the (previously) *forbidden zone* that had suddenly become the passion fruit of the Caribbean? Forty years of impermissible relations and banned travel as well as unauthorized trade would have U.S. tourists viewing Cuba as a hidden Mecca of a lost jewel waiting to be exploited and picked like a ripe fruit. And this much is known to be true.

It'd be forgotten the prohibitions enacted with 'THE embargo' were *ONLY* for American citizens and others subject to the control of the U.S. government. Which to those few might seem as if it were the whole-wide world! However, in reality, it's really just a very small percentage of the globe. The thinking might be, with riches untapped, resources plenty, an economy on the brink of disaster, and a living standard pre-barbaric, deals of a lifetime would be waiting to be had. Americans would see a gold mine waiting to be minted.

In the end however, they'd have to get there before the Cuban government and its people caught up to the rest of the world. The jet-setters would have to make it to the enchanted isle prior to their lifetime deals having gone the dinosaur way of distinction. Their profits gone before they were gotten and money spent without being made. Rising prices for the comforts of home and commodities never before had would be the rule of the day.

In the modern world, influx of knowledge travels at warp speed... knowledge that Cuban objects of art were being sold at cheap prices and transferred for pennies on the dollar! But knowledge is a two way street. It does have a price! One would have to think that at least some Cubans had computers and access to the *Internet*... or its citizenry had relatives living off the isle. Americans would be quick to forget the travel ban was *ONLY* an American embargo... and that the rest of the world didn't share in their politics. Americans would *ONLY* care that their government had terminated a blockade its design had created... resulting in the prevention of which could then happen. The rape and pillage of an untapped resource!

On the other hand, any loss of revenue generated by those lost travelers would be a severe hardship. It could translate into political instability for all the countries those lost travelers weren't traveling to anymore. Even if it was *ONLY* for a very temporary hiatus from the norm... say one year... the American political propaganda armada machine wouldn't, nor could it, survive the disastrous onslaught that could end up being fought on their own turf - the Western hemisphere! Or so those political-think-tankers would have everyone believe. And that is where they'd take us.

The concept would be to take a country like Jamaica! The thought would be about what would happen if they lost half, even a quarter of their tourists for one year. The point would be to point out the effect on Jamaica of losing those tourists. Tourists, Jamaicans had come to rely on to fuel their economy because they wanted to go to Cuba instead. It would result in their not having the dollars spent on travel for hotel, food, car rentals, and airline fares. Or for items like straw hats, baskets... and ganja! The resulting loss in revenue would filter through to the people. They wouldn't have money to spend on food, clothing and other items of necessity. And that could proffer an attitude of political reform. The think-tankers wouldn't have to go too far back in history to reflect on the political instability that country went through in a similar situation.

In the late 1970's, Michael Manley was Prime Minister of Jamaica. The voters switched to Seaga because the government was unable to feed the people. At the time, the change was called an example of the democratic process at work. It was overlooked the change came as a result of the American government pulling U.S. personnel off the island

and withholding foreign aide. Back then, the loss of revenue caused severe economic hardship on the people that brought about the change in government. In the present day, it'd be forgotten the change in political climate was contrived and artificially induced. The only thing that'd be propagandized would be the political (in)stability produced. In the 1970's, it was the plan and the plan worked as designed. But the same wouldn't work to the capitalists' *best* interest in the modern world. Or so it might be thought.

Instead, what might be said would be that political reform most likely wouldn't come through dialogue, but would result in insurgence! Insurgence because political leaders wouldn't want to relinquish control of their country! Nor would they be able to counteract or absorb the loss of tourist dollars not being spent in their country. America would have to rush in to save the day! The question is, would they? Even if they could!

The truth is, it wouldn't matter if America saved the day. America wouldn't be able to withstand the political implications of that kind of image... especially in its own backyard! It wouldn't bode well for our concept of democracy and capitalism! A democratic concept of capitalism that's been spread throughout the world by the leaders of the free world! Democracy and capitalism is the way of the world! Democratic capitalism is the way of the future! Look at what America has to offer the world!

Effects from the pending foreign economic situation wouldn't be confined to countries suffering from those lost tourist dollars either. It'd travel back to America's own front yard and involve America's political system as well. All fifty States and the District of Columbia, Puerto Rico, and every system that uses the dollar as a basis for their currency would be inundated. That'd include Cuba, too! Although, Cuba would benefit from all those U.S. dollars pouring into their banks! Maybe, Cuba would become the paper tiger of the West. How frightening would that be? However, no one in America would be spared!

The basis for those think-tankers' logic would be that no country would be able to buy the same amount of goods from America that American producers had come to rely on... except Cuba! And America doesn't do business with Cuba! There wouldn't be statistical data to compare those figures with, however. Cuba supposedly couldn't buy anything from America prior to the termination of 'THE embargo.' None-the-less, exporting and balance of payment ratios would go through the roof. The argument would be that the resulting effects would create pressure on the foundation of the financial structure of the American dollar. Those effects wouldn't just be felt internally, but globally as well.

There'd be conclusions of dire predictions designed to create fear and confusion. Depression equaling the great depression would be probable and could or, most likely, would cause worldwide political instability. That would be the good news. Because in the new millennium that could prove to be catastrophic! *The Domino Theory*!

The new age we're embarking on brings new forms of weapons for destruction as well as access to those vehicles of death. Each passing day the access grows. The countdown moves shorter every second! Iran, Iraq, somewhere in The Middle East, maybe India, or a South of the Border country will be where the war of all wars will begin. Some lunatic will gravitate toward a power of the will of the people. Only the mission they'll be on will be misdirected. One day, bombs will fly! And death will rein! The world will disappear! Or, in the least, change! And, probably, not for the better! Freedomers will cite the resulting political (in)stability as a basis for civil disobedience and world strife. It'll be a rallying call to arms. War is war!

Maniacal leaders will use religion as a rallying cry. Death will be welcomed. Idiotic followers will accept madness into their realm. It'll be spoon-fed in rhetoric. Death to the infidels! Only the infidels will be those doing the killing. How long will it take to strike back? How many will die before the dying will kill those doing the killing? Bombs will explode. Then, bigger bombs will kill more of those who profess to not want to kill. In the end, Jihad will come to those who seek it. It'll be the end to their end! And, in the end… they'll get what they want. An end to it all! Allah is great!

Those who profess 'THE embargo' is in effect to remove a tyrannical oppressed dictator who enforces his rule by placing those in opposition in jail or simply removing them from this planet know not of what they speak. While some may have been imprisoned or even killed, 'THE embargo' hasn't deterred leadership in the slightest. Even if some are subjected to harsh and evil treatment, it's merely the result of consequences to the means of achieving a desired end. And why should only one be singled out for such activity?

'THE embargo' has been in existence for almost forty years. Yet Castro is still very much in power! Discounting the first thirty years, with Russia an ally, a decade has passed and Fidel isn't looking to depart his perch. Probably a truer end will come through his death. But, until then, little will bring about a change.

To divert tensions away from any conflict of politics, the U.S. government, as it has been quick to point out, uses its own propaganda campaign against the normalization of relations with Cuba. It maintains 'THE embargo' has had the support of the previous seven administrations. Those administrations have covered the past thirty-seven years of political activity. That's not something that can be washed away as if it didn't exist. But, what would I know?

I know of some 3,700 American citizens who had their Cuban cigars confiscated by their government during the past year... from when this story began! I don't know their names, but I know who they are or represent! They fall into one of two groups. Those in one group tried to import hundreds, thousands, maybe even tens of thousands or more of those prized Cubanos. Maybe, they used a boat or, maybe, a plane. But there was clearly an attempt to evade American Customs' laws. Laws stating that not more than one hundred cigars may be included in your exemption!

The main reason freedom was risked or life endangered was due solely to greed! The power of the dollar! Capitalism! How ironic! Now those people have more concerns and deeper worries than to think about getting those stoogies back. Freedom Is Just Another Word For... Nothing Left! And with their freedom gone, they have nothing left!

The other group consists of those I more closely identify with. They're cigar smokers or their mates, friends, and relatives. They're just people who probably went to some foreign land with a good and noble intention. And while traveling abroad, purchased those illicit smokes! Then, they returned to their country with them. So they were Cuban! Some probably felt the risk worth the reward. Others could've thought the reward was worth the risk. But they all thought they weren't doing anything wrong. However, everyone, E-V-E-R-Y-O-N-E, was smuggling just the same.

Then... there was me! I read those government books that said '*Not more than one hundred cigars may be included in one's exemption... if purchase in Cuba.*' I relied on that literature! I obeyed their words... and followed the rules. Rules that the government printed for all to see and read! I didn't spend any money on my Cuban trip. And I only had one hundred cigars.

Most of those 3,700 and some people, like me, weren't arrested. However, they were told they were traitors and threatened with being arrested. Called conspirators against their government, they were treated like criminals. As if they'd killed little babies or slaughtered the innocent. Worse... everyone is doomed to be treated like an *Enemy of the State* every time they cross any border of their country to re-enter the country in the future! I'll bet everyone, when not arrested, didn't let the door hit their butt on the way out! They were just happy to not be going to jail... for cigars.

How would it be explained to their spouses, their bosses? Their life up in smoke! What had they been thinking? Were they crazy?

Every one of those 3,700 and some people received a petition. Their petition that allowed them to invoke the right to contest their right to have those Cuban cigars! But most were just happy to not be going to jail. They only wanted to wash their hands of the situation! The few who had been placed in prison for a violation of law had more to worry about and a lot more to think about than the return of any confiscated cigars. Then... there was me!

I obeyed the law! I was on the cutting edge, maybe. And, maybe, I even walked a fine line. A very fine line indeed! However, I obeyed the law... none-the-less! I read their books... all those government books! I read the books that told me to rely on what I read! I knew **IT'S ONLY CIGARS**, but I wanted them back! It was the principle of the thing!

Stephen thought we needed more information on the subject of 'THE embargo,' so we re-connected to the voice from WestLaw. The voice from beyond was told we were looking for the basis of the statute. The line of communication went silent for a brief minute. Then we heard, "This is amazing. Did you know 31 CFR Chapter V got its origin from the Korean Embargo Act... during the 1950's? It falls under the Wartime Maritime Legislation as well as the National Emergency Act!" Then the voice said, "This is really amazing!" Finally... the voice asked no one, "And they're still enforcing this stuff today?"

Catch-22

***

Stephen spoke with the voice from beyond for a few minutes. When he was finished talking, Stephen reached over his desk and pushed the button that disconnected the dial tone. We looked at each other for a long silent minute. Stephen broke the silence when he asked, "Soo, you were in Cuba in 1968? What was it like?"

I told him a slightly more detailed story of a condensed saga that could've been a ballad from a much longer tale. I briefly told him about how I knew the hijacking was going to happen… before it did. That is, while I knew I didn't know about it beforehand, I told him I had a feeling it was going to happen… before it did. I also told him how, after we landed, everyone on the plane thought those evil communists were going to kill us all! Then, I told him how I almost got arrested twice while on the island… and once upon my return! Finally, I told him how I brought back twenty-five, less one, Cuban cigars.

"My G-d," he screamed! "You were probably one of the first people to bring Cubans into the country after 'THE embargo' began." I nodded my head and a smile swept across my lips. Then he asked, "Slightly ahead of your time, eh?"

"Sometimes it's nice to be a trend-setter."

During the remainder of the time I was in his office, we examined the statute in detail. It was **'THE bible,'** 31 CFR, Chapter V! At some point I told him, "I feel, by the statute, I've complied with the law." It was the lawyer in me speaking. But what did I know?

We looked at every clause in the statute… clause by clause. We looked at what the government cited as their authority to confiscate. We looked at all the clauses in the statute that gave me the right, gives us the right to have those cigars. Clauses the government completely ignores. I recalled the events and conversations that took place on the night of April 18, 1997… well over 4 ½ months earlier. I told my lawyer that I told Customs the cigars were a gift from Andreas! I told him that I told them, and I clearly stated that the entire trip was a gift from Andreas. I also said,

"I want to give them back to him." Then I told Stephen, "My request was completely ignored." And I was told that, 'It didn't matter.'

I didn't have the statute, **'THE bible,'** when I went to Cuba in March 1997. I hadn't read it. Nor did I know its contents... especially about gifts! However, I did tell those G-men agents that the cigars were a gift.

But I was told that it didn't matter. I asked Stephen, "Am I missing something? Look at the statute, **'THE bible.'** Look at 515.544! Tell me if I'm wrong! They act as if it doesn't exist." But, of course, they would. And, they'll continue to do so in the future. That is, unless they're told, ordered, instructed to enforce the statute, every clause, including gifts, by an American judge in an American court of law. The government must be told to obey the law they're empowered to enforce.

515.544 - Gifts of Cuban origin goods.
> *a) Except as stated in Paragraph (b)..., specific licenses are not issued for importation of Cuban origin goods... acquired abroad as gifts by persons entering the United States. **However, licenses are issued upon request for the return of such goods to the donors in countries other than Cuba.***
>
> *b) Specific licenses **are issued** for the importation **directly from** Cuba:*
> *(1)... (2) of goods which are imported by a person entering the U.S., which are claimed to have been acquired in Cuba as a bona fide gift, subject to the conditions that:*
> *(i) The goods are of small value; and*
> *(ii) There is no reason to believe that there is, or has been since July 8, 1963, any direct or indirect financial or commercial benefit to Cuba or 'nationals' thereof from the importation. (39 FR 25317, July 10, 1974; 39 FR 28434, Aug. 7,1974, as amended at 49 FR 27144, July 2, 1984)*

We both read that clause. Then I asked my lawyer, "Am I missing something? Doesn't it say, doesn't 515.544(b)(2)(i) say, gifts are allowed if they're of small value? They defined the word small. It's in the **Know Before You Go** pamphlet. A hundred cigars! And, in the minimum, they have to give Andreas back the cigars. Doesn't 515.544(a) say '*licenses are issued upon request for the return of such goods to donors in countries* *other than Cuba?'* Andreas is the donor from a country other than Cuba! He lives in Jamaica! Contesting the seizure is my request for the return of the cigars to Andreas in Jamaica."

I looked at my shark and continued. "515.544(b)(2)(ii) is a **Catch-22** loophole, for them, because those words can't mean what they say… or there's no such thing as a gift. By writing 515.544, the government meant there to be gifts! However, if (b)(2)(ii) is allowed to mean what they say it'll say, that there can't be any financial or commercial benefit to Cuba or her 'nationals' from the receipt of the gift given, then it could've just said, 515.544 - Gifts of Cuban origin… ARE NOT allowed! NO exceptions! Instead, it was written the way it is… so one could have a Cuban origin gift. Except for (b)(2)(ii)!" And, I just wanted to know, could there ever be anything given where there isn't a benefit… somewhere along the path? From the creation of the object to the giving of the gift!

I quickly answered my own question. "I think not!" I knew a gift was a gift and if it's a gift, then there's NO benefit from the giver to the given. But the same can't be said as to how the gift became a gift. For the giver could've bought the gift. Although, to give a meaning of (b)(2)(ii) that somewhere alone the line that would produce a benefit to a Cuban 'national' somehow… then, there couldn't be a gift! **Catch-22**!

I told Stephen the clause was amended several times since the creation of the statute. "At one time 515.544(b)(2)(i) and (ii) were connected with an 'and.' But, then, the 'and' was changed to an 'or.'" The interpretation of 'or' and 'and' was questioned… in this situation. I felt it meant (i) and (ii) should be considered independently of each other. Like Kierkegaaard's Either / Or thing! And, as long as the gift was of small value, it didn't matter if there was a benefit to Cuba or any 'national' thereof.

However, I knew the 'and' meant (ii) had to be considered regardless the value. And that would mean there couldn't be anything as a gift. That is, if the wording was taken to mean what it said. **Catch-22**!"

I Fought The Law and The Law…

***

The lawyer in my lawyer said, "It appears they'll have to return those cigars." Then, we examined other aspects of the statute, **'THE bible,'** 31 CFR Chapter V, in detail.

I told Stephen I had issues with the enforcement of 'THE embargo.' Issues that tweaked the strings at the heart of the Constitution and the Bill of Rights! Our heritage! I told him I felt the government was infringing upon my rights guaranteed by the 5th Amendment.

Stephen didn't comprehend what I said. So I told him how the government was violating the Due Process Clause of the Equal Protection Guarantee under the law as provided in the 5th Amendment of the U.S. Constitution. Stephen's eyes opened wide! I told him, "And I know a thing or several hundred about how the government can violate the Due Process rights to Equal Protection under the law guaranteed in the 5th Amendment of the Constitution."

***

Time is a dream! Blink and it goes by in a flash. Poof… it's passed you by! Ten years had come and gone, but it only seemed like yesterday. With nothing to do except live with the time, I looked to free my mind in a search for escape. Freedom's just another word for nothing left to lose. And I had nothing left to lose. Hence the search!

I exercised my Constitutional right to a fair trial by law, but was told I had no right to expect anything… especially my right to the law! I was guilty and that was that. Never the two shall meet! Guilt, rights… and freedom!

It didn't matter and was, at most, a minor inconvenience that I was the only one in all the land to have to wait for the Supreme Court to decide an issue that all other courts were divided on. Every Federal District and Appellate Court from Maine to the Pacific Islands, from Alaska to the Virgin Islands, had but one objective when rendering a decision on the Constitutional issue. That objective was best described by His Honor, the honorable District Judge, James Burns of the District of Oregon who wrote in <u>U.S. vs. Belgrad</u>, 694 F. Supp. 1488, 1492 (June 30, 1988), '… inherent was a command to hear arguments promptly and to issue a decision quickly.'

It took time to find the fact(s) that I was truly alone. Only my court and Judge deemed it tolerable to not make any decision regarding my fate. Having nothing but time gave me the time to find I'd been treated differently than everyone else, when confronted with the same exact issue of law. I studied the rule of law and researched how history prevented that which had occurred. Then I sued! But, in the end, it didn't matter.

After the clock ticked all its tocks, I was sent on my merry way. Packing resentment and anger as well as frustration, I was awash in disbelief that the justice system harbored no justice… only retribution. This case was different however. It was a civil matter… not criminal! And, I wasn't alone!

There were thousands who were in the same boat as I. Only most, if any, didn't know it! Not to mention were the hundreds of thousands and, maybe, millions who were being persecuted unequally under the law. Even if it didn't touch them directly!

***

Stephen didn't understand how my Due Process rights of Equal Protection under the 5th Amendment had been undermined. I mentioned the clause, 515.560(a), in the statute and Stephen looked at it… while I read it out loud.

515.560: *Travel-related transactions to, from, and within Cuba by persons subject to U.S. jurisdiction.*
(a) *The travel-related transactions listed in paragraph (c) of this section are on a case-by-case basis for a specific license for travel within this section and may be authorized either by a general license or related to the following activities (see the referenced sections for **general** and specific licensing criteria):*
(1) Family visits
(2) Official business of the U.S. government, foreign governments, and certain intergovernmental organizations;
(3) Journalistic activity;
(4) Professional research;
(5) Educational activities

    (6) Religious activities;

    (7) Public performances, clinics, workshops, athletic and other competitions, and exhibitions;

    (8) Support for the Cuban people;

    (9) Humanitarian projects;

    (10) Activities of private foundations or research or educational institutes;

    (11) Exportation, importation, or transmission of information or informational materials;

    (12) Certain export transactions that may be considered for authorization under existing Department of Commerce regulations and guidelines with respect to Cuba or engaged in by U.S. owned or controlled foreign firms.

I questioned why those few select could go, but others couldn't. I told Stephen I thought the law was for everyone. E-V-E-R-Y-O-N-E! Not just for the select few. Stephen heard me say I had trouble understanding why Cuban 'nationals,' whom the law seemed to be written for, were allowed to go to Cuba provided they applied for a visa. But U.S. born citizens were prevented from traveling there, except for those select few.

I said, "If a law is written, then the law is for everyone. Not just some! A law can't be written for some... and not others. And those some are a minor few at that!" I told Stephen, "The Constitution and Bill of Rights says everyone MUST be treated equally."

I continued, "A law for some and not others, especially when the others are the majority, is not equal treatment under the law. It's a violation of the Due Process Clause of the Equal Protection guarantee under the law... as provided in the 5th Amendment of the U.S. Constitution."

I questioned the wording in the statute. Where it said... support for the Cuban people and humanitarian projects were permissible. My trip to Cuba was support for the Cuban people AND should have been considered a humanitarian project. Stephen rolled his eyes when I said what I said. But I knew he knew the intent of my meaning. His meaning was that the government wasn't going to accept my interpretation of the wording. Nor would the judges in their courts!

Then, I raised another issue about the legality of the law itself. I said, "If a law is based on a wartime situation and the National Emergency

Act... and those conditions don't exist... than it would seem the law shouldn't exist either." I told Stephen, "I could understand the situation if it was thirty years earlier. But in the present political environment, it seems passé.

Stephen's head nodded and I continued, "If no condition exists for a law to be in existence, the law should automatically be repelled. It shouldn't be forced on a populace to have to contest the change of what doesn't exist." I also told Stephen that I thought it was like prohibition back in the 1930's. Stephen seemed to be digesting what I said because his eyebrows rose higher than I ever saw them rise before. While it started to make sense to him, I could tell he thought I was so far out to lunch that I missed breakfast and dinner too.

Finally I questioned the clause, 515.307, certain persons **unblocked**.

    (a) *The following persons are hereby licensed as unblocked 'nationals:'*
    (1) Any person resident in or organized under the laws of a jurisdiction in the U.S. or the authorized trade territory who or which has never been a designated 'national;'
    (2) Any individual resident in the U.S. who is not a specially designated 'national;'
    (b) *Individual 'nationals' of a designated country who take up residence in the authorized trade territory may apply to the Office of Foreign Assets Control to be specifically licensed as unblocked 'nationals.'*

I wanted to know what **unblocked** 'national' meant and who were designated as such. My rational was that since I had never been designated as either a *designated 'national'* or a *specially designated 'national,'* I should fall within the group of those who were licensed as such... (a)(1) and (2)! Stephen didn't know what it meant, but said he would find out. Time would tell if he would or not.

I finished my tirade on another equal protection of the law issue. I said, "This clearly shows how the law is not being uniformly enforced. Cubans can go to Cuba... provided they were never designated as either a d*esignated 'national'* or a s*pecially designated 'national.'*" But being an American born citizen, I'm being discriminated against. And that is against everything that is American... as well as the law."

A week later Stephen had another conversation with Beth when she told him that the cigar petition, my petition, was being denied, turned down and rejected! And she told him the reason(s)! It was the same things she'd said to him the first time they talked! She said, "An official written response will be forthcoming." Then she said, "You should receive notification in the mail for the basis of denial within the following seven days."

Stephen said Beth seemed somewhat stoic and not at peace with herself. I couldn't have cared less. Stephen said she was slightly beside herself when she said we'd be receiving the rejection letter in the mail... within the week. But she also asked us to not appeal the decision. Apparently, it appeared an appeal would cause two cases to have been filed with the court. I questioned what that meant. Only Stephen said we should wait for the response before making a decision about what we should do.

We waited another four weeks. One month! Every time I called my lawyer, I got the same answer. "Haven't heard anything yet!" Then, one day the phone rang... at the house of a friend of mine who I was staying with.

Balthazar, King of the Gypsies, spoke into the mouthpiece for a few brief minutes. Then he handed me the phone and said, "Here... it's for you."

I put the phone to my ear and heard the voice say it was my lawyer. Then I heard the voice say, "We've finally received the official position on your denial. We've got all the gory facts!"

The following day, I walked into Stephen's office. His secretary gave me a photocopy of the government rejection letter. I read the single page response. At the bottom, I noted that the lady named Beth signed the letter. She said my petition was denied because, although I relied on what I read that was printed in the government literature, had I formally, or verbally, contacted the government prior to going to Cuba, the government would've told me that I couldn't go or do what I did. She stated it didn't matter that I didn't know I had to contact the government to find out I couldn't go to Cuba or do what I did. And it didn't matter the government never told anyone in their literature that contacting the government was mandatory. I was shocked!

On the other hand, I knew the government had to take that position. What? Allow Americans to go to Cuba! Because if they allowed me to go, then they'd have to allow everyone to go! However, I did find it interesting the government wanted to change the issue of my petition. Because the issue of my petition wasn't the issue of my petition that the government said it was when they addressed the issue of my petition.

The government literature said if no money was spent on a trip to Cuba then no violation of prohibition or restriction would occur. Although, the government literature didn't exactly say that, what it did say could only be interpreted to mean what it said. I didn't spend a penny in Cuba and I hadn't planned on spending any money either! Without the spending of money in Cuba, no regulation or prohibition monitored or controlled by the Office of Foreign Assets Control was violated. Therefore, no requirement was needed to contact the government! As the words read... 'should...' not 'had' to.

The government literature also said a limited amount of cigars, one hundred, as stated in the **Know Before You Go** pamphlet, may be imported into the U.S. It could be included in one's exemption. I imported exactly one hundred Cuban cigars. Not more and not less!

The government pamphlet, **Know Before You Go**, stated that if one hundred cigars were included in the exemption every citizen is allowed when entering the country, the articles that fall within that exemption could be verbally declared. I verbally declared all the cigars in my possession!

The statute, 31 CFR 515.544, said gifts were an exemption from the *generalized* confiscation policy of the statute. The trip and one hundred cigars were gifts from Andreas.

The statute, 31 CFR 515.544 (a), said gifts were to be returned to a donor from any country other than Cuba. Andreas was the donor! He didn't live in Cuba. Nor had he ever! Andreas was a German... who lived in Jamaica!

The statute, 31 CFR 515.544 (b)(2)(i), said gifts were to be returned to the importer... provided the gift was of limited value. The government **Know Before You Go** pamphlet defined limited as one hundred, and the statute defined limited as not more than one hundred dollars... in the value of the country where purchased! I had one hundred cigars.

The cost to Andreas for those one hundred cigars was less than eighty dollars. Everything was a gift! I didn't spend any money! And I was the importer!

The answer given to my petition also stated the government relied on, in their position of denial, the exact same portion of my passport I relied on. It was the sentence that said, '*Importation of Cuban goods is **generally** prohibited, except for... limited goods imported directly as accompanied baggage.*' What were they trying to say? It was hard to understand. What did the words **generally** and *except* mean? I imported those cigars '*as accompanied baggage!*' Was I missing something? By the government's own definition... the amount of those cigars were limited!

The last reason cited for the basis of rejection was the reason that really got to me! It's hard to understand why anyone would say something they know is so completely disingenuous as to never be plausible. Do they, the government, really think we, the people, are as stupid as they think we are? Do their minds really work? I told Beth that I flat out admitted to those Customs people I'd gone to Cuba when asked. When I told her that I went to Cuba, she gave me the same response I get from everyone... when they're told I went there. What? You went to Cuba? Why? What was it like? To say I wouldn't have said what I said when I said I went to Cuba was out to lunch. But they did!

The entire basis of importing Cuban cigars in the first place was based on the fact that products of Cuban tobacco were allowed... '*if purchased in Cuba.*' To say it any other way or that I wouldn't have acknowledged it when I went through Customs was total and complete insanity, lunacy... and stupidity. Then again, not having anything to work with, they had to come up with something. But what they came up with was off the wall and completely disingenuous. Was I missing something? It took the government, and their vastly under-intelligent legal-beagle minds, over one hundred and twenty-five days to come up with that answer! Couldn't they have said what they said in thirty days... as required by the law?

A Mission From G-D

***

Air Jamaica offered a super cheap airfare to Jamaica. I couldn't refuse! There was only one problem! The reservation and purchase of my ticket had to be by a certain date... and that date had already arrived. Needless to say, I made plans to return to Jamaica and begin the next phase of the Colossal Cuban Cohiba Cigar Caper. Soon, those five words would get shortened to the five 'C' thing... because it was too complicated to remember!

My flight was to leave within the week. I told my lawyer I was headed back down south... and for him to get ready for the next case. The real issue of the cigar thing! I also told him that I was going back to Cuba. But I told him that I'd do it right this time. That was... I was going to do it as it stated to do it in the statute, **'THE bible,'** 31 CFR.

Six months had come and gone since my last foray into *the forbidden zone*. It was a requirement of the statue! Actually the requirement was that six months had to pass between the importation of anything from *the forbidden zone*. Not with traveling there!

While in America, I attended several funerals for some people who once claimed to be a friend. One of the funerals was for a shark who I used to know in another life... many lives before. Back then, he professed to be a friend. But I knew better! His funeral brought a lot of old faces together. Faces I hadn't seen in years. At least several lifetimes... and, maybe, longer!

A girlfriend who I lived with for a year in one of both of our previous lifetimes some twenty-eight years earlier approached me. She questionably said my name. "David?" Looking at her face, and I looked directly into her eyes, I knew I had one of those dumb blank looks on my face. And when I just stood there not knowing who she was, she told me I should know who she was. "David, we lived together for a year."

"Saaaaaaaannnnnnnnnndyyyyy???" How embarrassing to spend a year of your life, in any lifetime, with someone and have no idea who they are! To my defense, I've discovered, over the years, that I usually had no idea who it was I was with mentally. I've also found that's true even when the past becomes the present. Let alone, when the present becomes the future!

At the funeral, I saw more than many sharks. However, there was only one flesh eating fish I was looking for. Shortly before the services began, I saw the face I went there to see. "Hello Richard!"

Richard and I knew each other from the good old days... over twenty-nine years before. Richard had saved me on more than several occasions. We'd been friends also. His hair was thinner and he was a bit heavier. But, otherwise, Richard hadn't really changed all that much. At least, not as much as Sandy had! Good G-d, Lord Almighty... I wouldn't have known who she was had she not told me who she was.

When the services ended, I watched the people mingle. Richard and I got together. We were talking when his partner approached. Richard introduced us! The partner said he'd heard of me. He asked what I was doing these days. I told the partner not to believe what he'd heard... and only half of what he'd seen. Then I told Richard and his partner what I was doing these days. But they didn't seem to believe it. I asked if they knew anyone into or anything about Customs and Importation law. Richard shrugged his shoulders and said I was the third person in the past week to ask him that question.

Richard's ride back to the city was ready. He told me to give him a call later in the week. He said, "We'll have lunch. We can talk about your case in a much better environment." Then he said, "Bring the literature! I want to see what you're talking about."

I knew he thought I was crazy! No! I knew Richard knew it! What he said or thought was just re-confirmation of that fact. I guess it's nice to know some things never change. Nor does time dilute their substance. For Cuban cigars, while vogue and in style, were definitely illegal to have... or import. Or were they?

Three days passed before I called Richard. We made an appointment to meet the next day at lunch. Twelve o'clock! Noon! He was in the same office in the same building he'd been in since I knew him way back when. It was nice to know some things never changed. The receptionist announced my name and told me to go back to his office. She started to give me directions. But I told her I knew the way.

Only two short days before our meeting, Princess Diana crashed and burned in an auto accident in France. It was the talk of the day. The night before our meeting, Richard was on the regional TV news. He's the local legal eagle used to discuss foreign law. In this case, it was the legal exposure regarding her death! Richard is probably *the* foremost legal authority in America on matters of foreign law.

His office was as chaotic as I remembered it. It was nice to know some things never changed. As I walked into his office, he looked up from his desk and asked, "So what's this about Cuban cigars?" Deja Vu!

And it was unanimous! Everyone who read all of that information came to the same conclusion. And it was unanimous!

Richard looked at my passport and said, "Yeah, OK! I see where you're going. But, what else have you got?" Then I showed him the **Know Before You Go** pamphlet, opened to page six. He read it!

"WHAT," he said very loudly! Then, he read further. Afterward, we had the exact same conversation everyone who reads that literature and I have. Finally, Richard looked at the law, the statute, **'THE bible,'** 31 CFR Chapter V.

I asked, "Have you ever read this stuff?"

He answered, "Of course not! No one ever reads this stuff."

He read section 515.544, Gifts of Cuban Origin Goods, and said, "It would appear those cigars have to be returned." Next, he read all the sections I referred him to. I asked him if the sections and words used meant what they appeared to mean. He said, "It would appear so."

He was beyond completely blown away too. Then he said, "You know, this is going to be very costly." He wanted to know if I really thought the government would allow me to undo 'THE embargo.' Thirty some years of totalitarian suppression! He said, "They'll fight you tooth and nail. They'll take this to the Supreme Court… if they have to!" Then, he said there was a magazine I needed to get.

I said, "Cigar *Aficionado*!"

Richard said, "Yes, that's the one. It'll be a political e`` ial publishing coupe for them. They'll want to help because they'll sell more magazines. This'll help! But you need to get to them to help you... or you're dead!"

Richard was told that was where I intended to go... eventually. Richard suggested in no uncertain terms that eventually might ought to be sooner than later. That was, if I was interested in pursuing it through the press. I told him, "I found their sight on the Net. And I've read the magazine."

I told him I'd seen articles about the owner and editor as well as numerous articles he'd written. I said, "Yeah, I know I have to get to the are we smoking man, but I have to wait until the time is right. This has to be played right. He has to be approached the right way."

Then, I expressed my belief that I shouldn't go to him myself. I said, "I'll need a messenger!" I need someone to introduce us." But, Richard expressed his belief that I just needed to get to him... and his magazine.

Leaving Richard's office I remembered that I always felt good leaving his office. This time was no different! It was nice to know some things never changed. He always made me feel better. When I left his office that day, I felt better about the cigar thing. I'm neurotic, but I think everyone is neurotic. What separates us is only the manner we manifest the neurosis. However, my neurosis was visually manifesting itself. It was nice to know Richard agreed with me. That he saw this cigar situation how I did. It was also nice to know that Richard let me believe I wasn't totally out to lunch. Or dinner!

Would that be enough? Hell no! I once heard it said that the road to hell is paved with good intentions. I knew the path I was on. And I knew I was heading directly toward the gates to purgatory!

I was on a mission! I thought... from G-d! My last three days in America were spent rushing around getting the things done I needed to get done. Halloween was approaching. The time of year children, any age, get dressed up with make-up and masks. Less than a month later, it'd be Thanksgiving. A date everyone gives thanks for all they have.

I thanked G-d I was heading down to Jamaica. And somewhere in the back of my mind was a plan to prepare my plan to import one hundred of Fidel's finest into America. But, the next time I'd do it, I'd do it the right way! It was going to be by the law! My plan was to use their words… against them!

Negril has always been a place of retreat for me. This story began less than two years after moving there. Psychological repercussions of a major operation and the recent extraction from a personal situation, as well as a desire to live in the warmth of a tropical climate created a change in location from where I was living! Freedom from mental restriction, plus the pursuit of getting a life or of being at a place in my life where it seemed as good a time as any, produced a change in my living standard. Being released from confinement wasn't the mental freedom I sought. The physical freedom I wanted was to free my mind and spirit from the bonds and chains of suppressed existence. Tyranny is tyranny!

Having little money and no means by which to employ myself mattered not in my decision! I left America for the Caribbean… shortly after snipping the noose from around my neck that the government called supervision and having a tumor removed from my throat. I observed with interest how a change in lifestyle produced a change in mental well being. And that produced a change in attitude that greatly improved my approach to restoring a long lost and departed spirit. But I've never thought of myself as a writer or as my mother had said… a revolutionary.

Life is a paradox! Every time I call my friend Balthezar on the phone I'm reminded of that fact. For that statement is on his telephone answering system message tape. Life is a paradox! And my life mirrored paradox.

The country I moved to is a paradox… as is the country of my birth! I moved to Negril due to its beauty, ideal serenity, and perceived sense of tranquillity as well as climate. In addition, is a constant movement and influx of people! However, Negril is a paradox… serene on the surface! The constant influx of people, a transient movement of a beach community, and the ebb and flow of the movement of the water produces a retard-like mentality bordering on a Groundhog Day type of life. That in itself is a kind of paradox.

Little growth in mental stimulation is ever achieved in Negril… let alone Jamaica! The occasional storm is worshipped because it offers change. Not only from activity, but with everyone's conversation as well! However, in an ironic sort of way, the easiness is therapeutic!

The beach is seven miles long. It seems to never end! The water makes a rhythmic motion. Each wave is collected and merged with the one before. The constant three-inch wave of water rolls over the white sand before slowly cascading to a stop. Add the receding mass of its base and all movement creates a hypnotic veil with one's mind. It's like a facial screen that lulls thoughts of reality to fade into a drug induced memory.

Everyday, I made it a ritual to walk where the water meets the finely grained earth. Walking the beach on my daily strolls, my thoughts consistently drift back to another time. My last night in Philadelphia on my last trip there! One lone tape recording keeps the accuracy of my memory honest. I sat with a seer, a mystic, and a fortune-teller. One of the cities' most well known psychics!

Balthezar is a King of the Gypsies. I'm not sure how many Kings Gypsies have, but Balthezar said he's one... and psychics don't lie! Neither do Gypsies! Balthezar told me my destiny the night he gave me some knowledge about the future... when he read his Tarot cards. But I've heard it said... '*a little knowledge can be dangerous*!'

Balthezar is a tall, bearded, rail thin American male of German descent with long brown hair. He looks to the stars to see what's on earth... and he doesn't use a looking glass. He said, "Shuffle the cards and keep them facing the same way I gave them to you. Otherwise, you'll change what is and it will not be what it was." I wouldn't want that! The cards reminded me of a deck of playing cards, except they're bigger and more difficult to shuffle. And every card is a picture that tells a different story.

A topic was required for the reading. The Cuban cigar thing was chosen to be the topic. Balthezar is a skeptic of the whole affair. He didn't understand the purpose. The reading was just as much for him as it was for me! The cards were placed in their place. I was advised, so said the cards, to seek out those who'd be of benefit and who'd benefit monetarily from an end to 'THE embargo.' The cards also said that I should seek out those who'd like to do business with Cuba. He read further! I was told to be seductive, but humble. Or was it humble, but seductive?

Suddenly, the mystic stopped his reading. He placed both his hands on his face and slowly moved them down to his chin... where he grabbed his beard. And in a louder than normal voice said, "My G-d, David! Do you know what you've done?"

Of course, I knew! The reason I had the reading was to see what the stars thought. I knew an almost four-decade-old distorted effort, something that millions of dollars and probably more than that had been spent to maintain, was turned into a joke. No! A farce of a joke! And I was standing at the humor door!

A political ideology was taken. A fervent movement backed by less than only a few million ardent followers was transformed into trivial merriment. 'THE embargo,' America's basis for economic sanctions against Cuba had been reduced down to the right to smoke a stoogie. But it wasn't just any cigar. It was a Cubano! And I had raised 'THE embargo' of Cuban cigars up out of the coffers of their humidors... where those smokes were able to see the light of humor. I mean, *IT'S ONLY CIGARS*!

"My G-d," he said. Then... he added, "*IT'S ONLY CIGARS*! I mean, *IT'S ONLY CIGARS*!"

The cost of a ticket from Montego Bay to Havana was seven thousand seven hundred and seventy-seven dollars. Jamaican dollars! Three times a week, Air Jamaica flew between those two cities. To me, it was just two more flight segments toward a free trip anywhere Air Jamaica flew. And I was a frequent flyer member! I hung up the phone after writing down my confirmation code.

My trip was set. I was on my way back to Havana. It was time to begin the next phrase. Only this time, it was going to be the right way. It was going to be by the way of the statute. And by the word of the law! This time, it was going to be under 515.560(g). I was going as a fully sponsored or hosted traveler.

Section 515.560 - *Certain transactions incident to travel to and within Cuba.*
(g): *For purposes of this section, all necessary transactions involving fully sponsored or hosted travel to, from, and within Cuba are authorized, provided:*

> *(1) No person subject to the jurisdiction of the United States shall make any payment or transfer any property or provide any service to Cuba or a Cuban 'national' in connection with such travel; and the travel is not aboard a direct flight between the United States and Cuba...*
>
> *(2) Travel shall be considered fully sponsored or hosted for purposes of this section, notwithstanding a payment by the person subject to the jurisdiction of the United States for transportation to and from Cuba, provided the carrier furnishing the transportation is not a Cuban 'national.'*

Section 515.560(g)(1) and (2) *specifically* authorizes travel to Cuba, provided the travel is NOT on a Cuban vessel (airline or boat), the crews aren't Cuban 'nationals,' and (if an airline) the flight isn't directly between America and Cuba. So, if one flew on Air Jamaica from Jamaica to Cuba and the crew was Jamaican, the Office of Foreign Assets Control or Customs or any other government official couldn't say one couldn't go to Cuba because the statute prohibited it. In fact, the statute *specifically* authorizes it! And, in authorizing it, the statute, if not explicitly then implicitly, implies a license has been granted for such travel and all that goes with the travel.

If it was said Cuban cigars could only be imported into the United States if they were acquired in Cuba on a licensed visit, an argument for claiming the return of any cigars confiscated was the fact that the travel was authorized and the cigars were acquired in Cuba! To wit: 515.560(g)... the authorized trip section, by the statute, to Cuba. And under 515.544 where cigars were acquired as a gift! I knew the government wouldn't like it. But words HAVE meaning.

515.560(g) can only be interpreted to mean what the words in that clause say! The words mean travel to Cuba is authorized if one doesn't travel abroad a Cuban vessel, use a Cuban 'national' crew, or travel directly between America and Cuba. It seems clear that people who travel to Cuba, authorized by 515.560(g), must also follow the rules as those who enforce the rules must obey what the rules allow. It's also clear that travel to Cuba via fully sponsored or hosted travel is *specifically* defined as an approved way of travel.

The government probably won't like it. Cuban 'nationals' probably will hate it, and the *Mafia* probably will detest it. But they're all obligated to obey the words of the statute, just as every American citizen is required to adhere to those same words. However, the federal court system is monitored by judges who are government employees! To forget that is simply ignorant! Who pays the judges' salaries? Every check written is from the coiffeurs of the Treasury Dept. of the federal government! Only the government enforces and interprets the statute how they want… with no rhyme or reason for what it says. Hypocrisy is hypocrisy! And hypocrisy is alive and well in the heartland of today's American politics.

The law is clear… very clear indeed! Travel to Cuba is sanctioned provided it's done in a prescribed manner. If it's done in the prescribed manner, then all spending rules must be adhered including the purchase of merchandise intended for importation into America. That was why a trip back to Cuba was planned. That was how my trip back to Cuba was planned. That was the way I was going to import Cuban cigars into America. At least, one hundred cigars anyway! And not any more than that in any six-month period!

There were three reasons why I wanted to do this. The first two were that *Truth* and *Justice* lay at the core of every American's thoughts. The third reason was that every American had the right to smoke a Cuban without fear of reprisal, in the form of oppression, from their government. That's the core of my basic belief system! Anyhow, **IT'S ONLY CIGARS**! Not to mention was the dinner and The Raffle! And, maybe, a book or a movie somewhere along the way!

I'm also tired of being held a prisoner of war on behalf of the politicizing of a populace for a land that isn't our land. It isn't even our war! While I have compassion for and can emphasize with the plight of those displaced souls from their land, our land was never meant to mean them and us. Their struggle isn't our battle to keep what was fought to have the right of. Nor should our rights be a basis for their political encroachment of those rights. Should it be our duty to hold others accountable for their actions, when we aren't held accountable for ours? And, besides, I couldn't figure out just who had died… and put us in charge?!

What had me thinking the most about it all was that should we be allowed to determine another sovereign's politics, then it would seem right that they should be allowed to determine ours! And I wouldn't want that! But, a more salient point is, whoever said our way was their way? For while people should be allowed to chose their own path, the hope would be that the path chosen would be the one that would include the option to choose their choice. Besides, who are we to force our way on them? Because if we force our way on them, we're no different than those we condemn for doing that to others. After all, tyranny is tyranny!

What do I hope to gain from this? First, I believe the first obligation of every citizen is to question their government. Tyranny, wearing any label, using any logo, going by any name, is tyranny all the same. I once heard it said that park sausage came in many different wrappers, many different packages, many different sizes, and many different shapes. And it's called by many different names. But park sausage is still pork sausage! No government, be it my government or any government, wants anyone to advocate an elevation of human consciousness. *Specifically*, as it relates to the government.

People are conditioned to do as instructed, programmed not to question authority, and told to obey without question... the government! To that end, America is no different than Russia or East Germany during the height of their oppression during the cold war.

The populace is taught that to question authority is a destructive anti-governmental, liberal, left-winged threat against order. And the structure itself! Those who have been and who are now our leaders have told us it's bad. Newscasters downplay protesters as knuckleheads and anti-government types. Their meaning is that Thomas Jefferson, Ben Franklin, George Washington, John Adams, John Quincy Adams and the like were anti-government types. The most rebellious of rebels! Revolutionaries all! I can only wonder where America would be today, and it might not have ever been... let alone what it is today, if not for those revolutionary type rebel hero's. So is rebellion bad?

It took people who questioned authority, who questioned their government, in their day, to make the American government the government it is today. So what makes them bad?

Today, to the American government, they're just bad! Today, more than likely, George Washington, Thomas Jefferson, and the rest would be put in prison for treason. The American government would prosecute them all because they'd be a threat to the same government that they helped create! Today, the American government would put in jail all those responsible for it's very own existence... for treason! Long live hypocrisy! It's alive and well in American politics!

America has become what it fought against. We're a country fighting what it isn't so it can become what it wasn't intended to be. That's one of the reasons why I'm doing this!

I see tyranny wearing a democratic logo with a capitalistic shield! I see a hidden czar, a faceless tyrant, and a nameless entity annexing authority... telling all to obey. But to obey what? In this case, it's a law that shouldn't exist. In the least, it's one that makes no sense! Why? Because THEY said so!

Then again, maybe, some green can grow in my garden. AHhh, yes, the truth comes out! I'm not so much the altruistic soul I might appear to be. This is the age of a new dawn. The new millennium is upon us. This is America! This is capitalism at its best. A book! Maybe, a movie! To know any more... you're gonna have to '*buy the rights*!'

The endless washing away of my thoughts by the countless waves occurred as I endlessly walked the beach. I've been told to write. I've a certain ability to captivate people when telling stories of experiences from throughout my life. I personally thought them boring. But what do I know? This IS my story. This is a story about America. This is a story about some American people. And, this is the story of how a nice... and, maybe, not so nice... Jewish boy from Villanova, Pennsylvania became enmeshed in the whole politically incorrect principle of protesting a thirty-something-year long struggle with America's neighbor to her South. Cuba!

Vintage Russian-built aircraft... Cubano Air. 'The only way to fly!'

The Partigas cigar factory in Havana.

The Havana skyline... from El Moro

Our hero, 'Havana Dave,' enjoys the view... and a fine Cuban Montecristo A.

A colorful El Moro Guard.

The cannon balls ARE real! So is the cannon

The pre-revolutionary line-up of imported American luxury cars in old Havana.

All proudly cared for with a simonized gleam...

and barely kept running with catch as catch can parts from other global trade tanks to lawn mowers.

Havana Dave in a meeting with his Man in Havana

A close up of the negotiations! Can anyone read lips?

Havana Dave making the great escape after the deal... in a Spanish Rick Shaw. Yet another form of transportation in this Island City.

Public transportation in Havana... 'The Camel'.

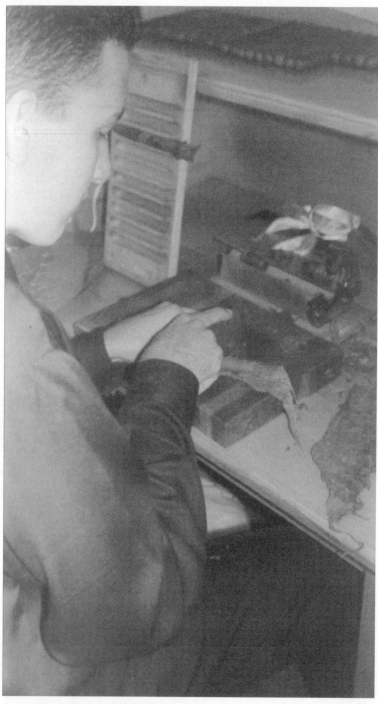

A true art... rolling cubanos

The process continues with

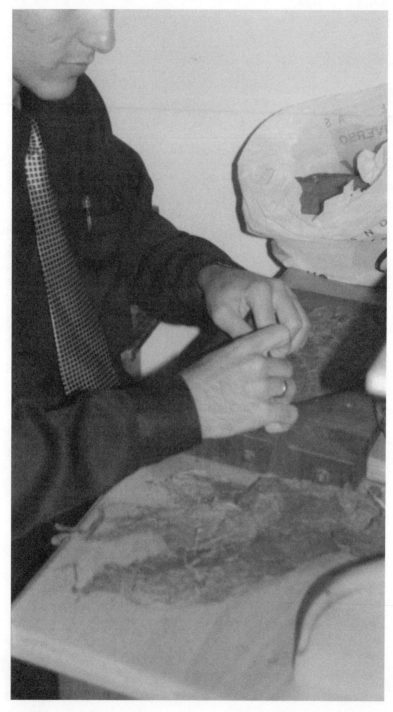

More of the process

Ah, the stories she could tell... if only she would.

The streets of Havana are always filled with music and the warmth of the beautiful smiles of the people.

Day or night... the music continues.

Colorful vintage costumes of a simpler time... and the beauty of Havana women has Havana Dave swept away.

Chapter 2
The Case Build-up

Back To My Future

***

While gazing out a window at thirty thousand feet above a city full of brotherly love, the full moon hit my eye like a big pizza pie... with lots of extra cheese. I've heard that's amore, but I was more interested in the cheese! The pilot's voice announced our arrival and within the next few minutes everyone was asked to fasten their seat belts and to put their seat backs up. The flight crew took one final walk through the cabin to make sure everyone had complied with the FAA regulations the pilot announced. I sat in my seat with my carry-on bag under the seat in front of me. Inside my bag was a cache of one hundred Cubanos... all Cohibas! Thinking back to my last episode with U.S. Customs in Philadelphia, I thought about what might take place within the coming hour. Time would tell! Then, I flashed back to my last foray into *the forbidden zone*. It had been quite an adventure.

Prior to leaving Negril, I called the shark to notify him that I'd be returning and asked him to be on call! One never knew what to expect. However, I expected the worse! He said to call if I needed help. Only I couldn't help think that he was more interested in the cache than my freedom. And it wasn't like I hadn't been there and done it before! But this time, it would be different... because I had been there and done it before. So ignorance wouldn't be an excuse... not that it'd been before. It was a statement heard in every law class... *ignorance is no excuse for the law.* Thousands of thoughts were racing through my mind at a warp speed of light when suddenly I flashed back to how I got to where I was. Even if no one else thought it... it had been quite an adventure.

***

Minding my own business, I was laying on the sand enjoying the sun... a cool Red Stripe in one hand and a cold piece of lobster in the other. Suddenly I saw a familiar face walking up the beach. Wearing a smile from ear to ear, she saw I recognized her. As she approached, she said, "David... everyone in Negril says you're the man to talk to about Cuba." Then, she kissed my cheek and said, "Hello... dear!" We dispensed with the usual polite formalities. But when I asked what she wanted to know about that island, she said, "I want to go! Will you take me? I'll pay!"

The following day we made reservations with a local tour operator who specialized in trips to Cuba. Two days later we were flying to Havana and I couldn't stop wondering about the alternatives. While America celebrated independence, in Jamaica... it was just another day in Margarita-villa. And in Havana, few know of freedom, except those far and few-between freedom-fighters who had come together to ride into their capital with a revolution's trophy dangling from the end of their pistols on the Eve of the 1959 New Year's celebration... almost forty years before.

It must've been quite a party at the Hotel Nacional. The interruption came when the loud speaker was grabbed by one of the revolutionaries who spoke into the mike, "Ladies and gentlemen... please excuse the interruption in festivities. The revolution has arrived! Now on with the party!" But, from the time we left to go to Cuba, it seemed more like a series of comic relief than a serious relief of comedy.

To enter Jamaica from America, U.S. citizens need only proof of citizenship (birth certificate and pictured driver's license). But to enter Cuba, a U.S. passport is required... even though Cuba's Immigration service doesn't stamp it. And Cuba doesn't stamp any U.S. passport unless requested because that'd be a signal to U.S. government officials that travel was conducted in *the forbidden zone.*

I never thought to ask if she had the proper travel documents and the tour operator never mentioned it. To me, out of sight meant out of mind... until the Cuban Immigration officer asked her to produce her credentials. She showed him proof of U.S. citizenship, but he just shook his head and spoke something under his breath... something in Spanish. I could only assume he said, "Damn Yankees!" It was obviously not a reference to some big apple ball club or a play long ago played out. Then, he left us at his station while he went off in search of who knew what for what seemed like forever.

Eventually, he returned and said she wasn't going to be admitted into the country because she didn't have the proper travel documents. In a polite manner, a protest was lodged because to do otherwise wasn't a wise thing... especially since Americans didn't have an Embassy to protest their unwise action(s) to. And if an Embassy had existed, the employees would only have asked why we were there. Then, they would probably have told us that we weren't allowed to be there. So I politely questioned their policy… and it was a good thing that *por tres anos éstudie Espanol en mi escuela.*

The Immigration officer wanted to hear little of what I had to say. I was told to enter the country and the girl was asked to wait in another area. And he said she'd have to wait in that area… until she left their island. What could I do? I told her not to worry… I'd figure something out. But inside my brain it was panic-city time. We separated as I passed through the Customs checkpoint. Immediately upon entry, I came upon a Havanatur tour operator who appeared from out of nowhere. He said he'd been waiting for us to enter the country. When I told him our problem he said, "No problem!" It was an universal language! He took her Havanatur tour travel coupons in his hand and walked into an area where travelers weren't allowed.

A very long twenty minutes later, he re-entered the area of the airport I was in. She was following… close behind. He said it was a good thing that we purchased those tour coupons because without them she would have remained in the airport until the next flight left to go back to Jamaica… three days later. That would've been a real bummer! And there wouldn't have been any alternative… because there wasn't another flight back to Jamaica for three days.

We boarded the Havanatur tour bus and were dropped off at our hotel. The tour operator said he'd see us the following day. Then, he told us to have a good day and to enjoy the nightlife. After we got into our hotel room the girl said she wanted to take a shower and clean off. I told her that I'd *soon come back.* It was a Jamaican term, but since Jamaica and Cuba claimed to be sister island nations it somehow seemed appropriate. And I heard the door close behind me as I walked out into the corridor.

I skipped down the steps that led out the lobby and onto the walkway one story below. At the intersection of the street and the hotel access, I decided to head down the street. No sooner had I traveled three feet off the property when a familiar face approached and said, "¡Hola, David! ¿Usted reguese aqui?" I couldn't believe it! And I wondered whether Paco lived up on the corner. But I knew better because I'd been to his house on my previous trip… with Andreas.

When Andreas and I last set foot in *the forbidden zone,* he actually found Paco on our first day there. He wanted to take a walk around Havana before the sunset. At the time, Andreas was off in search of a higher puff than any Cohiba could provide. As it turned out, the fumes he inhaled didn't soar too high.

On this trip, after the girl and I checked into our hotel, I needed anything that could calm my racing nerves. The circumstances surrounding our arrival... actually hers... had me reved up. At the time, I didn't know where anything could be found, but I knew if that place was like any other place something would rise up from somewhere. Then, all of a sudden, Paco appeared on the scene. To both my pleasure and displeasure, I found nothing had changed from my previous trip. But it was nice to know some things never change.

Paco was a young twenty-six year-old who was older than his years. He spoke little English, but knew everything I said. I was an old forty something who spoke little Spanish. The similarities ended there except both of us were capitalistic swains who knew a thing or ten about salable smuggled stuff. Paco sold the cigars that his brother, who worked in the factory, smuggled and said he could find anything one desired... as long as price wasn't an object! I wondered if brother meant blood or buddy, but Paco never answered which. However, I don't remember if he was ever asked. True to his word, Paco found whatever I desired... however the price I paid wasn't the price I wanted to pay. And there's a price to pay for everything!

A couple of isle hours passed in what seemed like New York minutes. Then, it was time for me to return to my hotel. I arrived just in time to see the sun set into the sea. Walking in the room, I saw she was dressed to the max. All I had on were blue jeans and T-shirt. She wanted to go out and see the nightlife... so off we went. She was dressed in a short skirt, sexy shirt, and heels. I wore blue jeans and a T-shirt. Every eye was on her when we walked out of the elevator. I felt her hold my arm in her hand and wondered what all the Cubans were thinking... *older man in grunge clothes with hot-looking young-babe in Cosmo wear*. But it felt good to know that they all wanted to be me. And not because I was an American!

Two days later it was time to head back to Jamaica. Ten boxes of Cubanos, purchased for a lot more than nothing and beyond a lot more prices, were stuffed into our bags. And while the price for stoogies in Havana may've seemed deer, it paled when compared to those in *Nueva York*.

We landed in Montego Bay and proceeded through Immigration. The officer asked to see my ticket... off the island. I told him no one ever told me I needed to have it with me, but he wanted none of that. I told him that before I went to Cuba I left my ticket in my house because I figured it wouldn't be needed... and I'd been afraid to lose it. But the officer wasn't having any of that. He said I couldn't enter his country without proof I was leaving the island. Then, he said I'd have to go back to where I'd just come from. Cuba!

I felt panic-city time arrive deep down inside the bowels of my being! I saw myself bouncing back and forth between Cuba and Jamaica... a traveler of no country. I protested to no avail. The officer's only reply was that I'd have to see his supervisor.

The supervisor asked to see my passport. Opening it up, he saw lots of Jamaican Immigration stamps stamped on the pages. His eyes rolled around inside their sockets. He said I'd have to have a ticket off the island prior to getting on the island. He didn't care if my ticket was back in my room back in Negril. In other words, I'd have to purchase a ticket to leave the country if I wanted to enter the country. My passport was kept while I entered the country to go to the ticket counter to purchase a ticket. But the ticket counter didn't sell tickets. I'd have to go to the ticket agent... where the ticket would cost me a higher rate of fare than normal. And there's always a price to pay for everything!

I waited in line for what seemed like forever before purchasing a one-way ticket off the island. The cost of the ticket was much more than any roundtrip fare, but it was the price I had to pay to enter the island. The supervisor gave me back my passport... stamped with another entry stamp alongside the others that preceded it.

I went over to the Customs area to pick up my bags and noticed no one was around to check my things. After a short while an agent appeared, but it appeared he just wanted to go home or wherever Jamaicans go when they aren't working. And he just waived me through. Suddenly, he stopped me and asked if I had any cigars. I said I did and he said I'd have to check any that were more than fifty into their Customs system. He seemed pissed that I was cutting into his time, but I really think he was just pissed at himself for having inquired whether I had any cigars. Paperwork is paperwork... in any country! I removed two boxes from my bags and checked them into their system. However, he did allow me to keep three boxes... which was one box more than I was allowed to have.

It took more than several long Southern hours to enter Jamaica... hours counted in any country! I was amazed to see the babe had waited for me. She asked what took so long. I told her my story. She told me they allowed her to keep all the cigars in her bags even though they saw all the boxes she had. She smiled that smile she smiled and said being a woman had its advantages. I didn't want to hear any of that and muttered something about pregnancy, menstrual periods, and having to deal with bulges in her chest when she ran. She laughed and said I was just being a guy. Then, she said something about those bulges getting her anything she wanted. All she had to do was do what solders were told what to do... *thrust that chest out.*

A few days after returning to Jamaica, she went her way and I went mine... never to see each other again. The last time I saw her, she was sashaying that cute little butt of hers down the tarmac... dressed in high-heels and a short skirt. In one hand was a suitcase packed with over one hundred and fifty long-necked Cubanos... all cigars! She liked pushing that envelope. Although we only knew each other for a short couple of months... in the end we were like ships that passed in the night. However, for us, it seemed more like birds in flight.

A couple of months later, the holiday every red, white, and blue-blooded American gives thanks for was only a couple of days away. So was the expiration of my ticket. The special deal of a ticket sale that I bought my ticket under, almost two months earlier, had a lot of restrictions... one was that the ticket wasn't good any longer than six weeks. I quickly made my reservation to head back to America and readied my plans to retrieve the Cubanos left at Jamaican Customs back in July... prior to my last trip back to the States when I went through Chicago. Back then, it had been a plan... and the plan had been laid out a long time before when I read my passport where it said, '*As of November, 1963, the purchase or importation of Cuban... goods... are **generally** prohibited, except for... limited goods imported directly as accompanied baggage.*'

I read those words and re-read them... over a thousand times. A couple of times before the umpteenth time, I knew what those words said. But I continued reading them over and over again... just to be sure. '*Cuban...*

113

David Weisenthal

goods… are **generally** prohibited, **except for…** limited goods imported **directly** as accompanied baggage.'

Since there were only a hundred Cubanos, I knew the limited part wouldn't be a problem… as per the **Know Before You Go** pamphlet. It said on page six in the section, Cigars and Cigarettes: '*Not more than one hundred cigars… may be included in your exemption.*' But I figured the *directly* aspect of the words couldn't be overlooked. Hence the plan to place those Cubanos in Jamaican Customs!

The words didn't say I had to enter America *directly* from Cuba… only that the cigars did. And they had to be with me *as accompanied baggage.* How to do that was the thought. The first time I flashed on the thought was when I first checked cigars into Jamaican Customs… when I went to Cuba with Andreas. At that time, I didn't want to lose the smokes and took the alternative avenue of choice… check them into Jamaican Customs.

When I went to Cuba with the babe back in July, I had to do it again. Thus the thought to traverse the cigars' travel directly from Cuba to America… even though I hadn't! Being placed in Jamaican Customs meant the cigars would travel directly from Cuba to America. It didn't matter where I'd been or for how long I'd been there. It also didn't say how long a time was given before the statute of limitations would expire.

Although it seemed a loophole in the wording of what it said to do, I did what it said had to be done so that it would be done correctly. And, when I was doing it, I knew it was going to be interesting! I didn't know about the fun stuff. But I knew it was definitely going to be interesting.

***

After the flight landed in Philadelphia I took several long, slow, deep breaths while getting off the plane. I was mentally trying to calm my mind as I walked through the airport. Immigration was a snap! When I entered the Customs area I immediately encountered a canine cop who sniffed every person and all their possessions for all the things that could be sniffed that could be considered contraband.

I passed the police hound without incident and proceeded toward the exit when a rather young-looking Customs agent stopped me. He seemed new to the task, but performed his work in a professional manner. He

114

asked to see my declaration card. Then, he asked some questions. One of the questions was whether Jamaica was the only country I'd traveled to on that trip. In that I hadn't gone to Cuba since before the last time I entered America, when I went there with the babe, what I said when I said it was the truth, the whole truth… and nothing but the truth!

The Customs agent looked at me for the briefest of moments before he handed back the Customs declaration card. He told me to give it to the agent at the exit door… as I left. And that was it! He didn't care… nor did he think further questioning or more inspection was warranted. Out the door I went after giving the Customs declaration card to the agent at the exit and not an eye looked in my direction as I did so.

David Weisenthal

Lotto of Love

***

Through the years, I've sailed the seven seas and seen more than most of the wonders on Earth. From incredible water-scene sunsets to outrageous landlocked sunrises, from thunderous hurricanes to mammoth earthquakes, from faraway peaceful looking horizons to near-missed almost fatal verticals. But all the while, I kept missing the boat with what I was in search of. Something akin to a day late and a dollar short... or ships that passed in the night.

There are many lotteries on this planet. Pick a number... win a prize. Mail in a coupon and feel like a winner! One hundred and one ways to avoid the military draft! Lucky at love, unlucky at cards! There was only one problem... I was lucky at cards. From the time I was first interested in girls, I've played the Lotto of Love... without much success. It seems my choice(s) for a mate weren't always thought out with much logic. Then again, maybe, I just used the wrong head to think with. And, maybe, there's truth with size!

My search took me high and low... past rainbows and over high seas. Yet, nowhere did I find what I was looking for. Back when I left home, I left in search of someone that somehow could make it all seem worthwhile. I sought another half of some unknown quantity... with a quality that was above reproach. She'd have to possess an inner beauty that would match her outer glow. And she'd have to exceed my wildest imagination before I'd even look in her direction.

Many times more than I'd like to remember I found myself waking up to a different beast that lay beside my soul... and what I saw was almost enough to make a grown man cry. Jackals, wolfs, snakes and vampires... all creatures of the dark, whether they flew, slid or walked. And all were horrors of the night! Day's light brought renewed hope that obtaining the object of one's dreams couldn't be so far out of reach. But each sunset brought the repeated reality that those dreams were further away than believed.

Each passing day brought a sadness that my dreams were actually slipping further away faster than they were getting closer. For although I was careful not to let the playpen become a lair sometimes the toys did get into

116

my den. It was almost reminiscent of having invited a guest or ten to dine. And not having them leave... when the meal was done.

Having spent many lifetimes in search of what I knew not, I never reached a summit of knowledge. Instead, I came to believe that I had to forego the remainder of the trek... and turned toward nothingness in order to ease my pain for not fulfilling the journey. Then, the day came when my number hit. I'd won a lottery and hadn't even played. But one can't win if they don't play. So a gambling man I had to be... once more. Only this time the game of chance was the Lotto of Love. I thought *to hell with the dice and diamond cards of clubs and spades.* I knew *hearts* was the name of the game and the shape that could only be the suit. And all those others could all be damned with any of those other jokers.

My Saving Grace

***

Life's travels took me near and far and I'd seen much in my time... however, I never found what I was looking for. Maybe that's why I seemed older than the years. But age is just an illusion. The century's last decade began with me sitting in some stir hole of a stockade that society passed for a prison of my soul. At the time I was involved with a girl whose eyes looked like a cat. It was probably why she called herself that name. However, she had everyone believe it was I who christened her. When I could least afford it she split with my spoils... after finding new game on her turf.

Although I'd grown accustomed to her presence, I knew I'd be better off without her. For, I didn't miss her as much as the lucre that lined my pockets. Besides, many times I heard it said *money made the world go round.* She had too! And being a product of some 'X' generation, she had little scruples and less integrity. So off she went with my pillage... and left only dust in its place.

Such be life that the more one looks for what they want the harder it is to see the object of their desire. The same could've been said for me. For, I was lost in a sea of abandoned dreams and looking naught for what I desperately sought. A quest for rejuvenation took me to some far off place in a way out locale... where the mind could take off when the sun dropped into the sea.

My stay was set in a newly built castle that reminded one and all of an old European relic of fable lore. At three every morning I'd lay on the stone floor outside by the water looking up at the sky with the cold face of the stone blocks that made that building what it was standing tall before my eyes. With the waves crashing up against the cliffs and the stars that loomed just out of my reach, I was grateful for the chance to live a life that included being included in the energy that made up that property.

Jamaica being what Jamaica is a man is required to show his prowess through conquests of the opposite sex. I was having difficulty with who I was and found the time I spent I spent alone. Jamaicans are physical creatures. On the universal level of existence, that is the lowest base of one's being. I discovered a core of my mentality could be raised through an evolution of heightened spirituality... and took refuge in any reading that included the elevation of my consciousness. Words of <u>Freedom From The Known</u> and the knowledge gained through <u>THE *KYBALION*</u> kept me full of hope there was something better to be gained though the lifting of the veil that covered the soul of my inner mind. But being a man I knew there had to be something else needed to spark my fire.

Negril is a small town with a Jamaican small town mentality. Having many opportunities to acquire property there over the years I should have, but never trusting my instinct I never did. Instead I chose to live the good life amid those who had made the plunge and because of my lack of substance I always questioned my intelligence... or lack thereof. I felt like a *duppy* of my former self. My outer body merely exposed the depletion from my inner core. It was amid this turmoil we found each other... or should I say, she found me.

Upon meeting, I knew she was a lovely Grace... but I also thought she wasn't what I was looking for. Only at the time I wasn't really looking for anything. And, maybe, that is the best time to find what one seeks. But there she was, staring me in the eye and beckoning me hither...enticing me with her knowledge and blinding me with her beauty.

The time we spent together always seemed valuable, so I wanted to spend time with her! The first time we met she graced my heart and I knew it then that she had a spirit like no other. Her eyes sparkled and I could sense an angel had touched her soul. When we first met I fought my feelings, but knew in my heart she'd always have a piece of me. I was grateful for having crossed paths with that maiden of Grace and although she was everything I ever wanted in a woman... I didn't think she was what I was looking for.

With a smile that heated the coldest frown, her warmth overwhelmed me and I soon melted into a pile of flesh. Being in no hurry to go fast we took time to discover our true feelings. Before I knew it, it was time for her to go and she headed back to a place that I'd left... just a few short years before. I watched her drive out of town... leaving me with nothing more than a few pleasant memories of the times we spent together. And, while I knew I'd see her again, I didn't think it'd be forever! But true love doesn't come with the first sight... and trust takes time to develop. Although I knew she was a true lady of grace, what I didn't know when we first met was how, over time, she'd be... **My Saving Grace**!

David Weisenthal

Unsolved Mysteries

***

The morning after the night I arrived in Philadelphia, I called my hippie shark lawyer to make an appointment. He agreed to see me later that afternoon. It was a first… getting to see him on such short notice. But I knew he wanted to see me! Then again, I also knew he wanted a Cubano and I knew he knew I had some! Entering his office, I gave Stephen the five smokes I set aside for him and he wasn't disappointed with their bouquet. I considered it benefits of the job, but the shark probably thought it was *quid pro quo*. However, since I was paying for the job, I didn't feel I owed him anything. Although, sharks always feel their clients owe them something! And it's usually more than they've agreed to be paid. Maybe, that's why they're sharks! Always hungry!

Shortly after sitting down in a big brown stuffed leather chair that wasn't quite as big as the big brown stuffed leather chair Stephen sat in, we began discussing my case. Stephen said the paperwork that contested the government's response to my contesting the seizure of my cigars had been filed with the U.S. Attorney's office… and we were waiting for an answer. As of then, none had been filed. What else was new?! I wondered how many times I'd have to hear that! Again, thirty days were required… by law! However, by the time our conversation occurred, over sixty-five days had come and gone.

I swore I heard him say something about being patient and biding my time, but my thought process was stuck in fast forward and patience was hardly a virtue I ever saw. In the end, I think Stephen thought the smokes would help pass the time, but I knew he didn't wear a watch. I also knew no one, other than me, was keeping track of the time… or so it seemed.

Before I knew it seven days had come and gone. When Thanksgiving arrived, I had little to show for my time in the North. There was still no word from the government. My mother was up in a city that never sleeps and I drove up to spend the holiday day with her. The day after the big turkey day feast I got in my car and headed back to the city of brotherly love. While driving down the toll-way freeway, I took off my overcoat and placed it in the rear seat.

An hour or so later I approached the exit-ramp and looked at the ticket to see how much the fare was. I reached into the back of the car to get the coat... where my money and passport were in one of the pockets. My hand groped and fumbled, but the coat was nowhere to be found.

My coat's disappearance was impossible or so I thought... because I never left the car. Nor had anyone entered it! However, in a blink of an eye that lasted less than a split of a fat apple second, I crossed paths with some weird black-magic evil-voodoo witchcraft that travels through time. I racked my brain for any logical thought and rationalized that it had to be *some sort of time warp or dimensional crossover.* It was the only thing that'd explain what had happened. Luckily, I had enough change in my pockets to pay the toll!

Immediately upon driving over the bridge bridging New Jersey with Philadelphia, I drove to the house of the King of the Gypsies. He explained the occurrence... *"Some sort of time warp or dimensional crossover. You're possessed!"* Then, he told me to not feel too bad because he had also experienced it... once in his past. However, that didn't make me feel any the better for my loss. And although some may call it denial or depression, I call it mental masturbation! Than again, it could've been anxiety or despair and, maybe, even apprehension or dread! But I feared it... all the same.

Adding to the scenario, one week later I walked into Phillip Mytank's office. Phillip Mytank was a friend of mine. Upon entering the door, his secretary handed me an envelope. The address had a U.S.P.O. seal on the front. However, there was no return address, postmark or date stamped anywhere on the envelope. I opened the parcel and saw a small bundle inside. It was an address label and Phillip Mytank's address was listed below my name. The address label was for a letter I was going to send via UPS to another friend that I never sent. In my wonderment over the missing jacket, money and passport, I failed to notice the UPS envelope with the letter inside that had also disappeared. But there it was... back in my face. Evidence of some strange weird black-magic evil-voodoo witchcraft that traveled through time!

121

Story of the Decade

***

Feeling naked as a newborn and unable to leave the country without the proper identification, I applied for another passport. I was told it would take time to process the application... once it was submitted. Having nothing but time left me the time to spend some time with the Lady Grace. I didn't have a problem with that since our time together had always seemed valuable!

A couple of days after returning back to the States was the first night I spent with her on my trip up north. Late into the night I thought back to the first time we had met and remembered how I knew it then that she had a spirit like no other. Her eyes were filled with an inner beauty that expressed her outer charm. I was grateful for having crossed paths with her. But although, over time, I knew she was everything I'd ever want in a woman... I still didn't think she was what I was looking for.

The light of day made way for the darkness of night... and the days quickly became a week that transformed into a month. Before I knew it, Christmas was only a few days away. During the day, she would toy with the tale... but at night I'd watch while she catered to her calling. She's a foodie who owns a much finer than very fine dining eatery. Somehow, I kept flashing on Michelle Pfeiffer when I'd see her tend to her trade and I've heard it said all who drink her special margaritas swear they're better than any swallowed south of any border. But, unlike the picture, I'm not Mel... and the sea was more than many miles away. Besides, the sun had already set... on another Tequila Sunrise.

The presence of her place makes one seem to not be on Earth. That was done by design! In fact, so accomplished was her aim, she has to remind one and all that she is indeed located on this planet. And, while her space isn't dubbed another who's known as Alice, one does recall a place where they can get anything they want! Well, almost anything!

My stay in America was in search of a way to get the story printed. I knew it'd make a great TV movie. I could see it all... with Danny DeVito playing the Bandito. However, the other players would be a problem. Who'd play the shark, me... or the leading lady? And there had to be a fair maiden… because sex sells. Then again, Michelle seemed like a shoo-in for the role. And more than several people thought Mel should play me. Only I like the Depp guy!

My psycho cosmic card-reading friend, Balthezar, King of the Gypsies, said he knew a writer who knew an editor who worked for a City Paper paper who could and would love to publish a story on the colossal Cuban Cohiba cigar challenge caper. The editor's phone number was given to me. I quickly called the number and made an appointment to meet with him the day after the day my call was made! The following day, Lady Grace and I drove into the city of brotherly love to begin spinning the yarn of a tale from a saga that could've been the Story of the Decade. And what a fable it was!

His office was filled with piles of waste. The desk was covered with mounds of news and papers from days long gone. It seemed like the set of some weird Walter Matthau movie and it was obvious that Felix Unger had never set foot in that wasteland newspaper bureau. But had he… then it wouldn't have had the same synthetic ambiance. I've heard it said on more than many occasions that *one man's trash is another man's treasure.* And make no mistake about it… Ed Ditor was an editor who treasured the trash he kept in his cubicle of life.

A modern-day hippie in grunge outerwear greeted us. Round and polly with dark curly hair, his smile bristled through a coarse beard. Ed Ditor rose up from his chair when we entered his space. Warm and friendly, he seemed truly interested in the tale I told. His hands never strayed from the strum the keyboard lay as his fingers weaved a yarn. And a cleaver one it was! Some questions were asked and answer's given. Then, he asked what I'd done with my life. I told him some things I'd attained before ending the dialogue with the time spent in those hellholes that passed for a human dump. A slight grin crept across his lips while his stout fingers continued to punch out the words. When I was done he said, "My deadline is soon, but it should make this weeks' news."

I left him copies of stories from three decades before when I first set foot on Cuba… although the news wasn't the news I remembered it to be. However, it was the news Lady Grace and I retrieved from the public library only hours before the meet with Edit Ed. The news was from three different newspapers. Each paper had more than several stories. And a different writer of unknown repute wrote every story! But reading all the stories by all the different reporters left me wondering… whose life it had been anyway.

Editor Ed Ditor finished the interview and said to call him with any new news… and to keep him informed of all the events. We shook hands… then bided each other adieu. With that, Lady Grace and I walked out from his sight.

Three days later Lady Grace and I drove near and far looking for sight of any City Paper paper. It took more than several stops to seek out the news because the news that was written had been gobbled up by lots of hungry fans. Then again, the paper could've just fanned the fuel that lit their fires. But perseverance paid off when we found the object of our desire. A short time later we stopped to eat and hungrily thirsted for the anecdote of our tale. We found the yarn and dined on the words while relishing the narrative delight that starry night. Then, later that night, we went in search of a stand in which to empty all the boxes of every paper in sight.

His logic was twisted like the pretzels he ate and he called the piece he wrote *Prezel Logic*. Being an editor of a City Paper paper in a city that made pretzels famous, Ed Ditor was no ordinary edit man. He liked inhaling the smoke he wasn't allowed to puff… regardless the brand. Ed Ditor saw through the ***Cigar Smoke and Mirrors*** to write a story that envisioned his vision. He wrote, 'A Philly man claims the nation's 34-year-old ban on Cuban cigars is just hot air.' And had anyone bothered to measure the heat of the air after his smoke rose, they would've seen that it rose.

'For 29 years Philadelphia raconteur David Fabler has had a very curious relationship with the island nation of Cuba. The relationship began on Dec. 19, 1968. The same day the U.S. tested an atom bomb 60 times more powerful than the one dropped on Hiroshima. As he was flying to Miami from Philadelphia, his Eastern Airlines Flight 47 was hijacked by a tall, trembling Negro accompanied by his 2 ½ year-old daughter. Nearly three decades later, Havana and Cuban cigars are still very much on his mind.'

'The U.S. government, which, despite all its atomic bombs, still considers Fidel Castro such a threat that the importation of Cuban cigars is a treasonous act. Customs agents searched the

Philly man's bags and discovered, then seized, a copious cache of contraband: 100 Cuban cigars, 15 Cuban mini-cigars, 9 Cuban cigarettes, 5 Cuban key chains, 1 Cuban wood jewelry box and 1 Cuban coin. It was a relatively small haul... especially when you compare it to incidents like the November 1996 seizure of 4,300 Cuban cigars, worth upwards of $215,000, by Customs agents in Philly. Maybe, the biggest single-bust ever.'

'Still, like hundreds of others coming into this country every year with an estimated $400 million worth of what are arguably the world's finest tobacco torpedoes, David Fabler saw his marvelous Monte Cristos, Romeo y Juliets, and Cohibas taken. But, apparently unlike anyone else in the history of this country's absurd 34-year embargo of Cuba, Fabler - who's sold antiques, analyzed finances for Chase Manhattan bank and served 51 months for conspiracy to smuggle pot - is fighting for the return of his cigars.'

'He's hired a lawyer, posted the required $2,500 bond and challenged the Treasury Department's Dec. 23, 1997, ruling that he summarily forfeited his goods, given to him by a friend... for his birthday. Fabler says the U.S. government has no right to keep him from enjoying his present.'

'Now that Fabler has challenged the forfeiture, it's up to the U.S. Attorney's Office in Philadelphia to pursue the case... or return the cigars. And it very well may be an unprecedented and unwinnable position for the government. Even U.S. Attorney's Office spokesperson Noah Levity can't remember a single case where someone challenged a cigar seizure. As of yet, says Levity, the Customs Service has not turned the case over to the U.S. Attorney's Office.'

The morning after the paper hit the streets my mother hit the roof of her house. She was more irate than mad because as my brother would say later, "*You spilled the beans.*" She couldn't believe I'd tell the world about my *vacation* spent away from life... out in some far off sphere. She didn't know what to think when I told her that I only considered myself to have been a prisoner of war. She was reliving my nightmare... and failed to see any humor struck inside the humor door. And, it was as though she seemed to forget, it was I who had survived to tell the tale.

Surfing the *Internet* Wave

***

Returning to America brought a continued quest to unveil any evidence of publicly lost stories from the history of time gone by. The search had begun a long time before... while I was down in Margarita-villa land. There, I discovered more than many anecdotes of previously unknown information that confirmed my vigil wasn't off the wall.

In Jamaica, the price to surf the *Internet* wave was a lot of money every month because the cost for phone service was more than pennies on the dollar. But, in America, it was only twenty dollars a month plus the local phone service charges... that, if using an unlimited local dialing service, was minimal at most. Obviously, in America, the search was a lot more economical in terms of out-of-pocket expenses. And that, in conjunction with what sharks cost and such, made my effort to continue fighting the good fight much more financially viable.

Time was of the essence as money financed the battle... and that was the nature of the fray for the government had a vastly unlimited amount to spend. Much more than I had... and, in essence, the government could've forced me to outspend the meager amount that had been earmarked for the struggle. Enough that I wouldn't have been able to have continued the combat! And, if they'd known just how meager the funds were, they probably would've... in an attempt to prevent the truth from ever getting out. Then again, maybe they did... and just didn't care!

On the day I finally received my traveling papers, I made arrangements to return back to Negril... much to the Lady Grace's chagrin. Part of her distress was in not understanding why I'd choose to leave. But one had to do what one had to do... and I had to return back to Negril. Five days later I was back in the land of sun and warmth. In the time between receiving my travel documents and departing the country, I went to the House of Customs to procure another copy of the book, **<u>Know Before You Go</u>**. My copy had disappeared a long time before... to some unknown locale. And, maybe, it went to the place where my passport went.

The last time I visited the Customs House was my third time. My two previous times there, the officials in charge of handing out the official government publications stated they were out of that *specific* book. But they did say they had some others. And they said they'd be happy to give me the ones I didn't want... in exchange for the one I did. On both occasions I thanked them for their courtesy, but declined their offer... although I did take a copy of every publication they had.

One of the publications was a U.S. Customs In Brief card. In brief, it was a one-page card that condensed the **Know Before You Go** book into a simple description. It was written in November 1995 and was Customs Publication # 506. In a 'Play It Safe' section, it said: *'This handout is only a brief overview of Customs requirements.'* Then it said, *'We'll be happy to send you a copy of our brochure* **Know Before You Go**, *which describes* **in detail** *everything that you should... **know before you go.**'*

Unlucky as three on a match or third time is a charm. Take your pick! Given those choices, I'd rather be charmed than matched. And I guess the third time at the Customs House was my lucky charm. I questioned if the new **Know Before You Go** pamphlet had arrived and was ushered over to a counter where all the pamphlets were kept. I was told the one in the case was the last one... so I quickly grabbed it. But no sooner had I removed it from the rack when another agent walked around from behind a desk with another copy in his hand. He said the one he was holding was the last copy... so I took that one also! When I left, I didn't turn around to see if another agent produced another last copy. I didn't care! I had both of mine!

Later that day I examined it and immediately noticed it'd been changed. The cover was different and the table of contents on the inside of the cover wasn't the same... however, other than those two things and the section(s) referencing Cuba, 'Cigars and Cigarettes' and 'Merchandise From Embargoed Countries,' there were no other differences between the two books. The new book was published May 1997... one month after I had contested the wording of the old book. One month! Coincidence?

The wording of the May 1997 edition of the **Know Before You Go** book stated under the 'Cigars and Cigarettes' section: *'Tobacco products of Cuban origin are **generally** prohibited.'* Page 21 of the newly revised document contained a new paragraph under the heading, 'Merchandise from Embargoed Countries.' It stated, *'The importation of goods from the following countries is **generally** prohibited under regulations administered by the Office of Foreign Assets Control... Cuba!'* It went on to state, *'Because of the strict enforcement of these prohibitions, those anticipating* *travel to any country listed above would do well to write in advance to the Office of Foreign Assets Control.'*

Just like that, the loophole had been closed... sealed and shut forever! Now, no one could read those words and contest the meaning of the words... for the meaning of those words had been changed to mean what they wanted those words to mean. And not mean what they meant when those words said what they said. Oh well... the time must have been ripe!

When I got back to Negril, the Bandito and I picked up where we left off... spending lots of Jamaican dollars seeking out hidden and lost information. And, although Jamaican dollars did seem like *Monopoly* money, spend enough of them and it digs into the pockets of good old American greenbacks. However, we were on a quest... and the quest was to let the world know about the struggle.

Somehow, it seemed the best way to let the world know about the struggle was to inform them of the story that had been written by that City Paper paper Editor Ed Ditor. For, although his story was my story, regardless whose story it was, it was a story of the century. Well, maybe, one for the decade! OK, it was really just a tale of the times.

Everywhere we went we hunted down information that pertained to the battle at hand. Whether at the beach or in the confine of our own shelter, the search went wherever one went at web speed in the push of a button. One place led to another and that led to others... and there was no end in sight. And we weren't satisfied with only seeking out the sights... so intent were we to spread the word about the great colossal Cuban Cohiba cigar challenge caper.

Sites were found whose purpose was the end of 'THE embargo,' one way or another. Whether protesting through hunger strikes or writing legislation, people all over the world agreed that 'THE embargo' was wrong and only hurt the Cuban people. One web site was the '90 miles to Cuba' petition. It had thousands of people from 45 states and 30 countries who made a pledge through their signatures to attempt a change in U.S. policy toward Cuba. Another web site was the 'Help End The Illegal And Immoral Blockade Of Cuba' petition. The Boston Committee on the Middle East created the site! They also had other petitions against

American policy... one that demanded an end to unconditional U.S. support for Israel.

There are many people in America who are in a position to foster an attempt to change the policy... members of Congress who profess a desire to see an end come of 'THE embargo.' And they're lining up to write legislation that brings about that end. Senator Christopher Dodd (D-Ct.) and Rep. Esteban Torres (D-Cal.) have argued that "The 36-year-old Cuban embargo hasn't worked because it hasn't toppled the Castro regime." Rep Torres said, "Instead, all its created is oppression and hardship... misery and discontent."

Rep. George Miller (D-Cal.) has proposed legislation under H.AMDT.163. It's an amendment to Congress that the government shouldn't prohibit the importation, sale or distribution of Cuban cigars in the U.S. Rep. Miller believes the time has come to put an end to the duplicity taking place, i.e., when members of Congress and the administration denounce Cuba through support of 'THE embargo,' but will light up... a Cuban cigar. Rep. Miller believes some people who actively support 'THE embargo' *are also enjoying Cuban cigars.* And he feels they shouldn't have it both ways.

The American people would be surprised at how many bills have been sponsored that propose an end to 'THE embargo.' Many members of Congress have sponsored bills. In 1998, Rep. Rangel (D-NY) introduced the Free Trade with Cuba Act, House Bill 3173... which was similar to another he submitted back in 1993. Basically, his Act amended the Foreign Assistance Act of 1961 and was intended to repeal 'THE embargo' on trade with Cuba. His Act intended to prohibit the exercise by the President with respect to Cuba of certain authorities conferred by the Trading With the Enemy Act (TWEA) as a result of a specified national emergency.

Rep. Rangel's Act declared any prohibition on exports to Cuba under the Export Administration Act to cease being in effect. It authorized the President to impose export controls with respect to Cuba... and to exercise certain authorities under the International Emergency Economic Powers Act only on account of an unusual and extraordinary threat to U.S. national security that *didn't exist before* the enactment of his Act. It also directed the U.S. Postal Service to provide direct mail service to and from Cuba. And it amended the I.R.S. Code to terminate the denial of foreign tax credit with respect to Cuba... as well as prohibit regulation or the banning of travel to and from Cuba by U.S. citizens or residents, or of any transactions incident to travel.

Another Act was the Cuban Humanitarian Act of 1997, HR 1951 IH. This Act was intended to make an exception to 'THE embargo' on trade with Cuba for the export of food, medicine, medical supplies, medical instruments or equipment. Several members of Congress and the House of Representatives co-submitted the bill. However, die-hard anti-Castro Cubans and right-winged hawks in Congress oppose the opposition of those who oppose 'THE embargo.' And they've thwarted any effort to end 'THE embargo.' In this instance, they amended the food and medical products bill to include a requirement that all sales be done with U.S. dollars and not allow any credit to be accepted... thereby muting all but any chance of trade between those two nations.

A basis for the 1997 Cuban Humanitarian Act was a recent American Association for World Health report that did a one-year study between 1995-96. Research traced the impact of restrictions on health care delivery and food security in the country. The report stated, "A humanitarian catastrophe could be averted for a health care system designed to deliver primary and preventive health care to all of its citizens."

In drafting the Cuban Humanitarian Act (CHA), the drafters looked at the misnamed Cuban Democracy Act (CDA), known as the Helms-Burton Act (HBA)... for guidance. They believed the CDA took 'THE embargo' policy a step further... turning it into a blatant international law violation. The CDA / HBA allows Cuban-Americans to sue (in U.S. Courts) anyone who does business that involves property confiscated from them... *before they became U.S. citizens.* CDA / HBA has the appearance of being an attempt to apply our laws outside the boundaries of the United States. The conflict is that that law can cause a violation of national sovereignty for every nation.

Legislation and petitions aren't the only way people want to express their displeasure with America's policy toward Cuba. People are also fasting. At one point, the 'Pastors for Peace' movement had people from more than 40 cities from around the world taking part in a group fast that was intended to show widespread world public support for lifting 'THE embargo' policy toward Cuba. The people who participated fasted for more than twenty-three days. And, if nothing else, at least they got to lose some weight.

American's have little knowledge about those who actively support an end to 'THE embargo.' For example, the American Anthropological Association and Muhammad Ali have spoken out. A consulting firm called Alamar Associates is an organization who lobbies Congress to end 'THE embargo' as well. Created in 1974 and based in Washington, D.C., Alamar has consulted with thousands of organizations, media outlets and people who are interested in doing business in Cuba and who want to bring about an end to 'THE embargo.' Space doesn't permit naming all of Alamar's client base, but some of their better known clients include: Deere & Co., Bell & Howell, MacGregor, Arthur Anderson & Co., Atlanta Chamber of Commerce, Ford Motor Co., Bear Sterns & Co., Bank of Newport, Bankers Life, Toro Co., Mobil Oil, Tampa Port Authority, The Boston Globe, Burroughs Corp., Billy Graham Association, General Electric, General Mills, Honeywell, U.S. Rice Federation, Price Waterhouse, International Harvester, Johnson & Johnson, Uncle Ben's Foods, Security Pacific National Bank, Massachusetts Lt. Governor, Texaco, Minneapolis Chamber of Commerce, Office of Boston Mayor Kevin White, Oklahoma Dept. of Commerce, Pillsbury Co., Philip Morris International, Seatrain Line, Prudential Insurance, San Francisco Chamber of Commerce, U.S. Import & Export, and Xerox. All Alamar's clients have one thing in common. They have all participated in the Alamar organized conferences and trips to Cuba that's intended to bring about an end to 'THE embargo' and supports doing business with Cuba.

The United States Chamber of Commerce is also in favor of lifting 'THE embargo.' They believe trade would benefit U.S. business and consumers as well as the Cubans. They also believe the rationale for 'THE embargo' is to push Cuba towards democracy. However, it's contradicted by the U.S. position that trading with China helped open up that country to liberalizing influences.

More importantly, many Americans are **generally** opposed to the continued policy the government maintains against Cuba. Numerous polls taken by an *aficionado* of cigar magazines, Cigar *Aficionado*, indicates the numbers couldn't be wrong. In one, their readers were asked two questions. The first was whether or not they'd like to see 'THE embargo' lifted. Not surprisingly, eighty-eight percent of the respondents answered "Yes!" The second question was what they'd do if 'THE embargo' was lifted. Twenty-three percent said they'd plan a visit to Cuba within the following twelve months. Ninety-one percent said they'd purchase Cuban cigars, if available. Forty-three percent said they'd drink Cuban rum, if available.

Twenty-eight percent said they'd invest in U.S. companies conducting business with Cuba. And only eight percent said they'd continue to reject Cuban products until Fidel Castro was no longer in power.

Another poll by <u>Cigar *Aficionado*</u> asked their readers if they had 'ever brought Cuban cigars into the U.S. (by having them in a vehicle in which they were riding, on their person, in their luggage, or shipped directly from another country.)' Some sixty-percent of the U.S. citizens who responded stated that they had done so in one form or another. And of those who responded and were non-American citizens, fifty-two percent said they also had. In a different poll, almost ten per cent of the U.S. citizen respondents indicated that they'd been to Cuba since 'THE embargo' was enacted back in 1963. However, it doesn't matter how the U.S. trade policy is looked upon… because it's contradictory.

The real reason for 'THE embargo' is a very strong anti-Castro lobby in Congress. And, although the government doesn't want to admit they exist, the *Mafia*. Not to mention are those Russian missiles that were based in Cuba… pointed at U.S. cities. However, much has changed over the past three decades.

Over the years, America has told Cuba that if they '*remove their troops from Africa, stop supporting revolutions in Central America and reduce military ties to Russia*,' then '*normalization of relations would be approved by Congress*.' By the 1990's, all those conditions were met! The Soviet-Cuban alliance was over as was Cuba's support for revolution. Not only was *Soviet* Russia gone, but so were the missiles. Cuba was no longer a threat, militarily or otherwise, to U.S. interests anywhere in the world. In fact, Castro had stopped exporting revolution and substituted revolutionary tactics with cigars and tourism. Therefore, 'THE embargo' has no more basis in fact. And what has America done in return? It has moved in the opposite direction! So much for honoring our word!

American politicians are caught up in the emotional battleground that Cuban-Americans have with casting Castro out of Cuba. Our politicians have lost sight of any sensible or practical goal that could bring an end to the impasse. So conflicting is the conflict that our own government is divided on the issue with Congress only recently voting to end enforcing the enforcement of 'THE embargo.' However, President Bush has stated he will not terminate it. And why is that? Maybe, there's an election to be run? Or is that won?

Today, the real reason for 'THE embargo' is politics. How many Cubans live in America? How many are U.S. citizens? How many can vote for a Congressman, Senator... or President!?" How many? A State's worth! Any doubt was removed in the 2000 election. The world watched while Florida's banana republic(ans) played a major role in how that State voted... and, consequently, the outcome of who became President.

Our Not So Secret Past

***

Since Cuba doesn't pose a military threat to America, U.S. citizens should have a Constitutional right to trade with the Cuban people... a right that U.S. Courts should recognize. Therefore, it's not just Congress but also the U.S. Courts that maintains this counter-productive attitude with 'THE embargo' on investment, travel, and trade with Cuba. There used to be a time when the U.S. Courts protected the rights every citizen had... rights that included trading with any country who wasn't an enemy of the State. And that included Cuba!

Between 1958 and 1983, the U.S. Courts were committed to supporting the citizens' right(s) in dealing with issues involving Cuba. On June 16, 1958, that commitment was put to a test in the U.S. Supreme Court. The case was <u>Rockwell Kent & Walter Briehl vs. John Foster Dulles</u> (President Eisenhower's Attorney General). That case upheld the citizens' right to travel when it held, '*The right to travel is a part of the liberty of which a citizen can't be deprived without due process of the law under the 5th Amendment.*'

On July 8, 1963 the Kennedy Administration tightened 'THE embargo,' using its authority under the Trading With The Enemy Act (TWEA) of 1917. The Treasury Dept. replaced the Cuban Import Regulations with the Cuban Asset Control (CAC) Regulations that implemented the essential elements of 'THE embargo.' TWEA allowed either the President or Congress to prohibit '*economic transactions between America and foreign countries or foreign nationals during times of war or national emergency.*' The '*national emergency*' pertinent in the regulations was declared by President Truman in 1950... **during the Korean War** because of the threat of '*world conquest by communist imperialism.*'

The CAC Regulations prohibited *unlicensed* commercial or financial transactions between Cuba and U.S. citizens, *unlicensed* import of or dealings abroad in merchandise of Cuban origin, and *unlicensed* import of goods made in 3rd countries with Cuban materials. No U.S. citizen was allowed to participate in *unlicensed* transactions with Cuba... *in U.S. dollars.* This prohibited spending U.S. currency for expenses in Cuba and for Cuban travel tickets. However, it didn't regulate foreign money being spent on those items or if foreigners spent their money to take a U.S. citizen to Cuba… as their guest.

In 1963, the U.S. Supreme Court upheld a citizen's right to travel. On May 3, in Zemel vs. Rusk (President Kennedy's Attorney General), the Court refused to order the State Department to *not* validate a passport for travel to Cuba. The citing was written by Chief Justice Earl Warren. It took 15 years for the government to change its way. In 1978, Congress remedied Zemel vs. Rusk by legislating that there should be '*no geographic limitations for passports except in time of war or other danger to the traveler.*'

On January 10, 1967, in U.S. vs. Lamb, the U.S. Supreme Court upheld a Federal District Court's decision on May 5, 1966, legalizing travel to Cuba for U.S. citizens… as long as they followed '*Treasury Department Regulations regarding the exchange of money.*' And U.S. vs. Lamb was the key as defined in 31 CFR Chapter V, 515.569… because the Regulations state that not more than one hundred dollars per day can be spent on travel related expenses.

In the case Regan vs. Wald, May 16, 1983, the First U.S. Circuit Court of Appeals in Boston **unanimously** ruled U.S. restrictions on travel to Cuba **invalid**. They ordered the District Judge to issue a preliminary injunction against the government regarding the Cuban Regulations. However, that was the final straw. It was the turning point upon which the government would have no more. And this was when the courts stopped defending the citizens' right(s) with regard to travel abroad.

On July 6, 1983, the Supreme Court granted a Reagan Administration request for a stay in Regan vs. Wald. All travel restrictions were left in effect until the entire court would decide whether to hear a full appeal. On June 28, 1984, in a 5 to 4 decision, the Supreme Court upheld the Treasury Department's Regulations on Cuban travel. The opinion was based on *grounds they were a part of* 'THE embargo' *rather than political control of the right to travel.* That was when 'THE embargo' exposed a policy of politics and politics became the rule of the day. At least, as it regarded Cuba! And nothing has been the same since! Might reigned over right… and right prevailed over the left and center! Catch-22!

Anyone who is interested in a non-political, unbiased overview of Cuban-American relations should read Cuba and the United States…

<u>A chronological History</u>. Written by Jane Franklin and published by an Australian company, Ocean Press, it presents the Cuban revolution in relation to its relations with America. It begins with background information before tracing the relations both countries had from the time they were colonies of European powers. The book details the chronology between these two nations in the context of global events and politics in a yearly format.

Other readings include <u>The Cuba Reader</u> and <u>Cuba's Ties to a Changing World</u>. Both were written by Donna Kaplowitz, adjunct professor of political science at Michigan State University and President of Cuba Research Associates... a Michigan-based consulting group. She served as Deputy Director of the Cuban Studies Program at Johns Hopkins University's School of Advanced International Studies from 1988-1992 and was the founder and Executive Editor of <u>CubaINFO</u>.

Another article written by Kaplowitz can be found on the Net is called, <u>Anatomy of a Failed Embargo: U.S. Sanctions Against Cuba</u>. It is a very comprehensive article that explores the longest-lasting embargo in U.S. foreign policy history. It examines 'THE (Cuban) embargo' and how it reflects the intricacies of the modern world: '*Struggles for self-indepen-dence; relationships between national, regional, and global sources of power; and, both North-South and East-West conflicts.*' Kaplowitz' work provides a historical analysis of 'THE embargo' and offers an explanation as to why it has failed to achieve its major objective - the ouster of Fidel... despite its longevity and exhaustive scope.

Wayne Smith is a former U.S. State Department expert on Cuba. He was the former chief of the U.S. Interests Section in Havana... between 1979 - 1982. When he left the Foreign Service in 1982, he was regarded as the department's ***leading expert*** on Cuba. When last heard, he was a senior fellow at the Center for International Policy. He's been quoted as stating that 'THE embargo' *has accomplished nothing.* "It's an illusion to think we can deal with private entities and citizens in Cuba. Sooner or later, if we want to encourage a government to move ahead with reform, we *must* deal with that government."

Mr. Smith believes the Cuban Democracy Act of 1992 and the Helms-Burton Act of 1996 conveys the wrong message... '*Threatening to sue foreign companies incorporated in other countries in U.S. courts if they deal in expropriated property or do business with Cuba.*' He was quoted as believing that it has caused serious problems between America and her closest trading partners and neighbors. Mr. Smith thinks these acts have alienated the U.S. from the world and spurred a worldwide widespread rejection of American policy toward Cuba.

To verify this, look at the last nine yearly U. N. resolutions that have overwhelmingly endorsed an end to 'THE embargo.' In 1999, the vote was 155-2. Only Israel voted with the U.S. to support 'THE embargo.' Prior to that, only Israel and the former Soviet Republic Uzbekistan voted to support 'THE embargo.' And both those countries did trade with Cuba when they voted to support 'THE embargo.' The reason U.S. allies were united in their support of the U. N. resolution(s) is that they considered their own sovereignty to be infringed by the 'extra-territorial' effects of 'THE embargo' with the punishing of non-U.S. companies that do trade with Cuba.

Mr. Smith believes 'THE embargo' is an idea whose time has passed. Why? "Because change has not only occurred in Cuba, but is well on the way." He cites economic reform as not only having begun, but as "... being irreversible and taking on a momentum of its own." Mr. Smith believes examples are the *'dollarization of the Cuban currency' and 'self-employment laws.'* Laws that have allowed farmers and artisan markets to open as well as a *'broadening of the foreign investment laws in Cuba.'* Mr. Smith believes *'the need to reduce the state sector of the economy is putting pressure on the government to expand the private sector.'* As a result, *'Cuba is on the way to a thoroughly mixed economy.'*

In the 1960's, 'THE embargo' was established for logical reasons. Fidel appeared to be a communist who allowed the Russians to deploy nuclear missiles... aimed at us. Buying Cuban cigars undermined *our* national security.

In the 1970's, the reason became Fidel's fermentation of revolution elsewhere. Buying Cuban cigars appeared to undermine somebody else's national security.

However, by 1998 Fidel didn't have nuclear weapons and he didn't exported revolution although there was a market for it... somewhere. And while Castro may still yearn for a Spartan as well as disciplined socialism, he's made room for shopkeepers and struck deals with foreign capitalists to modernize Cuba's tourism. There are renovated hotels, better telephones, nickel mines, and a new ultra-modern airport. But the State Department says 'THE embargo' policy will stay in effect until Castro allows Cubans' democracy and improves human rights. But in reality, 'THE embargo' is just a limit on the U.S. citizens' right(s)... to buy Cuban products like sugar and cigars, to sell our wares, to travel to Havana, and to even send or receive gifts.

Three objectives were at the root of 'THE embargo' when it was first enacted in the early sixties. One was to 'punish' Cuba for nationalizing *our* properties without just compensation and, possibly, to force Fidel into a compensation agreement. Another was to raise the cost of doing business between the Soviets and Cubans in maintaining an alliance and pursuing any policy that was determined to be detrimental to U.S. interests. The third was to reduce resources Cuba could pour into assisting revolutionary movements... especially in Latin America.

It's been said on more than many occasions '*the more things change the more they stay the same*'. Change is now happening in Cuba... however, the change isn't because of 'THE embargo!' The reason for the change is because Cuba has lost her *Soviet* saint. Unfortunately, no country has ever abandoned a political ideology because of an embargo... be it Russia, East Germany, Vietnam, North Korea, China, or any other repressed State in the world. This is common knowledge to everyone... except us in the States. And, it's a fact that at this time, 'THE embargo' is *only* carried on by the U.S. government.

Conflicting with 'THE embargo' policy is the U.S.' inability to embargo authoritarian States to act peaceably. America is a 'friend' with one of the *least-free* countries in the world, Saudi Arabia. The U.S. is also actively conducting business with Korea, Vietnam, and China. And although the American government may lecture China about human rights, the same U.S. government supports trade with that country. A truer reason Cuba isn't being treated like China probably has more to do with their 1.2 billion people... all those Chinese who want to buy U.S. products. Politics!

The only country that hasn't accepted Cuba as a communistic State throughout the world is America. There's something about Castro that seems to drive U.S. conservatives into a state of Castroitis! Despite America's numerous attempts to kill or overthrow Fidel, Castro has survived. Maybe, a reason the world doesn't seem to mind him still being in power is because they think it's nice to know there's someone around capable of thumbing their nose at Uncle Sam... and who manages to get away with it!

Despite the fact Cuba isn't the worker's paradise Castro envisioned during the revolution and his regime is more repressive than liberating, his government isn't going anywhere... regardless of the sanctions imposed. To state it again, the main reason the U.S. still fights Cuba is the very vocal and brutally belligerent throng of Cuban exiles in the States. Jorge Mas Canosa, before his death, and his Cuban American National Foundation (CANF) make a lot of noise and give a lot of money to both political parties... Democrats and Republicans alike! Mas had links to anti-Castro terrorists and wanted to be Cuba's next President. The last thing Mas or the CANF want is a normalization of relations with Cuba. And although Mas is dead, CANF is still very much alive.

In the early 1980's, the U.S. Senate investigated American intelligence abuses. It was disclosed that America was involved in at least a dozen attempts to assassinate Fidel. There was evidence that showed the U.S. had engaged in or sponsored a large number of acts of sabotage against Cuban property... and that *our* Cuban refugee agents were committing terrorist acts in Cuba. If that situation were reversed... if Cuban agents were doing the same things in America... Cuba would've been nuked years ago. However, it seems that when the American government does those things, the media coverage is barely noticeable.

A more salient example and equally troubling reality of hypocrisy in America's ideology of the Democratic political philosophy is the Northwood Document... basis of OPERATION NORTHWOODS. OPERATION NORTHWOODS was a memorandum commissioned in 1962 by the Joint Chiefs of Staff for Secretary of Defense, Robert McNamara, in response to a request from the Chief of the Cuba Project, Col. Edward Lansdale. The subject of this document is (titled) Justification for U.S. Military Intervention in Cuba. Obviously, top secret and only recently unclassified, it describes, in detail, how several various pretexts could be engineered in such a manner that an U.S. invasion of Cuba would be justified. The scenario(s) included staging assassinations of Cubans living in America, creating a fake 'Communist' Cuban terror campaign in and around Miami as well as other Florida cities and Washington, faking or actually sinking a boat with Cuban refugees, simulating the appearance of a Cuban air force attack on a civilian jetliner, recreating

The Maine incident by blowing up a U.S. ship in Cuban waters and of blaming Cuba with sabotage as the cause. And, I'll say it again, if those in the position of authority they're in are known to have done these things along with others including numerous assassination attempts of Fidel, then one could reasonably ask... what else is being done in the name of Democratic principles of freedom?

Unfortunately, one country's subversion is the basis for another's effort to look out for its own legitimate strategic interest(s). America regards Central and all of South America as well as the Caribbean as its own private dominion. It should be of little surprise that, during the last fifty years, the U.S. has been involved with subversive acts in Brazil, Ecuador, El Salvador, Chile, the Dominican Republic, Guatemala, Haiti, Nicaragua, Panama, Jamaica, and Uruguay... as well as Cuba. And if the U.S. was involved in any subversive acts abroad, quite possibly it may have been involved in subversive acts within the borders of its own country... as well. President John F. Kennedy's assassination brings all kinds of conspiracy thoughts to mind. Hell, why should borders keep those doing those subversive acts at bay? Wouldn't the same people be behind those same subversive acts?

Confusing the issue of 'THE embargo' is General Cigar Corp.'s apparent infringement of Cuba's Cohiba trademark protection with intellectual property registration. Cuba filed a challenge in U.S. federal court with the U.S. Patent and Trademark Office (USPTO)... claiming infringement and unfair competition as well as trademark dilution by Barcardi-Martini U.S.A., Gallo Wine Distributors, and General Cigar Co. When the suit was filed in 1997, the motivation was clear... skyrocketing rum and tobacco sales during the previous few years. The suit augmented a growing expectation that trade might soon open. And there was also a strong desire by both manufacturers and businessmen on both sides of the Florida Straits to corner markets and garner trademark protection

A hope in an impending break in 'THE embargo' was that Cuba took its case to the U.S. Courts. However, the following year, all the parties in the suit agreed to suspend litigation and entered into settlement negotiations. It was viewed as a novel approach to intellectual property battles between America and Cuba... given that any payment to Cuba or participation in General Cigar Co.'s business would require a license and could have been seen as a new form of trade.

It's interesting to note that settlement discussions did take place... thereby raising the possibility of an unprecedented payment to Cuba that might have signified a crack in 'THE embargo.' For, while 'THE embargo' allows U.S. registration by Cuban manufacturers, and hundreds of U.S. companies have registered trademarks and copyrights in Cuba, it bars the sale of Cuban cigars in America. Hence, Cuba has never registered the Cohiba trademark in the States... although it has held the Cuban registration since 1972.

The whole U.S. legal community is caught up with Cuban anythingism. On April 6, 1998 the National Law Journal published an article written by Pamela S. Falk, that was a special to the National Law Journal, entitled Visions Of Embargo Falling Spark U.S.-Cuba IP Battles. It began, *'Posturing for future free-trade era ignites suits over cigars and rum brand names and a flurry of IP registrations in both nations.'*

The National Law Journal followed the case between General Cigar Corp. and Cuba closely... and reported on it regularly. They aren't the only ones preoccupied, either. There probably isn't a person in America who doesn't know who a boy called Elian is. Every paper and TV station carried the custody battle news daily... and in some cases hourly. And cafés, bars, and restaurants promoting and advertising Cuban fare and drinks or ambiance is now a popular venue for Americans... everywhere.

In the fiscal year 1993-94, Customs officials said the number of Cuban cigar seizures was two hundred and twenty-one. That number jumped to over three thousand seven hundred back in the 1996-97 fiscal year, when agents confiscated over two hundred and forty thousand stoogies worth an estimated $3.1 million! This upsurge in confiscated cigars represented a two-and-a-half fold increase over the ninety-six thousand plus that were taken in the 1995-96 fiscal year.

In all the years 'THE embargo' has been in effect, it hasn't ostracized Castro's regime. Instead, it's provided Fidel with a scapegoat to blame Cuba's woes on. If the U.S. government really believed in economic freedom... then why does it perpetuate a policy that hasn't worked? Trade is a human right and people have a right to trade their work, products, and services with anyone... from the local druggist or artist to a Cuban cigar maker. The **only** exception is war! And America isn't at war... with Cuba.

Many Americans know they'd benefit by lifting 'THE embargo' and opening Cuba to trade. In fact, the one who has the most to fear from lifting 'THE embargo' is Castro himself. There's no better way to undermine Fidel than to flood Cuba's streets with U.S. tourists, students, and businessmen... with their ideas of freedom and business. Ending 'THE embargo' would end Fidel's scapegoat. And if Fidel kept American investment out of Cuba, he'd have to shoulder the blame. Then, with luck, he'd fall like a rock... like those from the Berlin Wall.

Pedro Pablo Diaz, Coca-Cola's vice president for communications for Latin America stated in 1995 that Coca-Cola was a big seller in Cuba before Castro nationalized the facilities there. He also said that Coca-Cola *'would be selling its' soft drinks in Havana in hours'* if 'THE embargo' were lifted. He added, "When the government of the U.S. decides it's appropriate, we're going to be there immediately."

Pedro Pablo Diaz apparently hasn't been to Cuba recently because at the time he made those statements, Coca-Cola **was** being sold on the island. However, being a vice president of Coca-Cola communications for Latin America, he should've known their soft drink was being sold in Havana... and has been for years. In 1997, when I was in Havana, Coca-Cola was present wherever one went and available to mix with their famous Havana Club rum drink that's known *'round the world.'*

Ernest Preeg is a former diplomat who wrote a book, <u>Cuba and the New Caribbean Economic Order.</u> He's stated, "What keeps Cubans from hosting guests at the Radisson has more to do with American voters than with Castro's ideology. It's much more domestic politics... than foreign policy. Cuban-Americans comprise a powerful political force in Florida, whose whopping 25 electoral votes gets a presidential candidate nearly a tenth of the way to the White House." Neither American political party wants to alienate Cuban-Americans... the most vocal of whom back 'THE embargo.' The 2000 U.S. Presidential election should erase any doubt. Surely it might've gone another way and another might've been elected had the Clinton Administration backed the cause of that little Elian boy's relatives.

In the three years between 1997 and the new millennium, the U.S. government relaxed and eased 'THE embargo' against Vietnam... that is the same trade embargo imposed on Cuba. The U.S. State Department has stated that 'THE embargo' will remain in effect until the fundamental goal of achieving '*a peaceful transition to a stable, democratic form of government and respect for human rights*' are obtained. However, during this same time period, the same State Department released their annual report on global human rights abuse… each year. Nowhere during that time had Vietnam's policy changed… let alone changed as much as Cuba's. In fact, the State Department criticized Vietnam for a lack of political freedom and for official government persecution of Catholic and Buddhist clergy. The report(s) also accused Vietnam of making arbitrary arrests, failing to distinguish in legal terms between peaceful and violent political dissent, and maintaining a legal system that didn't guarantee accused offenders' fair trials or due process under the law. All the things the U.S. government wants the Cuban government to assure prior to changing their policy regarding 'THE embargo.'

E-Mails R Us

***

In an endeavor to spread the word, e-mails were sent out… even more received. Message boards were attacked in an assault on the great cigar liberation front. Words were written about the life of a smoke and in a spec of supersonic galactic warp speed the fire began spreading like a blaze out of control. Trails were branded by the mark of a stoogie. The rough terrain was traversed with the stroke of a pen and messages were read about someone who was challenging a right for political reform. And where one went others would follow. It was a path that'd lead them toward their own favorite cigar brand freedom.

Immediately upon hearing the news, support started to pour in. People from all over the world wanted to voice an opinion and show they backed the cause. And, then again, maybe they just needed a good cause to support. Growing up, I always heard *silence was golden*. But, at this time in my life, I found the written word was platinum to my ears.

Within the first week of arriving in Jamaica, the wave that carried the *Internet* surf began flowing. A Petri of a cigar life dot comer wrote of it in the universe of cosmic existence, "It's a great story and online at www.citypaper.net/articles/010898/howcol.shtml." That statement was in response to one written by another… 'Recently read an article in a local Phila. City Paper paper that said U.S. government is being sued over legality of the confiscation policy with Cuban cigars. Check out the City Paper paper dot net, Pretzel Logic - Cuba Libre. Thank G-d for people like him. It's about time the smoke screen got lifted. Read the article and disperse the smoke.'

Someone calling themselves' *ToBeA*nnounced and who was at an earth link dot Net address, made a statement in the universe of Net existence. "If David Fabler has a legal defense fund set up with a legal individual donation level not to exceed $10,000 (hell, Clinton has one to defend his ML brand BJ's) I will be happy to contribute… although substantially less than that amount."

Before I knew it, the veil known as the government's smoke screen, 31 CFR Chapter V was rising up into the air like a bird in flight. As the days passed, messages were multiplying. When last seen they were flying around inter-galactic outer-space and in a spec of time I was hearing from people all over the universe.

An office manager from Global Exchange, an organization that promotes Cuban affairs and an end to 'THE embargo' sent an e-mail, "Dear David... I've forwarded your message to the people in the office who do work around Cuba. They will probably get back to you. I have also put a note that I looked at the site and that it looks very interesting... and I am sure they will find it so as well. Thank you for the info."

In another, a head of a dot Net communications company wanted the world to know. "Thanks for the link. The 1994 manual quoting is quite interesting." And there were more... many more. So many that it was more than enough to keep busy surfing up and down the Net highway... in an effort to smoke out that screen of a stoogie cigar puff.

A British citizen traveled to Cuba before going to America. He said he was going back again... sometime in the future. When he entered the States he had an encounter with U.S. Customs and wanted to talk about his experience. His name was Billy Clubb.

"I was interested to read about your attempt to challenge U.S. government's seizure of your Cuban cigars. I've got a similar story to relate but, as you'll see, my circumstance is somewhat different. I am determined to pursue the matter anyway possible. Shortly, I'll be going to America and I'm planning another trip to Cuba before entering the U.S. from there (via Jamaica). And I'd like to be as well informed as possible. I don't want to challenge what happened in the past, but to stop the same thing from happening to me and others like me... in the future."

"In 1996, I went to Cuba and when passing through U.S. Customs in Nassau I was asked if I had anything to declare. I said, 'Yes, 49 Cuban cigars.' I thought they'd be of no interest to the agent... and he made no remarks about them nor did he make any attempt to confiscate them. I assumed that was because I wasn't a U.S. citizen or resident... and that it was OK to bring up to 50 Cuban cigars into the country. However, on a subsequent trip, in 1997, I landed at JFK airport and had marked my Customs declaration card to the effect that I had been in Cuba. I was asked by Customs if I had any Cuban tobacco goods. 'Yes, 50 cigars,' I said."

145

"They seized them. They also took my passport away and kept me in the airport for 90 minutes. Since then, I've been on some kind of black list in the computer and every time I enter the U.S. my baggage is searched by Customs and I'm questioned."

"I'm British! I am not nor have I ever been a U.S. citizen or resident alien. I had told Customs that I was leaving the U.S. within that week to go back to Europe and that the cigars were for personal use. When asked, I freely declared them and I never tried to hide anything... yet I was treated more or less as a criminal."

"My question is, did I violate 'THE (Cuban) embargo?' Under 31 CFR 515.204, am I *a person subject to the jurisdiction of the U.S.?* Surely, I would think not! And surely, if NO ONE may do the things proscribed, the wording should simply say *no person* period."

"I note that the statute 31 CFR states, '*...prohibits, unless licensed, the importation of commodities of Cuban origin.*' The interesting point is the wording '*unless licensed.*' Title 31 CFR 515 lists who may go, and defines circumstances under which OFAC chooses to authorize on a case by case basis travel (for example) for professional research, educational, or religious activities. It's clear this can only apply to U.S. citizens... and to resident aliens."

"How can I, a non-resident alien wishing to travel to Cuba for educational purposes, obtain authorization from OFAC if I wish to carry out a visit to Cuba via the U.S.? Impossible! They have no jurisdiction over me. How can they allow their own (duly OFAC authorized) citizens to import $100.00 worth of Cuban merchandise... yet not me? It would seem that I could temporarily import $100.00 worth of Cuban merchandise if it is for my own use and not for resale. What is wrong with this?"

And I knew exactly what Billy Clubb was talking about. Because, although different, I was experiencing the same thing!

A Ceylon who may have been from Ceylon sent encouraging words. "Keep the faith. We're all fighting with you. Let us know how things turn out. Good luck!" Monte Python who might've been a movie star voiced his support. "Have read about the struggle in some news links with your lawsuit against Customs. I certainly hope you prevail against this really archaic law that does little to *punish* that bad, naughty Fidel. Maybe if

YOU could get elected to Congress YOU'D legally be able to possess all the Cubans YOU wanted, but just don't let Bill get his Monica on them."

A mad hero who called himself Madero and was from Honduro penned, "Gee do the rest of the other Central American islands seem overly U.S. ravaged? What about the Canadians, Mexicans, British, French, Japanese, Australians, etc? They visit the Bahamas, Jamaica, Puerto Rico, and the Caymans as well as Somoa, Tahiti and Bali in addition to Cuba without a single thought other than boosting any amount to those economies. I feel they do as much *damage* as the Americans. Boh dank once said something to the effect that Americans completely destroy any aura of the island nation, yet Canadians do more damage than the others... only because they can go there at the drop of a hat compared to other nations. Any aura damage will have been more than done before the U.S. ever gets to enjoy it - regardless of Bautista, Guevarra, Castro or any other Bozo-being in charge."

A Dolfin from some warm-watered winter locale sent best wishes. "Want to voice my support for freeing your Cubans from the evil forces. How can I help? Others can help by voicing their support too! Is there a government department I can write or e-mail to voice my opinion? Do they care? FINALLY an American who has the guts to stand up for his and our rights against the U.S. government on an unjust law! Please keep me posted on the progress of your case. And if there is any way I can offer support... I'd be happy too."

One day, while traveling at twice the speed of light, my travel through inner-space's outer-space exterior took me to a traveling man from some woe-be-gone forgotten hellhole spot. And those in charge had little better to do than to haul a Duke called Raoul off for the bust of neither's lifetime. The Duke beckoned me into his domain, but I really wanted no part of the story... although he eventually got to tell me all about his tale of lore. It seems that he wanted everyone to believe he was merely a victim of his own convictions however society has grown into a civilization of people who aren't responsible for their own actions. Maybe our parents were too lenient, but more likely is that the culture has grown a penchant for irresponsibility.

"I was set up by a disgruntled *ass-hole*," he stated! "The guy was in his mid-20's and came from an extremely wealthy Greek family. Dad torched his multi-million home about a year earlier. He got busted! But, when he posted bail, he split for Greece... where they refused to extradite him back to the U.S. He left the entire family behind (wife, 2 kids) and the wife went to the Fed Pen for 7-10." I wasn't quite sure what the wife had to do with anything. But, by then, I was hooked.

He continued, "That left one of the kids on the street trying to hustle. However, when the kid got into trouble he got himself out by giving up his bed so that another could rest in his place." Seems that's the way America's legal system works... rat out another to do your time.

So the case began! It was straight out of a Tequila Sunrise sequel! Apparently Raoul the Duke became a middleman for the two Debell brothers in the Bay area... Ding and Dong. Both brothers had tattoos on their arms that reflected their nicknames, Mikalo Angelo and Leonardo. As the story went, it became apparent that both brothers were trying to hide their tattoos, but one of the brothers quietly admitted the tattoos were the work of Ninja turtles... who the brothers worshipped back in the 1980's.

The Debell brothers and Raoul Duke eventually met at a place located down Havana way... alongside the pool at the Hotel Nacional. The Duke called Raoul heard his U.S. connections boast of their business... buying black market stoogies and smuggling them into the States via Mexico. His story had the ring of a tall tale with smoke screening the scene. Suddenly, the Dukester Raoul said the people he met at the pool in the Nacional said they took their clothes to be cleaned by some *friends* while they were on one of their *fishing* trips to Cuba. However, all that happened a long time before the brothers Debell began bugging Raoul Duke to sell their smokes for them. The Duke said the *set-up* involved a purported purchase by the *ass-hole*, except it seemed to me that the *ass-hole* was Raoul himself. Anyhow, all the guys met and the transaction went through the Duke... probably as a matter of convenience. I thought, how convenient!

The Duke continued his bizarre story with what he considered to be a situation that'd get everyone off his back. The brothers Debell wanted him to sell their cigars, which he wouldn't do. And the *ass-hole* was bugging the Duke of Raoul to sell him some smokes... which he claims he wasn't going to do either. So struck in the middle was he! But all they really wanted was the Duke's connection to his man down Havana way who worked at one of the Upmann factories and who desired to trade his factory brands to buyers up in the States. It seemed an easy solution to his woes, but Raoul got caught up in some lowdown showdown... at high noon.

However, no one's life imitated the arts because the characters weren't as smart as their counterparts.

The *Internet* wave kept growing as the flames fired the action. There was a posting from some smoothie she-head at a switch-head dot com address. She was really a he and he said, "I'm getting really tired of these anti-Fidel groups dictating U.S. travel policies. I don't think Castro is any worse than the Chinese government - and we gave them most-favored nation trading status. The main reason for 'THE embargo' is the strong lobby of Cuban-Americans, many of whom dream of returning to Cuba to resume the privileged life they had when it was a dictatorship."

In another, Lager De Beers from the Netherlands' De Beers wrote, "Cool story! Thanx! Maybe it helps to know we smoke Cubans all around our country (cigars that is)! We're democratic!"

At the same time the Netherlands' De Beers was heard from, someone who later became known as *Twenty-Buck Bernie* made his entrance onto the scene. "I'm interested in hearing more about this suit! I'm against 'THE embargo' and although I'm not a lawyer I can't believe 'THE embargo' could really stand the test of a solid legal challenge - Trading With The Enemy! I don't recall the U.S. declaring war on Cuba. I've often felt that if enough of us could get together we might be able to make a difference!"

Matt Dillon who may or may not have been an actor and could've been a descendent of an old wild-west lawman wrote, "I agree with you! Why should we be penalized for spending our already taxed money? Let the government spend or not spend their money on what they want if they want to make an economic statement. Tell me how your case is going! I assume it is a civil suit."

P. T. Cholera, not to be confused with a disease or the circus circus man, wanted to be *counted in for support*. His e-mail stated as much and since he was somewhat local to the case he thought he could add to the cause. Soon, thereafter, an e-mail was received from another in another area of the universe. "What's going on in this case? Curious people want to know!"

He was e-mailed back "The wheels of justice grind slowly… if at all. And they're snarling along at a snail's pace."

The Empire Strikes Back

***

Before I knew it, my 50th b-day was approaching. Lady Grace came down to the islands to share the event with one and all, but mostly with me. We were maintaining communication through the Net and had been sending messages back and forth... reading them when we could. However, her work prevented her from spending too much time looking at my mail and my phone access costs were impeding access to her correspondence.

'Paranoia strikes deep! Into your life it will creep! It starts when you're always afraid. Speak out and you'll be taken away.' I knew I was crazy to have lived my life the way I did... and it left me a child of *paranoia*. In my own way I spoke out and, sure enough, was taken away... for longer than too long. That is, until they thought that I had promised to repent my sins. But a leopard doesn't change its stripes. They know that! That's why all who are caught the first time are kept... so there won't be a second.

In my case, the time finally ran and they had to let me go. At the time, I didn't know where my direction would be, but there I went anyway. Then, I got ahead of myself because I became *paranoid* before my time. However, I had nothing to be afraid of... or so I thought! I also thought I didn't trust the government to just sit back and let someone undo their trade policy activities for the better part of the previous forty odd years. And I didn't know what I was feeling, but I knew that I was stuck in a *paranoid* state of mind.

A couple of days before the big day I received an e-mail from the shark. Suddenly, there was movement on the case... as the sharks were feasting on the material they'd been fed.

Subj: Re: Call from Customs Date: 98-03-06

David: A few minutes ago I got a call from Baltimore Customs. They had the Philadelphia article that quotes you as saying you smuggled cigars from Cuba to US way back when... therefore you knew it was illegal. He also got into the lie about what you were bringing into the country. Talk about tipping your mitt. I'm sure the US attorney would be pleased to know that they laid out their whole defense. I did get him to admit the page in the book was the wrong number. He told me the case would be in the US

150

attorney's office by Friday. I told him we've been hearing this for 6 months now, however I was glad he wasn't calling to tell me they'd be giving them back with the understanding of never doing it again because that wouldn't be acceptable. After I told him this he said that it's never been done before. I told him that wasn't true. And our conversation sort of deteriorated after he took the position that all pot smugglers are liars. I tried to explain what *crimenal faisi* is… that a rapist, killer or pot dealer doesn't make that person a liar, but he didn't get it. Anyway watch what you say to people. Peace the Sharko.

When I read it, I immediately e-mailed back.
Stephen… 2morrow's my b'day! What's happening??? I am impatiently waiting!!! Tell me more about your conversation with Customs! Did u get a name, department, position, etc??? Who exactly spoke with u???

Two days later Stephen sent a follow-up. 98-03-08 12:20:08
David… I'm going to Palo Alto on Tuesday. Unfortunately the petition still isn't done. I'm taking your file and will be optimistic in telling you that I hope to complete it within the next few days. I know you're anxious to get this filed. However, nothing will go forward until the government's Petition for Forfeiture is on record. The Petition for Return of Property will lock you in to some extent! It may be if the government files their Petition of Forfeiture first they will lock themselves in. It could be argued that strategically it would be better to wait, however I will not try and persuade you because I agree that…

And that was the end of his communication. However, a couple of minutes later another e-mail came through.
98-03-08 12:31:01
David… Sorry we got cut off for some reason. Lars believes I sent him the article when in fact I didn't. Lars Titon Helmsman is a Customs agent from Baltimore and apparently that office somehow became involved with your case… is all I know. He did say there was precedent, but he wouldn't give me the citation. The bottom line was simply that Lars Titon wanted to tell me not to pursue this because you will lose. In addition, he believes that because you were convicted of smuggling pot way back when and that you snuck cigars into the country many years ago you wouldn't

be believed when your testimony was interfaced with the customs agent at the time of your entry. Apparently the Customs agent will testify, when asked, that you verbally stated that you didn't declare anything. Furthermore, because you snuck cigars into the country before... you had to know it was illegal. If I'm able to prepare the draft of our petition while I'm away, I'll forward it to you... via e-mail. We'll see if Lars Titon Helmsman speaks the truth when he said this case will be in the hands of the U.S. Attorney for the E.D.Pa by March 10. Lars is a Customs agent who's apparently taken an interest in David Fabler. In that he has scrupulously read the article in the City Paper paper and may've done some additional investigation of you, although I wasn't sure if he was subjectively characterizing the information contained in the article.

I wanted to know who Lars the Titon cigar Helmsmen detective agent man was. Maybe he was Matt's brother, but I thought the P.I. series died when Dean bought the farm and went to Scotch heaven or wherever the Martini man went when he left... this world. Then, I wanted to know what that Lars Titon cigar Helmsmen G-man Customs agent man wanted with me. I also wanted to know who had stuck a bone up his butt, but knew I couldn't deal with it because I was out of the country. However, I knew it'd have to be dealt with sooner or later. In the meantime, I showed the e-mails to Netman as well as the Bandito and the graced lady of my life. One and all were all blown away by it all. I should've known it then or seen it coming. What had been the first clue? The empire was striking back. War had been declared.

The time passed quickly. In an instant, another month came and went. Amid an atmosphere of *paranoia*, weird evil-sadistic black-magic voodoo was taking place... shaping the events of future occurrences. Suddenly the lights went out! The cord got pulled and the electronics went silent. There were no more e-mails as access to the account set up to receive the e-mail(s) and communicate with the world's populace had been shut down. The empire was striking back. War had been declared!

Passwords were entered and registered, but not recognized. What was, wasn't any more. The worldwide wait was terminated! No longer was I sitting and waiting for access to the *Internet*... because I couldn't gain access. The access was denied. My passwords weren't activating my account. Someone or something had changed them and all I knew... it wasn't me or mine. Nor *us! Them* was more like it! Who, what, and why were the 'W' questions needing to be answered. And every answer came back to that G-man Lars the Titon cigar Helmsmen Customs agent man. The empire was striking back. War had been declared!

I went to Netman, but he couldn't offer any help. I immediately knew it was time to go. The empire was striking back. War had been declared!

I knew I needed to be where I could fend for myself… as stupid as that may have sounded! Within days, I made plans to return back to the States. Besides, the summer was near and there wasn't any reason to remain where I was. Warm winds were beginning to blow across the North Shore. It seemed a good idea to be where my friends were… even though the government was no friend of mine. So off I went! The reception I got when I returned was anything but friendly. The empire was striking back. War had been declared!

A few years earlier, I couldn't wait to leave the place I left. At the time, I could've said the devil made me do it… but he didn't. It was just something I needed to do. So, I did it! Then, the time came when I decided to return back to where I left. At the time, I could've also said the devil made me do it… but he didn't. I just met a woman who I wanted to be with. And to be with her, I had to be where she was. Since she was at the place I left… and couldn't leave it behind… I went where she was.

Returning back meant I had to decide what I wanted. Back when I first left, I did it because there wasn't anything left there for me. I left in search of something, but eventually never found it. However, I did find the girl I was searching for… even if I didn't know it.

Returning back meant I had to decide what I wanted. That was difficult because I had no idea what it was… except I knew I wanted to be with her. Although, I also knew I wanted to be in the sun, sand, warmth, and water. Decisions… decisions! What to do?

In the beginning of May I boarded a plane back to the States… without any cigars. Cubano or otherwise! It was probably a good thing! Upon my return, I was singled out and separated from the rest of the pack because my name was recognized by the Customs agent man… who knew who I was before I even got there! His exact statement was "Mr. Fabler, Customs requests to see you over at the secondary counter once you've picked up your luggage." I could only wonder whether I had an option. The empire was striking back. War had been declared!

My possessions were searched and examined. Then I was questioned for more than several hours about my conduct and other things that didn't have anything to do with anything even remotely associated with cigars. Cuban or otherwise! And it was obvious. The empire was striking back. War had been declared!

Beyond no shadow of doubt… had any cigars been found, Cuban or otherwise, I would've been treated like the criminal I was. Arrested on the spot! Thrown in prison! The key thrown away! And it wouldn't have mattered what they were… Cuban or otherwise! That was the point when I knew my e-mails had been intercepted by those who were opposed to the action(s) of my petition. I could feel it! I also knew my passwords had been changed by *them*. I'd been hacked. The empire was striking back. War had been declared!

The plan had been for the Lady Grace to pick me up at the airport, but at some point she began thinking I'd missed my flight… due to the length of time I spent *chatting* with Customs at the secondary counter. She had a hard time believing my story about being singled out… for stoogies. She said, "David, its not like it's drugs. I mean, *IT'S ONLY CIGARS*!? Right!?" I knew she was right, but I also knew she wouldn't understand until she'd experienced it first-hand and witnessed the carnage… with her own eyes.

The following morning, I called my hippie shark lawyer to set a time to meet and late in the day on the day that followed my call a meeting had been set. Before our meeting the next afternoon, I stopped by the apartment building where I once lived and saw a lion of a doorman… Leo.

A tall, lean man of African descent, Leo was middle aged and middle class. He was a security officer in the city's court system prior to his present position providing security working the doors of the building he worked in. And in his business he saw lots of cops… come and go.

Leo shook my hand. Then he asked, "David, what's goin on?" I told him not much since the last time we had seen each other… some six months earlier. But I did tell him that I was still continuing the struggle over my confiscated cigars. Then, I thought about what had happened with my e-mail service and at Customs when I last entered the country. And I told him about that too. He told me he wasn't surprised. But I was. And I asked him what he meant.

He said, "Less than three weeks ago, two guys showed up here asking lots of questions... about you. They were *packing*... and were dressed in expensive suits." I asked how he knew they were *packing* and Leo said, "I know when someone's *packing* or not. Remember, I used to work the city court security system. They were definitely government types. What's happening with you... and them?" Then, as an after-thought he added, "Oh boy, you better watch yourself..."

I told Leo about the suit, but it wasn't like he didn't know anything about it. It had been the better part of a year since Leo personally handed me the envelope that contained the six pages that were the right to contest my right to have my right to have those cigars. And those six pages was the beginning of the case that'd be called, **U.S. vs. 100 Cuban Cigars**.

Leo had that envelope with those six pages because, on that April night over one year earlier, when the government seized my cigars, I gave Customs the address where Leo worked... when I entered the country. I did it because, at the time, I still received my mail at that address. Since Leo handled the security at the door he also dealt with the people who delivered the mail and packages and, in particular, the package that had been sent from the Dept. of Treasury, U.S. Customs service... certified mail. Leo enjoyed the smokes the government said he couldn't enjoy. And he believed it was much ado about nothing. But he also believed the government wasn't to be taken lightly.

I asked Leo what the G-men agent men asked about me... and about what he told them in response. Leo told me they wanted to know if I lived in the building... and who I saw. He said he told them that I didn't live there anymore... and, then, they wanted to know how long it had been since I moved. And where I moved to! Leo said that was when they asked who I used to see... and what I did.

Leo told me that he told them that he had bad eyes. That, he said, was the reason he no longer worked for the city's court security system... as it was a requirement to be able to see what people were *packing* in court. He also told me that he told them that he took the job that he had because all he had to do was open and close the door. Leo said they hung around for a few minutes before walking outside and standing around in front of the building for more than several long minutes. Leo said it seemed as if they didn't know what to do. Leo finally said that they left after several minutes, but not before leaving an impression with him.

About an hour later I was sitting in the shark's office. He told me that there was still no word from the government on the motion we filed after Customs made their determination that the cigars weren't going to be returned. I was pissed. I thought this was the way the government was going to avoid letting me have my day in court. Stephen told me to not worry. But it wasn't his fight he was fighting. And I wasn't really sure if he was fighting my fight either. I told Stephen that I was pissed because the government couldn't be trusted. They were all liars… and thieves!

I questioned the shark about who that Lars Titon Helmsman cigar smoking Customs agent man was… and how he knew of me. I also questioned the shark about why that Lars Titon cigar Helmsman had such a bone stuck up his stump… about me. The shark told me what he told me when he sent me those e-mails around my birthday… several months earlier. Afterward, I told the shark about my most recent bout with Customs. But he just shrugged! He said something to the effect of asking about what did I expect! Then, he said that we were at war… and that I was the enemy. He also said that I should be careful with what I did because if I got busted for anything, anything at all, they'd probably trade… '*tit for tat!*' It had become very apparent. The empire was striking back. War had been declared!

When I got up to walk out of his office, Stephen told me to not worry again. I knew he wasn't. However, he didn't have as much to worry about as I did. He wasn't David Fabler and he hadn't been singled out by Customs when he entered the country. It wasn't his e-mail(s) that he couldn't get anymore. Nor was it his account that had been hacked. And Customs wasn't going around to his old places of residence asking people questions. Stephen didn't know what to say, so he said it again, "Don't worry. Leave that to me!" But I was!

Thirty years before, my father died an untimely death. On the upcoming July 4th holiday, I was going to be as old as he was on the day he died. It had been several years since I'd last been to his grave. At that time, I knew I wouldn't be returning there again until the day when I'd be as old as he was on the day he died.

Lady Grace had never seen a City of Motors. On the anniversary of America's birth and me having lived to be as old as my father on the day he died, we went off to see the Motor City. Somehow, a day that represented both birth and death seemed appropriate. In her past, the Lady Grace was wed to a Greek... and the only thing to see in an auto town was Greek-town. But I went to my birthplace to see my departed dad. And I wasn't interested in sightseeing in any town... be it Greek, Chinese, or any other nationality!

It was Saturday and Saturday is the Sabbath. And, on the Sabbath, the cemetery is closed. With all the commotion about all the hoop-la regarding the great colossal Cuban Cohiba cigar caper I forgot that the cemetery is closed on the Sabbath. Actually, it never crossed my mind until I was in front of the cemetery and the gate was closed down shut tight. I was dazed and confused! I turned to the Lady Grace and asked what day it was. She said, "Saturday."

"SSHHhhittttttt!" Suddenly, I found myself praying for G-d to grant me the power of access. I looked around, but no one was there. I didn't know what to do. However, I knew I wasn't going anywhere without seeing my father. I had visions of being arrested for breaking and entering dancing around inside my brain and knew it'd be difficult to explain that I only wanted to see my dad. I could see it all so clearly! Grave robbing was a serious offense. Then, I heard the sharks' words dancing around somewhere inside my head... '*tit for tat*'

I saw a house that seemed affiliated with the cemetery. I got out of the car and walked toward the sounds of voices I heard coming from the rear yard. I stuck my head over the neck-high fence and inquired as to the possibility of getting in to see my father. The response I got was anything but friendly or even acceptable. It was simply "We're closed for the Sabbath." And "Come back *another* day."

A lot of money had been spent and we had traveled a long way... *another* day wasn't acceptable. Besides, *another* day wouldn't occur for *another* day and the plan had been for us to be in *another* place... many miles away.... when *another* day came! Time was becoming the essence. I tried to explain that to the voices, but they weren't convinced. Reason seemed to be going out the window, so I tried *another* approach. I lashed out at their indifference and lack of understanding! I knew they could relate to that reasoning.

A deafly silence ensued for one very long minute. Suddenly, I heard "All right, all right already! Do what you want. Now, leave us alone!" Then, I heard "You could be more polite, you know!" I also heard a warning "Don't do anything you shouldn't!" And I received *another* warning... although I didn't understand what it was about. "Don't disturb anyone either!" I quietly thanked G-d for his sympathy, intervention, and compassion! As I quietly walked to my father's grave, I wondered who would be disturbed if I disturbed anyone... and how they'd complain. But looking over my shoulder back at that house, I knew who the who being complained to were.

Lady Grace stayed in the car while I sat by my father's grave for some fifty minutes. Then, in a flash, I knew it was time to go. When I left, I left with Lady Grace and we left the Motor City. We headed up North of the border to the city where the Bandito's hometown is... Toronna. That's Canadian for Toronto!

The time skipped by and in what seemed like less than an instant it was time to go back to the States. We returned our rental car at the Toronto airport. Lady Grace went through Customs without incident prior to clearing Immigration, but the same Customs lady wasn't thrilled with me returning Stateside. After all, I was an *enemy of the State*. I had to empty everything out of all my pockets out on the counter and open my suitcase. Then, she asked if I were on drugs and said that she'd know if I lied.

"Drugs?" I asked. "No!" I said!

She said I could be tested. I told her she couldn't do that... but in any case, I wasn't on drugs. She stared at my eyes. Not knowing what I should do, I stared back. Then, she asked if I'd ever been arrested or spent time in stir. She told me she could check it out. I knew she already had and it'd be stupid to lie. Besides, I had no reason to. This was only cigars! Not drugs!

Although I felt it none of her business, I told her about the *vacation* I took courtesy of my government. And to get that *vacation*, all one had to do was to have been arrested at some point. More to the point, they'd have to have been found guilty… of something. Whether or not they were guilty of what they'd been convicted of. She wanted no part of my logic and continued looking into my eyes for several long minutes prior to saying that I could move on to Immigration. By then over an hour had ticked off the clock. I thanked her for her courtesy and left her in my past. Or so I thought.

In the meantime, Lady Grace was patiently waiting for me by the plane and the plane was impatiently waiting for us to board. When I got to the Immigration post, the officer immediately asked if I'd cleared Customs… something I had to do in order to get to where he was posted. And I knew he knew that I had. Not satisfied with my response, he marched me back to the gatekeeper lady from Hell.

I saw the humor door open slightly… and had the slightest bit of a chuckle when I heard the Customs lady say she'd done everything possible and questioned "What else was there to do?" And everyone knew what she meant with what she asked! Then, she told him she'd rigorously searched every piece of clothing after he made her tell him how I'd been examined.

I found it interesting the female Customs agent was more thorough than any Customs agent I'd seen before. However, her thoroughness was lacking. For, if I'd had a mind to, I could've done whatever it was she was looking for me to have done. Yet, after producing many different forms of identity, she still wasn't satisfied with who I was. She asked if I ever lived in Pennsylvania and couldn't understand why my driver's license was issued in New Jersey. I told her that my sister lived there and that I used her address as my address instead of changing my address every time I moved… which had been often. She wanted no part of my logic. Instead, she just ordered me to open all my bags and to take everything out of all my pockets.

Two hours slowly ticked off the clock before I was allowed to proceed to the international section of the airport where the Lady Grace was waiting for me. The flight had been announced a long time before and she was worried about my whereabouts. Everyone had boarded the plane… and I was nowhere to be seen. When she saw me, she said that she would've continued waiting… in order to make sure that I got out alive. Prior to that experience, Lady Grace wasn't sure if the stories I'd tell her about those departments of law and order were being made up. But when I didn't come out for over several long hours, she knew although I was a son of a Fabler by birth, I wasn't a storyteller by nature.

On the flight back to Philadelphia Lady Grace made me promise to see the shark and to have him put an end to the unfair harassment. I laughed because I knew it'd never change, but I made that promise because I needed the security of knowing it could. Two days later, I sat in the shark's office and told him about the tale of my return to America. I said, "Now they're looking for drugs and asking questions they have no right to ask. This is getting out of hand!"

Stephen just looked at me. He asked, "What did you expect? How did you think they were going to act?" Then he said, "This is war! You're the enemy!" He also suggested something. "Maybe we can file a Freedom of Information request." However, he qualified his suggestion with a statement. "But I don't know what good it'll do." And he projected an after-thought. "Anyhow, realize every time you come into the country, you'll be subjected to this type of treatment. So, for G-d sake, don't do anything... STUPID!"

"STUPID!? Like what?"

Stephen said, "Like anything that will get you busted and question your character. That's what they're doing... using one thing against another." Then, he said it again... and he said that in this case, which was my case, that if I got busted for anything, anything at all, they'd probably trade... '*tit for tat.*' The empire was striking back. War had been declared! And... I was the enemy!

Rebel Without A Cause

***

Sitting in that big stuffed leather chair in front of the shark's desk, I told Stephen "Enough was enough." I also told him that I was fed up with all the government bull and that I was going to start a web site… one that'd tell the whole story. Stephen thought it might not be such a bad idea. In addition, I told Stephen that I was going to get in touch with various web sites to promote knowledge about my petition… in order to gather support for the cause. Stephen had no opinion. He just shrugged his shoulders and raised his eyebrows.

Then, I told Stephen that I was going to start a legal offense fund. And it was going to be a lot like all those legal defense funds every President America ever had had. I told him I'd be very offensive too… and that the government had no idea how offensive I could get. Stephen just stared at me and smiled. I didn't know if he was taking me seriously, but I told him I was serious. The shark showed his teeth because he liked the rebel in me… with or without a cause!

When the meet was almost done, I told the shark that Lady Grace was planning to have a special dinner type event. And that it'd be a cigar dinner event of the year kind of thing. I also told him that he was invited… in order to help show support for the cause. Then, I told him the event was going to be Cuban. That was, that it'd consist of Cuban food, music, coffee, liquor… and, of course, the finest cigars. It was going to be a Cubano Noche special event! Finally, I told the shark that Lady Grace was going to gracefully give some of her proceeds from the great Cubano Noche *IT'S ONLY CIGARS* dinner feast fest to help counteract all the shark fees his fees were chewing up. I told him that while it wasn't going to be THE ultimate cigar dinner event of all time, because that'd have to wait until we got the cigars back, it was going to be a cigar dinner feast not to be missed. However, I told him the date had yet to be announced when I said, "*Soon come.*" And I knew he knew what I meant.

The last thing I said before walking out of the shark's office was that the T-shirts were "*in the works.*" The T-shirts were black cotton short-sleeved pullovers with a cartoon-type caricature-image of Cuba's long-standing leader, Fidel, on the front. Smoke was rising up into the air from the stoogie he was smoking. It was titled 'Cohiba Libre!' On the back were cartoon-sketched words written in a manner that showed the humor of it all. *IT'S ONLY CIGARS*!

The T-shirts had become a reality only a short few weeks before. That was when I met with an old hippie who had become a priest... many years before I met him. The priest received his vestment papers from a <u>High Times</u> magazine ad back when he was a young hippie. Back then, his hair was longer... and it was darker than the silver white it was presently. Flying high and having nothing to do left him with nothing to do other than to respond to that ad. And, although every marriage he pledged over the years remained true to their vows, he kept his daytime job.

Fob, a G-dly type man, made T-shirts by day and arranged new lives at night... on the nights when he wasn't making T-shirts. He told Lady Grace and I the *IT'S ONLY CIGARS* Cohiba Libre T-shirts would be ready by the night of the great Cubano Noche smoked out affair.

After walking out of the shark's office, we drove over to see that old hippie priest. He called earlier that morning and told us the T-shirts were almost ready. The T-shirts were to help sustain the legal offense fund. Anything to aid the cause! And there were many people on the Net who voiced support by stating they'd buy the T-shirt... once it was on the market. We had pressed Fob the G-dly cloth man to get the T-shirts done prior to the Cubano Noche *IT'S ONLY CIGARS* dinner feast fest. It was coming together... although slowly, and time was becoming essential.

Keeping my word with the shark, within two weeks after I met with him, I met an *Internet* Whiz kid that I trusted would get the web site up and running. I told Net Whiz that I wanted the web site done within the month following our meeting. An exhaustive search was conducted and the name of my dot com web address was finalized. Since it was *only* cigars being talked about, it somehow seemed appropriate the name of my site was - *IT'S ONLY CIGARS*!

I still couldn't gain access to my e-mail account and questioned Net Whiz about it. He had few, if any, answers. The *best* he could offer was to create a new account. He suggested I continuously change the password(s) with newer and more difficult ones. That would eliminate the problem(s) from happening again... or so he said. The next day, I created two accounts with two different passwords on two different web site providers. I had everyone send and post to one. When a post was received, I immediately forwarded it to the other. And no one knew about the other. My thought... *never more*!

When I wasn't meeting *Internet* Whizzes, T-shirt makers, and the shark, I was spending more than several hours every day sending messages... and reading e-mails. In the span of inter-galactic outer-space, the news was flying across the airwaves... traveling at the Net speed of *Internet* sound. E-mails were sent and received... and the news was getting posted on various cigar-related bulletin boards. And many people from different walks of life started standing up... wanting to be seen, heard, and counted.

One member of the silent, and maybe not so silent, plurality was a cheese-head from a deep-freeze State of a Pack. Bernie was a betting man who annually bet twenty bucks on his team to win the big one... although it seemed like it had been more than twenty years since The Pack last played in THE game. If nothing else, *Twenty-buck Bernie* was loyal... to a fault. *Twenty-buck Bernie* believed in standing up for what he believed in. And there were many ways to stand up for what one believed in.

Over the past several months, I'd grown a kind of kinship with *Twenty-buck Bernie*... even though we'd never met. Through our brief e-mail transmissions, I came to realize *Twenty-buck Bernie* was a true soldier and a loyal compatriot. He believed in what was right. And what was right, to him, was that the American citizen didn't have their constitutional right(s) usurped... unconstitutionally!

Twenty-buck Bernie liked what he heard... enough to tug twenty bucks from his pocket and put it where his mouth was. True to his word, *Twenty-buck Bernie* forwarded his twenty bucks for the cause. In the space of a few weeks, the legal offense fund got funded and although it was only twenty bucks... it WAS twenty bucks! Suddenly, at only twenty bucks per person, only another nine thousand nine hundred and ninety-nine people were needed to finance the battle at hand.

I let the shark know that *Twenty-buck Bernie* was sending twenty bucks for the legal offense fund. The shark said he'd deposit it into a secure account. I assumed that meant his bank. Then, the shark instructed me how to word any future dialogue about the fund so I wouldn't run afoul of the word of law. And he reminded me about what he'd said... when he said, "Don't give them any reason."

David Weisenthal

Another not so silent stoogie smoker hailed from the far West Coast. He boasted of having a web site dedicated to informing his readers about what was news in the news. His claim was that if it had anything to do with cigars, Mike would post it to his board. Cigar Mike posted a bulletin of the news of my case on his board and said that the news was news to him. Cigar Mike's web page allowed him the opportunity to vent his *Rantz* on whatever he wanted to fume at. And Micky told me to keep him posted because he wanted to keep his readers posted about the news of my story.

A small *aficionado* from some stoogie smoking story spin mag made his presence known when the junior minor pager paged me about news of my case. He said, "We should meet." Within a couple of weeks a meet was made. The meet took place up in the big apple... where their office was. The building was locked down tight on the upper floors. Apparently, the smokers needed protection... probably from those who might've known what was being stoked and wanted to sniff out some too. Anyhow, the meet was set in a downstairs café down on the street. And why we didn't go higher may've had more to do with him having been too afraid to reveal a source to those who were higher up the ladder of print. Then again, maybe he just wanted to make sure the air was clear.

Many questions were asked and copious notes taken on a small notepad that had a lot of space to take a lot more notes. He said his boss had interest in the tale and an article could come of it. It had all the makings of a true-life real serial. Finally, he asked why I did it. I told him of the three basic core things that make us what we are... '*Truth, justice...and every American's right to smoke a good Cuban.*' I figured he knew that meant inhaling... not death. But if one did inhale, then it probably did mean death... in the end. And in the end, we shook hands and went our own ways with Lady Grace and I going up the street while he went up the elevator to tell the tale.

When all came to pass the tale was never told, but they did manage to get a few T-shirts that I was told were loved enough to wear around the office! And, maybe, a basis for the pressless press was due to a junior minor paper pager not being an older major smoke king stoogie hound. Then, I remembered what the Bandito said when he said that he'd have played... if given a piece. But I did make a note to further note, that if in the future were any other meet set, I'd have to make sure that I got a piece... for a piece too.

164

Bucks come in different forms and each has a different picture! The face on one didn't have a Hamilton or Washington, but a son of a Buck of a Rouldolph. I first met Bucky, or maybe he first met me, in a watering-hole saloon-town bar. I was there for a few brews. And I never did find out why he crossed over the line that marked the doorway to his outer world of reality. But there he was anyway.

A chance encounter, a coincidental meeting, a fortuitous conversation add up to the lucky sperm law. Bucky told me what he did... and what he did was interview people for a local TV station. I told him what I did... and what I did was sue the U.S. government over Cuban cigars. He said that he liked smoking stoogies, but had never tried a Cuban... and damn if he didn't want to.

After several whatever Rouldolph was drinking drinks, he said he'd like to know more about the great colossal Cuban Cohiba cigar caper. I told him it could be arranged and we agreed to stay in touch. We also agreed a TV interview might be a perfect source for public information. We soon separated. But unlike two ships that passed in the night, we kept in touch... with an intent of doing a TV interview. And I knew Buck the Rouldolph man would enjoy a Cubano Noche *IT'S ONLY CIGARS* dinner feast fest.

The Duke called Raoul kept registering in. Time after time, he told one and all, but mostly me, about his dealings with the men from Customs. He said it was as though they tried to portray him as being a big time stoogie swapper of some North American trader for Cuban cigar contraband. But it really sounded as though he wanted to ring a bell about his fear and loathing of being from a small-town gambling-hall of some medium-sized Mecca-town... down Vegas way.

From near and far, posts were posted. Whether they agreed or not didn't matter because the topic was something that required dialogue to decide the course of the issue... and everyone seemed adapt with speaking out on the issue. All, that is, except someone who claimed to be a captain of some long lost cave dwelling men and his sad band of ditto-headed cronies. For, while they could orate at great length on various matters, they knew little of what they spoke. And, although the news was spreading and most approved the action(s)... not everyone agreed my action was the action to take. Especially, those Neanderthal cavemen denizens that were awaken from their deep sleep to emerge from the cave they had been hibernating in.

The one who said he was the captain of all the cavemen had many things to say. However, he didn't have any idea what they were... and neither did most of those who read his rants. I was confused about what he really wanted to say when I read his first response to one of my posts. But after reading the post, I only wanted to know if he'd been elected or appointed. The captain responded that he'd been elected in a general election... although he said '*no one voted.*' Then, he said '*All the ballots were on parchment marked with charcoal.*' And it seemed, to me, to be the devil's work!

It didn't take long to realize that the captain and his ditto-brained butt-headed dodo pals wanted me to stop all the action(s) being taken. They were attacking like there was no tomorrow. I became public enemy *numbero one* and their radical ranted vents being fired, although not all were aimed at me, were directed in my direction. And if one didn't know any better, they might've sworn all those ditto-heads were government double agent mole spies.

Luckily, the attackers seemed to be few in number and their attacks seldom heard. And their sentiments posted were far apart. More importantly, the supporters greatly outnumbered the counterparts. In fact, it could've been thought all the posts were of one lone person... that captain of the cavemen dwellers.

One such posting was a message that said, "The law may be wrong." It continued. "When it is wrong, people must get involved to change the law." I was confused because I thought that was what I was doing... getting '*people involved to change the law.*' His message went on, "But the law says no importing from Cuba. I personally don't think you have a leg to stand on." I looked down and saw both my legs still supported my weight... and decided to write back. But before I could, another stood in my steed.

He wrote, "So how would you suggest people get involved if the law is wrong... and by your own suggestion 'the law may be wrong?' How better to allow the legal system (i.e. the courts) to decide the legality of the issue? Sounds to me like this guy is pretty cool... using the courts to decide whether the law is wrong. I don't know the law exactly as I've never read it, but I'd think if he didn't have a leg to stand on he might've fallen... already. Hey, who was it that said the first rule of the populace is to question the government? Oh yeah... Thomas Jefferson! But then, who was he? Just another hot-headed radical revolutionary! This guy is just doing what Tom did... and my hat is off to him! I think we need more heroes like this!" What more could I add? I decided to remain silent! Sometimes, it's better to think one's mind... than to actually speak it!

The captain of the underworld cavemen didn't want to be dismissed so easily. He had a voice and his voice wanted everyone to hear the rants he lavished on everyone... not just me! "Our country's policy is trade with Cuba is forbidden. Why should anyone be allowed to violate that policy? I'm neither validating nor criticizing that policy, but as long as it remains in effect, no one has a right to bring in Cuban cigars. There's no way this case will be won. But I suspect someone else is footing the bills. What is being said, in essence, is that you don't care what our country's policy is... you want to have your little forbidden candy. And, if prevented from subverting that position, you'll cry to your Big Brother. BTW... I love Cuban and other cigars, but I don't pretend our country should change its policy to suit my whim. Save it for someone else!" Then he added, "There's too many hypocrites in this world for me!" And, he closed with a good-by note, "Get lost... jerk!"

Another stood up to defend the cause and responded, "Then leave!" He added as an after-thought, "Do you have an ax to grind for some unjustified reason? This case has been documented by secondary sources and he has been kind enough to keep folks here updated as to what's happening. If you're not capable of grasping the significance of this case then that, I'm afraid, is your loss." There was nothing more I could add. So once again... I let others do the talking.

Before I could think about responding to the latest inflammatory citing the captain or his ditto-brain ass pals sent out into the universe, a barrage of responses went flying across the Net so fast it made my eyes spin. As fast as I read one, another appeared... and they didn't stop. "Thanks for the updates, Dave... don't let Cap Negativity detract you from keeping others updated."

"To Capt. Ass-hole - Get a life... jerk!"

"Capt. Cave, what you need is to crawl back into your cavern... you frustrated old man. About time someone told that jerk where to go!"

167

"No Dave... DON'T save it for someone else! I WANT to hear it!"

"Hey, Capt. thanks for your (non)contribution. But your last posting at 23:05pm was, at least, five minutes past your bedtime!"

"Dave, your posts sound great. Don't listen to the few idiots who don't want to hear about your exploits. PLEASE KEEP US UP TO DATE!"

"Dave, thanks for your post(s)! I'm rather interested in your case. I think you're trying to fix some power abuse U.S. Customs is committing. I agree it's right to not allow them to pass the formal legal limits... even if this kind of creativity may be dangerous in the long run. I also imagine you're having fun. And, most important, you allow yourself to have even more fun enjoying the great Capt.'s flames! Now go... CC!!!"

I wanted to keep silent because I knew it was the golden rule, but something inside my head told me otherwise. Looking back, I knew it was the devil, but I did it all the same.

"Sorry Capt. Cave... I paid 4 my legal costs myself. However, people have asked 2 help fund a legal offense fund... with the promise that I b very offensive. And I will b very offensive 2 get the smokes back. Also, a line of Cohiba Libre *IT'S ONLY CIGARS* T-shirts r in the works! Anyting 2 aid the cause. Besides, isn't this the way of capitalism? Although 2 get serious 4 1 moment, *IT'S ONLY CIGARS* we're talking about... not WW3! So b4 this whole world goes up in smoke we need 2 take a deep breath! Oh, and if I lose I don't have a Big Brother 2 run 2 except... Big Brother & The Holding Company or the government! And I don't tink the G-men want 2 hear from me... besides, those other guys disbanded a long time back! Such is life... but mayb a book or a movie! What u tink????"

The cavemen dweller's captain didn't really know what to say or how to respond so he just said, "Oh great freedom fighter of the great Cuban Cohiba cause, may you long continue to wage the tremendous battle and blast your ego all over this board. LOL!"

JJ, who I wondered if he was an actor, said, "Way to go Dave. Knowing the government, you probably won't ever see them again. They will find some way to ensure that you don't come out ahead. But strike one up for the little guys anyway!"

One who pondered being a Prevailing Justice wrote, "Everything sounds great! Think what you are doing is beyond commendable... please keep us posted and up to date!"

An Anxious Anxious wrote, "The more I read from / about you, the more I'm coming to like you! You're convinced by your reading of the law that you were treated unfairly by the government! It would've been far easier to just accept the loss and move on. I applaud your efforts and congratulate you on making your point to the government!" What more could I say, so I continued to tell everyone what was happening!

A few days later I received an e-mail from someone who wanted to know how the legal offense fund was going. "How is the 'offensive' fund going? I know many who want to send a Nanny or three. Please advise as to who to send $$$ to."

Near summer's end, I made my way up an old elevator shaft in a building that housed the American Civil Liberties Union. I went to see them because they were organized and specialized in helping the common citizen fight the oppression of tyranny. Since they opposed the oppression of tyranny I thought it might be best to enlist their services. And who better than the ACLU?!

The ratty old elevator never stopped rumbling and grinding, but it did finally stop at the button I pushed that signaled the floor that that organization was on. When the door opened, I entered the area of those freedom protectors. I also made a note to walk back down to the street... twelve stories below. I didn't want to push my luck!

Not two steps out the elevator door, I knew I had to be in the wrong place. I could see no one was there, however papers were thrown about... on tables, chairs, and the floor. The phone(s) were ringing, but no one cared... as no one was there to hear the ringing. No one, that was, except one lone old man who sat at a barren table and who seemed oblivious to the ringing that filled the stale office air.

I approached the old man. He was quietly talking on the phone while the other lines continued to ring. The ringing would finally stop... only to start again, less than a few seconds later. All the while, the old man continued his conversation... and ignored the ringing phone(s) as well as my presence.

I heard a loud thumping sound and turned to see the elevator door open. A middle-aged bearded man walked out into the dry musty area. He walked passed me without stopping to inquire why I was there... so I stopped him. I asked a question that he seemed less than interested in answering. For what wasn't even a fat apple second, he mulled it over... then told me I had to speak to the old man on the phone who was ignoring both me and the other phones that were ringing. The bearded one left the area through a door that led him out from where I was standing. The door closed behind him... leaving the old man, still on the phone, and I alone once again.

A long few minutes passed before the old man hung up the phone he was talking on. I continued standing there, thinking he'd address me. But after several minutes of silence, I knew I was mistaken. The phone lines continued to ring, but he didn't answer them.

After what seemed like forever, he looked up at me and asked if he could be of assistance. Not wanting to seem intrusive, I had pretended to look at some papers that had been clipped to a bulletin board. When he finally addressed me, I immediately stopped looking at those papers on the wall and turned to the old man. I told him I was looking for an attorney to help assist with my situation.

The old man asked, "What did you say?" I repeated myself... a little louder. The old man asked again, "What did you say?" I repeated myself once more... a little louder than before. The old man said he couldn't hear me. Then he said, "I wear a hearing aid, you know?!"

I repeated myself for the fourth time. I told him what I said and I said it loud enough for the old man to hear what I said. Suddenly, the old man said, "You don't have to scream. You know, I can hear!" I looked at the old man before looking up at all the corners and under the tables to see where I knew the camera(s) had to be. I also knew our conversation was being taped and recorded... and I was waiting for the release form to sign. I figured I was in some sort of movie. Little did I know! Only it wasn't the one I wanted to be in.

I told the old man I needed to see an attorney. He asked why. I told the old man I had a civil liberty case that needed legal assistance. He said that in the whole State of Pennsylvania there were only two attorneys who worked for the ACLU… one on each side of the State, some three hundred miles apart! I could only ask, "Two attorney's!? That's it? For the whole State! Two attorneys?" The old man simply nodded his head. I asked, "How does anything ever get done around here?"

The old man answered, "Not often." Then, he asked what my case was about.

When I finished telling the old man about my case, he gave me some papers to fill out. He told me to write my case down on the papers that he gave me. It took the better part of two hours for me to finish writing out my case and to fill out their forms. When I was finished, I gave the papers back to the old man. He briefly looked at them before telling me that someone would get back to me, but he didn't know when or how. Then, he told me that I could use the same elevator I came in with… to leave. I didn't hang around… and I didn't use that elevator either.

The day after the day I went to the ACLU, the Lady Grace and I received a phone call from Fob… the old hippie turned <u>High Times</u> priest. He said the T-shirts were finished. That night we entered his shop and paid him his money. Then, we walked out with our first order of Cohiba Libre *IT'S ONLY CIGARS* T-shirts. Later that night, I e-mailed all who had inquired that the T-shirts had arrived! *Twenty-buck Bernie* immediately notified me that he was sending his twenty bucks for a shirt… and he couldn't get it soon enough. I wanted to thank G-d for people like *Twenty-buck Bernie.*

A couple of days later, *Twenty-buck Bernie* received his Cohiba Libre *IT'S ONLY CIGARS* T-shirt and he immediately sent an e-mail that said how cool and clever he thought it was. He said he put it on… even though it was less than twenty degrees where he lived up in the boon docks of a back bush out in the cold tundra of the upper Midwest. He was proud of his purchase and the support he gave to the cause… and that was cause enough for *Twenty-buck Bernie* to celebrate wearing that cigar-smoking figurine chest- cover for all to see. And see it, they all did!

The only thing *Twenty-buck Bernie* was sorry for was that he couldn't make it to the Cubano Noche dinner feat fest of the year. But that event would've cost *Twenty-buck Bernie* a lot more than the twenty bucks he allocated himself to spend on anything he could afford.

Road To Jurisprudence

***

Shortly before the fall, I received a call from the shark who said he received a government motion for summary judgment. That meant the government was asking the court to order the cigars forfeited based on a Customs predetermination. Stephen said it could happen, but he also said the petition we filed was floating around somewhere inside the halls of justice... and it'd have to be dealt with somehow.

The shark suggested we meet... and a meeting was scheduled for the following day. The shark confirmed my belief that the reason the government didn't want us to file way back when wasn't because there'd be two cases floating through the halls of justice... as the government said there'd be, but because they'd have filed their case! And only their case would've been the basis for a judge to determine summary judgment... without a court hearing to hear or determine the basis of my suit.

Late in the afternoon on the day after the day that the shark called, I met with my hippie shark lawyer. He told me the government ignored my petition and instead filed a motion of their own... which explained why we hadn't received any response from the filing of my petition. Their motion was titled **U.S. vs. 100 Cuban Cigars,** and was for summary judgment of the seized articles taken on the night of April 18, 1997... almost seventeen months earlier.

In their motion, the government argued there wasn't any basis for the return of the articles taken and asked the court to bypass the legal system. In essence, the government didn't want the day to come when I'd have my day in court. I asked the shark about the possibility of it happening and was told it could. Then, he told me that a judge had already been assigned to the government's motion.

Stephen said that His Honor, the judge, was as anti-governmental as any judge could be. He said that he ruled from his heart, not his head... and not from his superiors. The shark suggested we move to merge both cases into one and take our chances with His Honor, the judge, who'd been assigned to the case. Especially since we could do a lot worse with whoever would be assigned to our petition! However, I wasn't sure if I should agree.

The shark said that His Honor, the judge, had already set a date to meet in his private chambers. The date was four weeks later... October 1st. The shark also said we should prepare for that day as if it'd be my day in court. Stephen said he'd argued several cases before His Honor, the judge, and liked my chances. Stephen told me that His Honor, the judge, had long white hair that flowed over his black legal collar and he danced to a different step then the beat of the government drum.

The shark said his name showed an independent style of his way... Freemen Ruhle! And with all judgment thrown out the window, I decided to accept the way of the land and proceed down the path of justice that had already been chosen. It was the Road To Jurisprudence!

Thirty days isn't a lifetime, but during that time the wait seemed like forever. Everyday took several to pass and the weeks felt like light years long. Preparing for my day in court took every second of every minute of every hour of every day during those four weeks... from here to eternity. And I wondered if it was some sort of sadistic form of vindictiveness that forced me to forgo the sleepless nights that plagued me all night long... every day of the week during that month.

I continued reading and re-reading all those government books... in order to make sure I hadn't missed or misread something in the wording. I also continued reading and re-reading the Regulations... 31 CFR, Chapter V. At all hours of the day and night whenever I read something that I thought I missed, I'd immediately call the shark to discuss it. And by the end of the month I was surprised his number hadn't changed. But it was nice to know that some things didn't!

When the afternoon of October 1st arrived, the shark, Lady Grace and I arrived at, His Honor, the judge's chambers before the government minnows. We signed in as the plaintiff... because I was the plaintiff. The government wasn't suing me as much as I was suing them... to get back my prized imprisoned Havana stooges. And being imprisoned wasn't a good place to be. For, I knew a thing or one thousand one hundred and sixty-two about being imprisoned. We sat around for about ten minutes before two people entered the outer room to the judge's inner chamber. I immediately knew one of the people was Lars that Titon cigar smoking Customs Helmsman... who showed up with another government wannabe anybody.

The mackerel seemed dazed and confused besides bewildered and, maybe, stunned when he saw where we had signed in in the sign-in sheet. He questioned the spot of our signing in… and the shark told him I was the plaintiff in this action. Then, the shark got into the art of legalese when he told the carp that he'd signed in in the proper sign-in place. But the government flounder just continued questioning how we could sign in the sign-in spot where we signed in. He couldn't get over it. And for over five minutes it was back and forth with the shark and the sturgeon about where on the sign-in form we had signed in.

The trout didn't want to sign in in the defendant's sign-in spot and he kept harping to the shark about where, on the sign-in sheet, he'd have to sign in… because we'd taken his spot to sign in. I had to suppress my snigger over the trite matter, as I didn't want to offend the clam anymore than he already was. But, in the end, I knew it wouldn't have mattered… one way or another. Amidst the disputed discourse, the judge's aide showed up to see if everyone was present.

Immediately, the crab protested about where we had signed in in the sign-in form, but she told the shrimp to just sign in… and to get over it. Reluctantly and dejectedly, he signed in in the defendant's sign-in spot on the sign-in form and the judge's aide then took it back into the inner room.

Five minutes later, the door opened and the judge's aide re-appeared. She said only the sharks were to enter the inner-chamber… and both fish got up from their seats and walked through the door. Through the door frame, a tall stalwart figure of a man was seen standing behind his desk… in the rear of the room. In a booming voice, he spoke out for all to hear. "Mr. Shark, how are you? Won't you please enter?" It was a statement to the man from Customs as much as a question to the shark. And, pointing toward a seat in front of his desk, he said, "Please be seated." Then, he asked "And who is this with you?" As the door closed behind the sharks, the judge asked "Are you the man from Baltimore?"

The judge's long white hair flowed over the white collar of his shirt… as the shark said it would. And, although he was only seen for the slightest briefest moment, it could be seen that he maintained similar characteristics to that Back To The Future nutty professor. Lady Grace and I looked at each other. We both thought the same thing when we saw him! Without either of us saying a word, the look in our eyes told everything needed to be said… but wasn't. Lady Grace and I continued looking at each other with eyes opened shut while the Customs girl fish just sat there.

Finally, the silence broke while the G-man stoogie man, the shark, and His Honor, the judge, were all mulling around behind closed doors. The Customs girl anchovy, Lady Grace and I began having a pleasant conversation. I might've been a bit confused, but the Customs girl seemed somewhat taken back with all the activity her government was going through… over my smokes. However, I knew she'd have to do what she'd have to do when she was ordered to do what she was ordered to do. It was in her job description!

The conversation Lady Grace and I were having with the Customs girl was abruptly interrupted less than five minutes after both sharks disappeared into the room with His Honor, the judge. The door opened and that Lars Titon of a cigar Customs agent G-man Helmsman re-entered the outer-room. The door closed behind him and in a blink of an eye the four of us were silently sitting in the outer-room. And the deafness was stifling! With the door closed and Lars the Titon cigar Helmsmen Customs agent G-man man sitting out in the outer lobby, the shark laid out the argument to His Honor, the judge. It was the same argument I raised with the shark!

After what seemed like hours, but was only some fifteen minutes, the door re-opened and Lars the Titon cigar agent Customs Helmsman G-man man was asked to re-enter the room… by the judge's aide. For the next thirty minutes, Customs girl, Lady Grace, and I remained silent while tocks ticked off the clock. The mood never quite seemed the same thereafter. Suddenly, the door opened again and both sharks re-entered the judge's outer office. The meeting had come to an end!

Before I could say anything, the shark motioned for Lady Grace and I to leave with him… and we walked out the room. Down through the elevator and during the entire way out of the courthouse nothing was said. Standing out on the courthouse steps, Lady Grace took a picture of that Lars Titon cigar smoking Customs agent man as he walked across the street. And standing out on the courthouse steps, he reminded both Lady Grace and I of a brother of some frazzled TV shrink.

While standing on the courthouse steps, the shark was asked about what took place behind those closed doors. Curious minds wanted to know! The shark said His Honor, the judge, ordered Interrogatories and

Depositions and listed the case for trial in the beginning of January… three months later. In short, we'd won the day! I was going to have my day in court! Long live freedom… for Freemen Ruhle had ruled that day!

I asked for a more descriptive description about what took place. The shark said His Honor, the judge, asked what my case was really about… since it only involved 100 smokes worth less than a hundred dollars in value. Stephen said he told His Honor, the judge, about what happened to me when I entered the country. Then, he said he told the judge about the men who showed up at my old address asking all those questions and about my *Internet* access… or the lack thereof! Stephen said he asked His Honor, the judge, if he believed in coincidence(s)… and that was when His Honor, the judge, ordered Lars the Titon cigar Customs agent G-man man to leave the room.

The shark said that when the door re-opened and the man from Baltimore was asked back into the inner chamber, he immediately asked His Honor, the judge, to dismiss the case. But His Honor, the judge, wanted nothing to do with that request. Instead, he took charge of the meeting and replied "I don't know how you do things down in Baltimore, but this isn't how we do things up here." Then, he ordered Interrogatories and Depositions be taken prior to the date he ordered the case be heard… in the beginning of the New Year. And he said to both sharks "If this guy wants to have his day in court, then he shall have… his day in court."

The shark was beside himself when telling his story… and basking in glory. He said he'd never experienced anything even remotely close to it before. The shark said it was like having a one on none hearing, with only one side being heard. Ours! And the judge never once bothered to question Lars the Titon cigar Customs agent G-man man about what the government's position was. In fact, he didn't care what the government's position of the law was… or the legality of the situation. All he was interested in, after having heard the shark's sordid story, was to allow me to have my day in court! G-d Bless America!

I wasn't sure if I understood what had transpired, but knew that I'd lived to fight another day. Although this wasn't the battle to end all wars, it did mark the day that on any given day anyone could win… because I'd won. Round one of the resistance went to the resistance. We were on our way. For round one went to the little guy! And somewhere, someone associated with the other side had to be wondering why it wasn't a slam-dunk shutout smash hit... game, set, and match!

Within hours, Lady Grace and I were out celebrating the victory over the evil forces... with dinner and a bottle of bubbly. Later that night, I got on the Net and sent a message that reflected the event(s) of the day. "Earlier 2day was the 1ˢᵗ hearing in fed court 2 retrieve my Cubans seized upon my return from Cuba last year. Finally! The g'ment wanted the case thrown out. However, His Honor, the judge, ordered a trial date instead... scheduled 4 the 2ⁿᵈ day of the New Year. It's so nice 2 know, with all the crap about poker smoking in the Oral Office... justice is alive and well in America. G-d Bless America!"

Immediately, responses began flowing in... with most showing support. However, those cavemen from another dimension also showed up... although they continued to not know of what they spoke. And why should I have expected anything any different. Sometimes it's better to know some things never change.

The Anxious Anxious wrote, "Dave... way to go! I was one of those with the one legged comment, but I also told you about the hypocrisy with three gallon toilet seats. I'm glad you're making progress and look forward to hearing your updates. Thanx!"

A pal whose number was 3000 wrote, "Great to hear this news! I'm sure everyone here was pulling for you! Well, almost everyone! I, for one, would love to help you celebrate your victory over the evil empire by enjoying one of those hard to get Cubans. It isn't often one gets to enjoy a fine Cuban, let alone one that has gone through so much. PLEASE keep us posted." And with his post, I immediately knew there'd be interest in the ultimate cigar dinner event of all time. Then, I remembered The Raffle... and it all started to make sense.

Someone whose name was lung cancer or, maybe, had survived the diseased cell-war frontal-assault stated, "Congratulations! Hope it all works out in your favor!"

Ceylon from Ceylon chimed in "Congratulations on the upcoming trial date (man, never thought I'd ever say that). I'm wishing you the *best* of luck against Customs. Wouldn't it be great if we could really bring some common sense to the enforcement of 'THE embargo?' By the way,

I'm not knowledgeable with the legal process here. How long should the case last and when can we expect a decision? If the court rules in your favor, what kind of change(s) can be expected and when would they go into effect? Thanks for your sacrifice!"

Although the news flashed at Net speed, it was quite apparent everyone wasn't up with the update(s). Almost a week later, I saw a posting from an Ethan Allen on a cigar board that asked, "Wasn't a preliminary hearing scheduled Oct. 1st in Philly? I haven't heard or seen a peep... anywhere. Anyone heard anything?"

I instantly responded that the hearing had occurred and what the results were. Then, I gave the address of the web site that was now finished and promised it'd have all the news... on a regular basis. I thanked Ethan for his interest... and questioned if he was a relative of that long past patriot cabinetmaker.

During the first two weeks following the October 1st hearing, the shark and I were busy preparing the Depositions and Interrogatories that had to be dealt with in the near future... as Freeman Ruhle ruled. We had several issues and lots of questions, but I also knew the government had their own as well.

Then, one day, the shark received an Affidavit in the mail from one of the government agents, Almen Notruful. His Affidavit indicated that he'd been in attendance the night of April 18, 1997... and that he'd witnessed all the events that took place. He also indicated that agent Busta Narco approached him for information about the situation that I had created... by my presence that night.

The Affidavit by agent Almen Notruful stated he was employed as a senior special agent with the U.S. Dept. of Treasury, U.S. Customs Service, Office of Investigations, Strategic Investigation Division, Philadelphia, Pennsylvania. His Affidavit stated, "On April 18, 1997 David Fabler arrived at Philadelphia Int'l Airport on Air Jamaica flight number 019." Agent Notruful said, "During Customs' processing of David Fabler, he was referred to a secondary examination where Customs inspector Busta Narco conducted a routine interview with Mr. Fabler." Agent Notruful said, "Mr. Fabler was asked by Customs agent Narco if he'd acquired any merchandise during his trip." Agent Notruful stated, "Mr. Fabler said he hadn't acquired anything during his trip to Jamaica and he presented a

Customs declaration that indicated the same." Agent Notruful also stated, "Mr. Fabler informed agent Narco that he stayed in Jamaica during his entire trip."

In addition, agent Notruful averred that "An examination of Mr. Fabler's luggage revealed the following items: 100 Cuban cigars, 9 Cuban cigarettes, 1 Cuban wood jewelry box, 5 Cuban key chains, 1 Cuban coin, travel tickets to and from Cuba, and a receipt from a Cuban hotel." Agent Notruful also averred that "Mr. Fabler, at this point, advised Customs inspector Narco that he used his driver's license for identification to enter Cuba."

Finally, agent Notruful stated that he "…declared under penalty of perjury that all the information contained in the government Complain for Forfeiture was based on reports and information **known to him personally** and / or furnished to him by agents of the U.S. Customs Service." And that "…**everything contained therein was true and correct** to the *best* of his knowledge and belief."

This statement and the way the Affidavit was worded indicated to me and others who read his statement that agent Notruful was present during my encounter with Customs on the night of April 18, 1997. And that was important because we'd been seeking the names of those who were present during the encounter that night. Suddenly, I had the name of the supervisor agent Narco went to who told me that I was '*under arrest*.'

From the beginning, when Stephen first got involved in my case, he asked on several occasions if I knew the names of any of the agents who I interacted with on the night of April 18, 1997. I told him I never got their names, except for agent Narco… who signed the forfeiture list I received. Until agent Notruful's Affidavit arrived in the mail, the shark had been less than successful in finding out who the other agent's names were who were in attendance that night. I think the proper term might be called stone-walling.

Every time (and there were many) that the shark asked the government for the names of their agents, their responses were totally unresponsive… to the point of denial or refusal and even complete indifference. Their responses had been our request wasn't necessary or they'd cite some long forgotten secret g'ment secrecy law designed to protect the agents. But I knew they only wanted to protect the case. However, when His Honor, the Honorable Freeman Ruhle, ruled… it was another day!

In response to agent Almen Notruful's Affidavit, I had to ascertain in my own Affidavit what the *true* facts were… as I remembered them. The process required more of an effort than I thought it would and also required numerous visits and many conversations with the shark and his newly hired sharkette, Sue R. Hammerhead. Allthough Sue R. was a shark in her own right, she wasn't as proficient a flesh-eating predator as her superior was… after honing his craft through experience.

Finally, after many faxes back and forth, and even more telephone calls, my Affidavit appeared complete. The only thing missing seemed to be my signature… and that was a formality. I drove into the city to sign the form, but never saw either shark on the day I penned my name. And this is what was written:

"On or about March 5, 1997, I left Philadelphia and traveled to Jamaica where I resided for part of the year. On or about March 19, 1997, Mr. Andreas Dueling, a German citizen and a resident alien of Jamaica, another friend visiting Jamaica and myself went to Cuba… as a birthday present to me. Mr. Dueling bought my airline ticket and paid for my hotel. While in Cuba, Mr. Dueling also purchased several gifts for me… including 100 Cuban cigars."

"The total cost of the Cuban tobacco products, alcohol and other miscellaneous items did not exceed $100.00. At the end of the trip, approximately three days later, I returned back to Jamaica."

"On or about April 18, 1997, I arrived in Philadelphia from Jamaica aboard an Air Jamaica flight. Andreas Dueling was also on the flight and was present while I was detained at Customs. Mr. Dueling also had 100 Cuban cigars."

"Prior to leaving for the weekend in Cuba, I reviewed a book that had been given to me during a previous trip abroad by a U.S. Customs agent in Philadelphia. The book was titled **Know Before You Go** and is a publication of the U.S. Treasury Dept. On the back of the book, it stated that it was revised in 'April 1994.' On the first page of the **Know Before You Go** pamphlet, it stated '*This book will help you understand our mission is to protect your interests… you're our customers and we* *hope to serve you well by making your Customs clearance as pleasant and unobtrusive as possible.'"*

"Page two of the book stated that Customs declaration forms should be prepared '*in advance for presentation to the Immigration and Customs' inspectors.*' It went on to state '*you may orally declare to the Customs inspector the articles you acquired abroad if the articles are accompanying you and you have not exceeded the duty free exception allowed.*' The **Know Before You Go** book further advised that a written declaration would be necessary only when… more than 200 cigarettes or 100 cigars were included."

"On page five of the **Know Before You Go** book it stated, '*Articles totaling $400.00 may be entered duty free, subject to the limitations on liquors, cigarettes and cigars.*' Page six stated under the heading, 'Cigars and Cigarettes,' that '*Not more than 100 cigars and 200 cigarettes may be included in the exception.*' On this page, the book stated, '*Products of Cuban tobacco may be included, if purchased in Cuba. See page 20.*' I, then, referenced page 20, which stated nothing about products from Cuba… cigars, cigarettes, or alcoholic beverages."

"In addition to the **Know Before You Go** guide, I also referenced the Treasury section of my passport. It said, '*As of November 1963, the purchase or importation of Cuban… goods… are generally prohibited, except for… limited goods imported directly as accompanied baggage.*' My passport didn't define what **generally** prohibited encompassed… however it did define the exceptions. '*Informational materials and limited goods imported directed as accompanied baggage.*'"

"On page two of my passport under the heading, Customs Service, it stated that the **Know Before You Go** book gives '*current information about Customs requirements and how they apply to articles acquired abroad.*' On page 6 of **Know Before You Go** it stated '*Products of Cuban tobacco may be included, if purchased in Cuba.*'"

"Upon my arrival at the Philadelphia airport on or about April 18, 1997, a Customs agent stopped me and asked if I had anything to declare. I responded that I had '*tobacco products and alcohol as well as other miscellaneous items… none of which exceeded my exemption limit.*' The agent, then, directed me to a secondary search area. At the secondary area, I met an agent that I believe was agent Busta Narco. He requested my declaration card and asked what I had to declare. I told him '*tobacco products, alcohol and miscellaneous other items... all of which were within my duty free exemption.*'"

"Agent Narco opened my attaché case and pulled out the four boxes of Cuban cigars that my friend, Andreas Dueling, purchased for me in Havana. Agent Narco confiscated the cigars. When I asked agent Narco why he was confiscating those items he responded that they were contraband."

"I told agent Narco that the Customs **Know Before You Go** book stated it was permissible to have Cuban tobacco products. Agent Narco produced a copy of the **Know Before You Go** pamphlet and asked, 'Where in this book does it say you can have Cuban cigars?'"

"I told him on page six where it stated '*not more than 100 cigars and 200 cigarettes may be included in your exemption*' and that '*products of Cuban tobacco may be included*' as long as they were '*purchased in Cuba.*'"

"After agent Narco read those words he stated that '*those words did not mean what they said!*' Agent Narco left me alone and returned with someone who I believed was his supervisor, agent Almen Notruful. Agent Notruful advised me that the only way I could keep the Cuban tobacco products was if I'd gone to Cuba and purchased them there. Then, he asked if I went there. I responded that I had. At that moment, agent Notruful stated that I was '*under arrest*' and ordered me to turn over my passport. While reaching for my passport, he kept yelling at me that I was '*under arrest*' and that I had to give him my passport. After the 3rd demand, I reached over and gave him my passport... whereby agent Notruful forcibly yanked it from my grasp. When agent Notruful was asked why I was under arrest he stated '*You're a traitor!*'"

"Agent Notrulful took my passport and left me with agent Narco who was thoroughly searching my belongings. A short time later an uniformed Immigration officer came into the area and asked where the Cuban 'national' was. Agent Notruful told the Immigration officer, '*There is no Cuban 'national.' It's just him.*' Then, he pointed toward me. After looking through the passport, agent Notruful was told by the Immigration officer to give me back my passport... and that I didn't do anything wrong!"

"Following the luggage search I had to endure a clothed full body search, being verbally abused, and falsely told they had found drugs in my bags. Only after being asked if I'd agree to be X-rayed was I released. However, the X-rays were never conducted."

"The agents never returned any of the gifts acquired in Cuba. Although, the agents did return a carton of Marlboro cigarettes that were purchased there! The agents also confiscated the 100 cigars my friend, Andreas Dueling, brought into the country as well. However, his cigars were returned to him when he left the country… several days later."

"To date, I've filed a Petition for Remission or Mitigation of Forfeiture, a Petition for Return of Property and the attached Answer to the government's Complaint for Forfeiture. Since the date my property was confiscated, the Dept. of the Treasury, U.S. Customs, has issued a new and revised version of the **Know Before You Go** book. The paragraph under Cigars and Cigarettes now reads: '*Tobacco products of Cuban origin are generally prohibited.*' Page 21 of the newly revised document contains a paragraph under the heading Merchandise from Embargoed Countries. It states, '*The importation of goods from the following countries is generally prohibited under regulations administered by the Office of Foreign Assets Control (OFAC)… Cuba!*' It goes on to state, '*Because of the strict enforcement of prohibitions, those anticipating travel to any of the countries listed above would do well to write in advance to the Office of Foreign Assets Control.*' And there were no other changes!"

Cubano Noche

***

The Cohiba Libre *IT'S ONLY CIGARS* T-shirts were selling like hot-cakes on a cold winter morning. In fact, they were so hot we ran out of the first run by the night of the third day. We received the 2nd order a few days prior to the Cubano Noche dinner feast fest at Gracie's Restaurant. Lady Grace thought it'd be a good way to provide funding for the legal offense fund that the shark was setting up.

Twenty-buck Bernie sent in his twenty bucks for the offense fund and he was the first to contribute to the cause. *Twenty-buck Bernie* also anted- up his twenty buck fee for the Cohiba Libre *IT'S ONLY CIGARS* T-shirt… and he was the first to acquire one. He was always the first one on his block to do anything… if it involved twenty bucks or less.

You can get anything you want at Gracie's Restaurant. Well… almost! It's hidden just over a half mile past the Olra railroad track… out near the middle of nowhere and in-between a place close to someplace else. Olra didn't dine there prior to touting the tune of his beat. He couldn't have… it didn't exist. Then again, somewhere out in the cosmos, it was always there. It's like a pearl in an oyster… or a gem of a stone! And the proprietress is an honest-to-goodness to-live-for real-life Goddess. Guess that's what makes her place so special.

Were Mae West alive today, she would've wanted to be known as the lady called Grace. In fact, there isn't a man not enchanted nor any woman not enamored by her essence. She's a real restaurateur with true taste. Her wit, charm, and elegance speak volumes for the eatery she crafted from little more than nothing else. Whatever one brings through her door instantly departs when passing though the glowing white arched gateway. Magical in nature and intrinsic by design, she somehow knew just what makes worrisome thoughts disappear. She crafted a twenty-first century café and placed it on Earth well before its time! For truly, whoever enters her bistro leaves where they were for that night… and possibly longer.

The woman has an intense spirit, but is possessed with a warm and gentle heart. Kind and gracious, Lady Grace's sense of taste is coupled with a fashioned enlightenment. The woman knows what she wants and isn't timid about having it. The wisdom she bears is as though it's been passed down through the ages… from before the eons of time. Needless to say, Lady Grace knows how to put on an event. It's her business!

A long time before, she said she thought it'd be a good idea to have a Cubano Noche Cohiba Libre *IT'S ONLY CIGARS* dinner feast fest. I agreed! Although my original thought was to have the Cubano Noche dinner feast fest after I got the cigars back… not before! However, when the government refused to provide an arena to continue the contest, I found myself the proud owner of a hundred Cubanos… minus the five I gave the shark. Since I wasn't in the business of selling smokes, my options for disposing of them were limited. Having a personal stash was out of the question. While I've been known to be a midnight-toker, I don't smoke stoogies… never have! So, what better way to have them enjoyed than to have a Cubano Noche Cohiba Libre *IT'S ONLY CIGARS* dinner feast fest… and help promote the struggle?

Finding a facility to put on the Ritz wasn't difficult because one was available for the asking. Adding to the benefit was Lady Grace's offer to raise funds at the fundraising event she agreed to have. She offered to contribute proceeds from the event to aid the cause. And to achieve the ultimate turnout, a mailing was sent to her regular guests. It soon became an SRO sellout.

The shark said he'd attend… as would his sharkette, Sue R. Hammer-head. Edit Ed said he wouldn't miss it for anything. I wondered if that included death, but never gave it another thought. Edit Ed thought some people should be invited who he thought would be good for publicity… and said they'd be his guests. Of course, it went without saying the shark and Edit Ed didn't pay for anything. Not even the smokes! Nor did their guests!

One of the people Edit Ed wanted to invite was a publisher of a local smoker mag. That meant a photographer who'd bring along his camera… to film the festivities. I wondered how much it would cost if the film ever got into the wrong hands! Blackmail! White male! Did color matter? Then, I wondered *did the guests have guests*?

Lady Grace said she'd need a little time to prepare the gala event. Perfection took time! And Lady Grace never did anything that wasn't perfect. On the Net, she researched the El Bogadito del Medio menu… the restaurant Papa H made famous. She also studied the mojito mixture…

the drink Papa H made famous at the restaurant he made famous. To put on a gala Cubano Noche dinner feast fest, mojitos and Cuban food were a necessity... as was musica and cigaros!

Lady Grace crafted a bill of fare straight out of an El Bogadito del Medio cuisine. Cold, light, and very toxic mojitos were provided. They complimented the Hondurans that were given out to smoke on the patio... when the guests first arrived. Before the beginning, it was decided to wait until the evening's end before bringing out the *best* of rest of the *best*... the build-up would be worth the wait! And to thwart those from missing out on their presence because they got drunk as a skunk before they went, warm hors d'oeuvres got served in the cool evening air to wet taste buds... and to spark anticipation for fine food that'd soon be coming.

The menu was vast and the spread varied, from conch and shrimp appetizers to black bean soup, a lobster salad and entrees of pork or a Creole pollo. It didn't stop there. Included was a banana flan and coffee ground from Cuban bean as well as Portos... and liquor too. All the invites and menus were written on cigar leaf parchment paper... in keeping with the theme. Throw in the Cuban musica and it was truly a Cubano Noche dinner feast fest to remember.

The people who attended Cubano Noche walked different paths of life. From businessmen to construction workers... and everything in-between! They all had, at least, one thing in common. For one night, they were all in the same place at the same time, doing the same thing for the same reason... to eat and smoke a Cuban! Cigar... that is! Not kill one!

One attendee, who owned several smoke shops, said he was planning to go to Cuba within three weeks after the regal affair. Attired in black tie and sneakers, his handlebar mustache framed a poker face that spoke volumes about who he wasn't. Truly a cover that foretold a different book than the words written about his story!

Herman Smudge said I could call him Herm or Herb, but I didn't have to call him Smudge. Herm pumped me for info about *the forbidden zone*... and asked lots of questions about acquiring cigars. Then, bringing them back! However, I couldn't stop feeling that he should've known what he was asking about. Either that or be *paranoid* to think that he was some sort of secret Customs G-man agent man. I preferred the former... at Lady Grace's urging.

Another in attendance was that TV personality who was a son of a Buck. His nose turned red after a bottle of wine or three martinis... whichever he drank first. Rouldy told me that he'd provide TV coverage of my case and said he'd like to interview me... a few days before my case was to go to court.

One who didn't attend was that Lars Titon cigar smoking Customs agent man. But he was never invited. Although, I knew that wouldn't have stopped him from crashing the gate. At some point I had a small thought about inviting him, but the idea quickly got squashed! For, in the back of my mind, while I thought it might be funny or add humor with many jokes made, I knew there'd be concern some uninvited government personnel might also show up to interrupt the carnival celebration. Besides, I also kept thinking that some G-men personnel were already there... however, they'd been invited! *Paranoia strikes deep...* Herm was in the house!

Mother Nat contributed to the cause with weather that couldn't have been finer. Warm and tropical with a slight chill in the night air! The mood was jubilant as the court victory, only weeks before, added to the triumphant exhalation that was still fresh in the air. An all girl band provided the musica! And although not all the Chiquita's were Cuban, in fact none were... they played a swinging Samba beat.

A Honduran cigar vendor was present who provided non-Cuban smokes. He said they were his treat, but I knew he really wanted to drum up business for non-Cuban brands. Heraldo invited a guest to accompany him too... more freebees for the freebees being given away! Only Heraldo probably thought it was *quid pro quo.*

Heraldo's guest was Rafael. Rafie's pleasure was anything that included Portos from any Portuguese port. Rafie was a Portuguese Portos rep who promoted his country's wares. I'm not sure if Rafie was from Portugal or Spain, maybe Mexico or Puerto Rico and possibly Cuba, but he spoke some strange Spanish speech all the same.

Rafael came baring freebees... an extremely rare vintage of Portos. Only two hundred and forty cases per year were imported into the States. Or so he said! More than most of the attendees knew the Portos being offered and were amazed at their good fortune. More freebees for the free-bees being given away! Few could believe such a wonderful freebee was being bestowed… with compliments to the fantastic Cuban meal Lady Grace had crafted.

The festivities began long before the sunset and when the sun did set, behind the mountain off in the distant horizon, everyone was invited inside to dine to their hearts content… while musica continued to play all night long. After feasting on fabulous food and drinking delicious drinks as well as great grapes, night's end was in sight. The shark stood up and spoke some words about *the good fight*… and Edit Ed stood up to voice his tongue.

Rouldolph Buck told everyone who was listening that he was going to interview me and he said he was saying it *'for the record.'* The cigar vendor even spoke his mind, but what he said wasn't what he wanted to say. Then, Lady Grace came out of the kitchen for a grand finale. It was Cuba's finest… the ones I bought back from Havana. They had entered the country the only time the government didn't search me when I returned from abroad… almost one year earlier. I gave them away so that they could be given away again. A loophole, in case Inspector Crouseau appeared on the case.

The Portos and Cubanos were a fitting conclusion to a fine evening. When the musica ceased playing and the lights were turned down… few wanted it to end. And when the end to the end finally arrived… no one left. Finally, after several more hours of milling about everyone was told the party was over and the lights were turned off. Begrudgingly they departed, but not before the event was an event to remember. Indeed, it was a splendid soiree that had occurred one very fine night… and could have only been pulled off by a woman of class. Enter… Lady Grace!

The Offer

***

The scent from the Cubano Noche dinner bash feast fest was still lingering in the air. The musica that throbbed to a samba beat was now making me feel more like a zombie than a mortal and I could taste the mojito tang over the mint of my toothpaste. Although several days had passed, the thick haze hadn't quite cleared and my brain was swimming in a pool of papa's hooch. It all felt like the morning after the night before, but the sun had set countless times since the last stoogie got smoked... and I was still gyrating through a clouded stupor.

The phone's exasperating peal brought me out of a dark funk. I slowly fumbled for the stirring machine. By the fifth ring, I finally pulled the annoying device off the hook... and quiet reined again. I dropped the talking device on the bed... several inches from my ear. My eyes were closed and I quickly began to fall back into a bottomless pit when I heard a buzzing sound flying through the room. I wanted to stick my head under the pillow, but put the receiver over my cochlea instead. Off in the distance, there was an insistent sound. The shark's raspy voice was hovering above my unconscious state! Suddenly, both my eyes opened. "David, we've received an offer!"

I sat up in bed... my headache was gone. All illusion of sleep had disappeared out the window with those five words. I wanted to know more... because knowledge was power. Then, I couldn't believe I was hearing what he was saying.

Time was required to temper my nerves. Jokes were fine, but it was closer to the end of October than the first of April. The last thing I remember saying to Stephen before I hung up was, "It's in the statute!" Then, I lay back down on the bed and pulled the covers over my head. I slowly sank back into a sea of pain. The ache swelled through my body like the incoming tide. In between beats of a pounding tempo, I repeated the same mantra I made to myself the last time I inflicted such masochistic havoc on my being years before... *never more*!

It took a couple of hours to dig myself out from the hollow I was stuck inside. I got up from bed and forced myself to begin re-entry into the human race. With my clothes on and two large cups of coffee in my stomach, I finally started to feel like a person once more. After reading the daily news, I searched for the papers that showed me the way. The papers were 31 CFR Chapter V... the 7-1-96 edition. And, in particular, the section known as 515.544... Gifts of Cuban Origin Goods.

I found the Cuban Asset Control (CAC) Regulations and examined the section that was key to the situation... 515.544, Gifts of Cuban Origin Goods. I needed to read the words for a thousandth time in order to feel sure I hadn't mis-read them. When I was finished reading, I was sure I hadn't! And when I was done reading, I picked up the phone and called the shark to tell him I hadn't misread the words I had read.

The section, Gifts of Cuban Origin Goods, read under subsection (a), *'Except as it is stated in paragraph (b)... specific licenses aren't issued for importation of Cuban origin goods... acquired abroad as gifts by persons entering the United States.'* Then it stated *'Licenses are issued upon request for the return of such goods to donors in countries other than Cuba.'*

Although I didn't have THE license to import the Cubanos I'd brought into the country that the CAC Regulations said I had to have in order to import them, those same CAC Regulations said I was entitled to have a license. It was a license to return the Cubanos to donors in countries other than Cuba. And, for what it is worth, I thought I had a license (implied)... I just didn't have a license (written). In short, The Offer wasn't an offer. And I wasn't offered anything I wasn't entitled to have ... by the wording of the law!

I heard Stephen's voice and read the statute to him. Although it wasn't that I felt he hadn't read the statute, I knew he didn't know the statute as well as I did. Only I wasn't sure I knew the statute as well as I thought I did. So I read it to him and asked if I was correct in my understanding of what the statute said I was entitled to.

When our conversation was finished, I hung the phone up knowing nothing was going to come of The Offer... because it wasn't like the government was offering me anything I wasn't entitled to. The Offer was required... by the statute! And I was confused about why I should accept what was already required.

Stephen said he'd study it some more, but I knew there wasn't anything to study. And I stopped short of refusing The Offer... until I knew exactly what my refusal meant. Then, I asked the shark to have that Lars Titon cigar smoking Customs G-man agent man put The Offer in writing... before I'd even consider (not) accepting it!

Two days later, The Offer flew across the fax lines. Lars the Titon of a cigar Helmsmen Customs agent man stated I could have those Cubanos returned to me... in any country other than Cuba. And, although he never mentioned not returning the Cubanos to me while I was in America, it was understood the States were taboo too.

The Offer stated The Offer would only be good for three days... before the government would begin playing hardball. I had a chuckle from the government threat and had to laugh at the heart of The Offer, but kept quiet just the same. Play hardball? Hell, the last time I played hardball was some thirty years before... in high school. Back then, I pitched and tossed fastballs whatever-some miles-an-hour past opposing hackers. Hardball... I used to play hardball! But somehow, I knew this would be different.

In three days, I knew I'd be somewhere other than where I was... and where I'd be would be in a place where I wouldn't be able to tell the government, the shark, or anyone else what I'd want. Even if I wanted to accept The Offer! And after I got The Offer in my hands, I drove over to that editor, Ed Ditor... and showed him the gory proposal.

Smoke it, Don't Poke It

***

Less than one week after the great Cubano Noche smoked-out dinner feast fest of the year, I met editor Ed Ditor a third time. The first time resulted in his article, ***Cigar Smoke and Mirrors***. Then, I saw him at the Cohiba Libre ***IT'S ONLY CIGARS*** legal offense fund contribution gala Cubano Noche dinner feast fest... and he told me to get in touch if anything new developed. That evening I told him about all the new things that had taken place... except for The Offer, which hadn't been offered yet. I ended with the Depositions and Interrogatories that had been ordered... and the January date when I would have my day in court. He said to call him later that week. And on the day the shark received The Offer over the fax, I drove into the city to pick it up... and to meet with that Edit Ditor.

In between watching the last puff get smoked and waking up to one of the worst headaches of my life, the U.S. Head of State made news with his numbered ML brand bj's and a smoke act that went off in a Monica love nest. Pres-man Bill made a statement to the press insisting his ML brand bj's weren't related by nature. And while that may've been true by nature, by human sexual instincts... they were at least distant cousins. How many times removed was the only question. His refusal to discuss what actually took place with those stoogies in the Oral Office had people wondering what actually took place with those stoogies in the Oral Office. But my question was... how many stoogies were involved? And in one way or another, Pres-man Bill had the press do most of his talking for him. Although most of their chatting wasn't what Pres-man Bill had in mind. Another who talked more than anyone wanted was the girl who branded the infamous smoking act that caught the world's ear! I thought the timing couldn't have been better! For Cubano cigaros weren't only in the news... they'd become front-page headlines!

I filled Edit Ed in on the events that had taken place. I gave him information about the Net news and the Deposition hearing. We talked about the harassment Customs was giving me whenever I'd enter the country. And we talked about my upcoming court case... and the date it was to take place on. Three days later, I searched high and low for a copy of the City Paper paper to see what edit Ed had to say. That's when I saw his article... ***Smoke It, Don't Poke It***.

It was more ***Pretzel Logic***. Although twisted, it had a ring of truth. Even though it was more on the Pres-man Bill and what he did with those Cubanos in the Oral Office at one in the morning than it was on my case in hand. And somewhere lost in his wording was the humor that filled the spaces. But somehow I could identify with all that... all too much!

Within the week that followed his article in the City Paper paper, I saw an article that appeared in another paper. It stated that a cigarette company was being fined for admitting to smuggling cigarettes into other countries... in order to avoid paying taxes or levies and import duties. Maybe, they should've kept quiet... and saved their bucks!

I found the article humorless because it was the least they'd done. Even though they admitted their guilt... they did it! And I could only wonder, having done that, what else they'd done... in the name of capitalism. Then, I wondered if a cig company could spend time in stir. But they did admit it... and having done that they'd probably do it again. However, it did help explain how all those American made and produced cigarettes made their way into the depths of socialistic totalitarian Cuba... without the U.S. government officially knowing they were there. Only, I knew the government knew all along... not only that they were there, but how they got there.

David Weisenthal

Mark Ken Tyme

***

The day after the latest blast bounced off the block, my hippie shark lawyer received a call from a small Mako shark who said he was Mark Ken Tyme. The Mako asked the shark how he could contact me. He said he'd once been a friend... from days gone by. The Mako left his name and number and told the shark to have me call. Later that afternoon, the shark called and said we should meet... the following day. Just before the shark hung up he said he had some other business to discuss... and he mentioned the Mako's name. However, when I asked for the number, he said he'd have to look for it.

The following day, I drove into the city with Lady Grace. Before going to the shark's office we stopped by my mother's house. She was beside herself with my name being in some printed press news. It was a flashback to another time. And that time wasn't a good time for her.

When she read the first article, she hit the roof of her house. But when the second article hit the street, she went out of her mind. It seems that article served to fan her fire and flame her passion. Remembering the past can sometimes be very painful!

After the shark and I were done discussing the things he felt needed to be discussed, he fumbled through his papers for the scrap piece of paper with Mark Ken Tyme's number scrawled in the corner. It took five minutes to find it. I was interested in seeing Mark Ken Tyme because we hadn't seen each other in over twenty-five years. Not since he went to some southern state shark school somewhere down south while I went off in search of a wacky weed-bush down in some South American jungle. And although curiosity had gotten the better of me, I knew it had really killed the cat... and no amount of satisfaction would ever bring it back.

I picked up the phone and dialed the number. When the ringing stopped, I mentioned his name. His secretary put me through and we spoke for a minute or two. Then, we made plans to see each other... a couple of hours later. Finished with our chat, I turned my attention back to the things at hand. The shark said he laughed when he read the story... and he had fun talking with editor, Ed Ditor. He also said people were calling to ask questions about the case. I asked the shark if he had found any court decisions regarding Cuba... and stoogies. He said he hadn't, so I pointed out the ones I'd found in my travels. Kent & Briehl vs. John Foster Dulles (June 15, 1958); Zemel vs. Rusk (May 3, 1963; U.S. vs. Lamb (January 10, 1967); and, Regan vs. Wald (May 16, 1983). I also pointed out the end result of Regan vs. Wald before the Supreme Court (June 28, 1984).

With the meeting over, Lady Grace and I went to see the Mako... who was Mark Ken Tyme. We walked into his office and saw a plump, some would say fat, man with sparse hair who greeted us. However, he was much taller than I remembered. But the years didn't seem like they'd been kind to him. I introduced the Lady Grace to the Mako... and within five minutes he was dissecting her business. Like the true shark he believed himself to be, he ingested her essence and spit out his crap. Only it wasn't like she couldn't fend for herself. And she just wanted to know why he thought he knew her so well. Then, she wanted to know... if he knew her so well, why didn't he do it as well.

The time dragged on... and it didn't come to a close until an hour or three later. Mark Ken Tyme relived story after story... from his good old days. I never liked living in the past, but it seemed that Mark Ken Tyme never let the times go. That was one of the things that separated us... and I knew it was one of the things that'd mean we'd never be friends. And if truth be known, I think I knew it back then... and that's why we never stayed friends.

Suddenly, Mark Ken Tyme began talking about the time when I went off to some South of a border bush jungle down in some strange southern land. For a quick few seconds, I racked my brain in search of which time he was reminiscing. Then, I thought it didn't matter. Nor did I really care. So I quickly moved on.

Mark Ken Tyme recalled the time that I left him my two-seat coup of a shit-fired sports car. I didn't recall the situation, but figured it happened anyway. He said he drove it all over town and even slept in it too. Hell... I'd slept in it also, but not because I wanted to! In those days I had to. It was a product of the times.

No money and no roof forced the existence! He said he couldn't believe I could've, or would've, been so giving. He also said it stayed with him throughout his life! I thought I did it... but hadn't given it another thought.

Lady Grace and I quietly sat while he told the tale. I found myself having to stifle a yawn. Then, I thought *'paybacks are a bitch.'* All I could think of was how I'd look in his brand new Porsche. I think it was called *quid pro quo.* Being a shark of any kind, I knew he knew the term!

Mark Ken Tyme suggested we get together again. I told him that Lady Grace and I were getting ready to head down to Negril... and knew we never would. He asked where my home was. I said Negril. I figured the distance would insure what otherwise might happen. He told us he once went there, but I left it at that. I really wasn't too interested. And knew, if I persisted, the time would continue to drag. I also knew Lady Grace and I had better things to do with the time spent.

Mark Ken Tyme and I shook hands and bid farewell. Lady Grace invited him to dinner, but instead of accepting her offer he told her that he'd been to her place once before. Then, he said it was before she owned the place he called joint. I guess it's true that one can lead a horse to water, but it's also true you can't make it drink. By the end of that meeting, I knew that I'd spent my life living through times of being a Fabler... while he had merely lived his life Mark Ken Tyme.

Havana Dave

***

A few days after meeting with Mark Ken Tyme, Lady Grace and I headed toward the land of Ackee and Saltfish. We needed time away where our batteries could re-charge. Stress can be a drag! I took the ***Smoke It, Don't Poke It*** article with us because I wanted to get an independent opinion from one who'd know of such things. However, I should've known.

"Havana Dave!? It fits you like a birthday suit," the Cohiba Bandito said. A slight smirk traced across his face.

I thought about what the Bandito said. Then, I thought, '*what did he know*?' I knew he thought it fit like a birthday suit, but I wanted to know what a birthday suit fit like. "I don't know... I think it gives the wrong image."

"Image? What image? F**k the image! How many times do I have to say... The Raffle!?"

He always thought in terms of bucks. Why not!? It seemed the world revolved around the stuff. I just needed to get with the program. But terms like truth, justice, honesty, rights, and integrity kept filtering into my brain... clouding it with thoughts of nobility! However, I was anything but noble. Then, I read the story again... Havana Dave! It really wasn't such a bad concept. And it could make an interesting character in a movie plot. *Havana Dave Smokes Em Again* (*as he fades off into the sunset*); or *Havana Dave Goes To Court (or Hollywood).* Maybe, *Havana Dave and The Bandito ride-em high*! But the best of all would be **U.S. vs. 100 Cuban Cigars**. I could see it all so clearly then.

I could also see the article that had just been flashed in the press. It was the second of such that chronicled the story of the century... well, maybe the decade. O.K., the year! The line across the head of that weekly City Paper paper stated ***Smoke It, Don't Poke It***!

Somewhere in another thought process the author intellectualized his presence with some twisted form of ***Pretzel Logic***! And people in

Philadelphia were crazy for pretzels. The twisted kind they could eat. But his story did have a good twist.

> 'Havana Dave, all decked out in island white, pulled a fine Cohiba from a big plastic bag full of fine Cohibas and placed it on my desk… a souvenir from his latest foray into *the Forbidden* island of Cuba. Havana Dave is single-handedly challenging this country's ban on the importation of cigars from Cuba… a misguided 37-year-old national policy created in the edginess of the Cold War and continued by the stranglehold anti-Castro Cubans have on our country's Caribbean policy.'

I re-read the story and thought '*why not?*' I knew I had to have thousands of reasons, but they were tossed aside as I fed on the hype. I mean… money's money. Then, I thought back to where it all began. Down a single-lined gravel lane less-traveled than other roads. Through the dirt and polluted smog, I thought it all seemed like some foul smoke screen of a story filled with ***Cigar Smoke and Mirrors***. And, why not!? Even Edit Ed thought so when he penned the news of the story called by that name. Writing in a breeze, his fingers tapped like the wind. In little more than a blur of an instant he spun a yarn of a tale that he wanted to tell. Then, with a stroke of a pen, a hero rose up from the ashes of humor… Havana Dave!

The Mask

***

Traveling to Negril was easy… and the packing was light. I knew, when the trip was over, my bags would be less than full because the plan had been to leave the Cohiba Libre *IT'S ONLY CIGARS* T-shirts on the island with friends… who would sell them. And that'd leave lots of room for rum, coffee, ackee… and other things. All of which would be declared upon entering the country.

Prior to leaving on the trip, the screws were being tightly turned. The government wanted to compromise me… anyway possible. Then, they thought, regardless the way compromised, the issue would go away. To them, nothing mattered more than ending the challenge. Because they didn't want the case going to court! Any court… and, especially, Freeman Ruhle's court! Everyone seemed to know that he wasn't the most governmental friendly decision-maker. Everyone, that was, but me! But that was what I'd been told. And from all appearances, it seemed that was the way he was.

I knew the government was going to open up a whole new hole… upon entering the country. They'd probably enlarge it too. I wanted to make sure nothing would be found that wasn't supposed to be found. Although one never knew what to expect with those guys… other than to expect anything! So the lady Grace and I came up with a distinct disguise… something to throw those government Customs agent G-men off the scent.

Upon entering the country, I passed through Immigration without much fanfare. No one said anything! But there was just one slight small indication of things to come. They stamped my declaration card twice… probably in case the first stamp wasn't seen by anyone. Approaching Customs, I dunned a new pair of plastic eyeglasses… complete with a rounded nose and Groucho Marks mustached mask. It was straight out of a comic book. Probably, the same one that the Cohiba *IT'S ONLY CIGARS* T-shirts came from.

Lady Grace and I stood by the conveyer belt waiting for our bags. I canvassed the room and saw every agent monitoring every move I made. I wondered, with their attention directed on me, '*how many smugglers were making it through.*' When our bags finally arrived, an agent immediately walked over to me. He never bothered to ask for my declaration card. The only thing he wanted was to *politely* direct me toward the secondary counter… where Narco the Customs agent man was stationed and waiting. I thought it interesting… because Lady Grace was directed toward the exit door. We were traveling together, but they were only interested in me. And what was in my bags! However, she was asked about the company she kept.

I took my bags and walked over toward the secondary counter. Prior to reaching that area, three different agents approached me. None of the agents asked for my declaration card, but everyone wanted to get in on the action. They were chopping at the bit. Like wild horses… the first time reins are placed in their mouths! Each agent asked me to go to the secondary counter… only everyone said a different counter number. Maybe, the intent was for me to not follow orders… so they would have justification to do whatever they wanted. I didn't give it another thought. And while not one agent looked at my declaration card, they all mentioned my name. *"Mr. Fabler, Customs would like to see you over at counter number…"*

I got the picture after the 2nd agent approached… and wondered what took me so long to get with the program. When the 3rd one came up to me, I told him that I could *'only go to but one counter.'* That agent just looked at me like I was crazy. Little did he know! Then, he instructed me to go over to secondary counter number four. What I found most interesting was that none of those agents said anything about my mask. Apparently, they could see through the veil of my disguise!

I stood in front of the secondary counters for a minute trying to decide which one to go to. I looked off to the side and saw supervisor Notruful standing off by himself watching every move I made. I knew his face, and with that… his name. But it was his Affidavit that gave his name away. I also saw agent Narco standing at one of the secondary counters. I decided if anyone was going to be the odd man out… it would be him. He had already had his fun… now it was my turn.

I looked around the room and saw every agent's attention focused on me. And I felt like they were waiting for me to make a desperate break. Maybe, they thought it would be for freedom. I could see the headlines in the morning papers… Stoogie-Smuggler Shot Attempting To Flee Customs At Airport. Or on TV… News Story. Live at five!

I finally picked a counter to approach. It was the one that none of the agents told me to go to. I thought *'screw them all.'* At the counter, the agent told me to place all my bags on the counter… and to give him my declaration card. Then, he asked why I was wearing what I was wearing. The agent wasn't amused with my answer when I told him what I said, like Groucho on TV, that if he said the right word… he could win a cigar! He just asked me to remove The Mask. And like all the others, he knew my name well in advance of my arrival… when he said *"Mr. Fabler, what do you have on your face?"* And after my answer, *"Mr. Fabler, please remove The Mask!"*

The secondary counter agent was very precise with his questions. He wrote down every word I said except the Groucho guise. And he searched my bags thoroughly… taking everything out. All my clothes were unfolded and every page of every book opened. Finally, near the end of his inspection, the agent asked what this was all about. I told him, but knew he already knew. I also knew he only wanted to hear what I had to say. But when I told him, he seemed surprised… and said in a question *"All this… for that!?"*

Right then, I knew he wasn't a loop in the loop. Just a drone doing what he was told! Finally, the agent told me I could leave… and, as I did, I saw him take my declaration card over to that Notruful supervisor and hand it to him. The following morning, I entered the U.S. Attorney's office and received a stick-em label pass that allowed me access into their inner-most offices.

The Highway To Justice Is Just A One-Lane Road

***

Freeman Ruhle had ruled the Depositions were to be scheduled for the beginning of November. He also ruled all the Interrogatories were to be completed prior to the date he set for trial. But he didn't say how long before. About a week prior to the Deposition hearing, we received the government's 1st set of Interrogatories. They had questions and more questions. Some went back thirty years. I questioned the shark about the basis of some of their questions. It seemed the government was going past the scope of what the case was about. He advised me to just answer everything... and he'd decide what to send them in response. In response, he sent them everything I answered. Go figure!

Their questions were about past addresses, employers, professional experiences... and the like. They asked about anything that'd make it easy for them to fill in the spaces of my life! They also asked about my priors... arrests and convictions. I told them that although I only had a couple of arrests, they could rest assure I had more than a few convictions. However, I wasn't sure if they'd be interested in my politics. Then, I told them about the forty-two month sabbatical... spent locked up in those hell-holed hollows. And just because my politics didn't agree with their politics! I thought, '*what the hell!*' I knew they knew... what difference would it make. Besides, I was sworn to tell The Truth, The Whole Truth... and Nothing But the Truth by threat of imprisonment, fine or both.

I thought it **ALL** beyond unbelievable. Because when we received the answers to our Interrogatories almost everything on every page was blacked out! A large black magic marker covered **ALL** the print on **ALL** the printed areas on **ALL** the pages where we were seeking information. While the government complied with His Honor's, the judge's, order to provide answers to **ALL** our Interrogatories, **ALL** their answers weren't able to be read... and there was only a scant few weeks left until the case was to be heard. And that wouldn't be enough time to do anything about the lack of honesty on their part.

The only lines left open and not blacked out were the ones for my name and where the event took place. They also listed the items confiscated... and a couple of names of officers. But what they said, when we questioned their blacking out of everything that was blacked out, was that it was security related. I wondered what could've been so security related... and couldn't relate to the security they were relating to. However, the government does what they want whenever they want. And they wanted to black everything out. So they did!

I couldn't help think that if I'd done what they did **ALL** hell would've been raised! But I didn't. Probably because I didn't have any forms that could've been blacked out! I only had my answers to **ALL** their questions. And they had **ALL** those black lines throughout **ALL** those forms for **ALL** their answers to **ALL** my questions. Go Figure!

David Weisenthal

DEC-15-1998 20:05   ASST CHIEF COUNSEL BALTO

FP? CASE ACCT I997110600001101

FISCAL YEAR:* 1997 TYPE:*   TOTAL: 01

TOPIC:* FAILURE TO DECLARE CUBAN CIGARS

VIOLATOR BUSINESS NAME:

ID #:   TYPE: CITIZENSHIP: US DOB: 03071948

VIOLATOR LAST NAME: FABLER   MIDDLE NAME:

FIRST NAME: DAVID

STREET:* 125 S. 16TH STREET   APT/SUITE: 601

CITY:* PHILADELPHIA   ST: PA CNTRY:* US ZIP: 19103

PERSONAL SEARCH: 04181997 1947 ARREST: SEIZURE: 04181997 1920

                              NAME-TITLE-AGENCY

PORT:* 1100

DECLARATION TKN BY: MARGO/P-CUSTOMS INSPR-C

ARRESTING OFFICER :

SEIZING OFFICER :   MARGO/P-CUSTOMS INSPR-C

SUPERVISOR   :*   KUDEMANN/D-SUPVY CUSTOMS INSPR-C

PORT DIRECTOR   :

** INCIDENT IS APPROVED - 06/19/1997, FP&F CASE ACCEPTED :

204

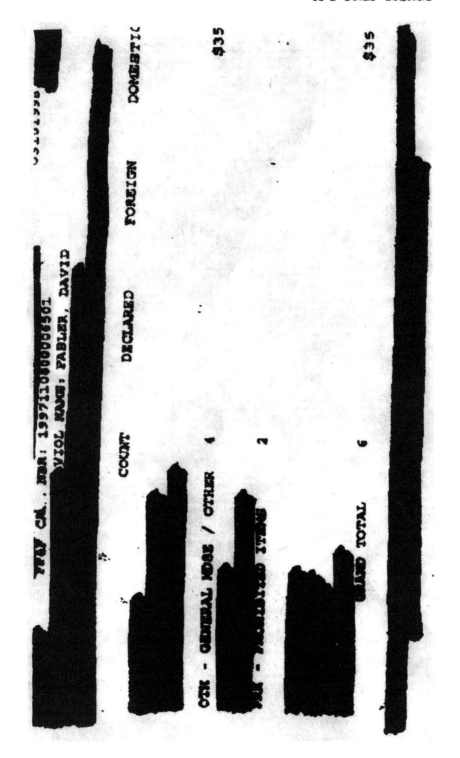

David Weisenthal

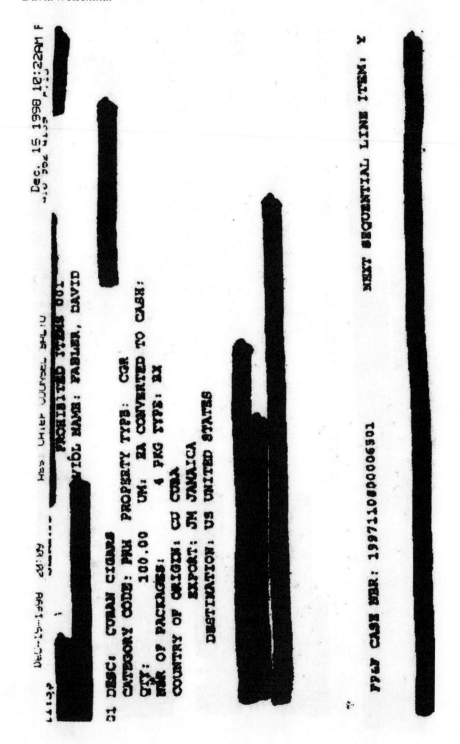

DEC-15-1998   20:06   ASST CHIEF COUNSEL BALTO

FTF CASE NBR: XXXXXXXXXXXX

VIOL NAME: FABLER, DAVID

(ENTER "X" FOR MORE:

DISCOVERY DATE:* 04181997

ITINERARY INFORMATION: IN/OUT BOUND:* I   DATE* 04181997 TIME

FROM* CU CUBA   VIA JM JAMAICA

CONVEYANCE INFORMATION: LOCAL USE:

TYPE: C - COMM AIR

FLIGHT # * VIS AIRLINE CODE JM BILL OF LADING #

David Weisenthal

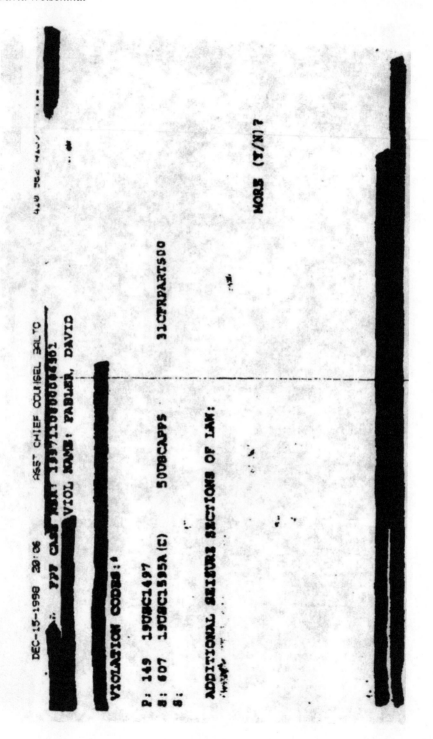

Dec. 16 1998 12:21AM

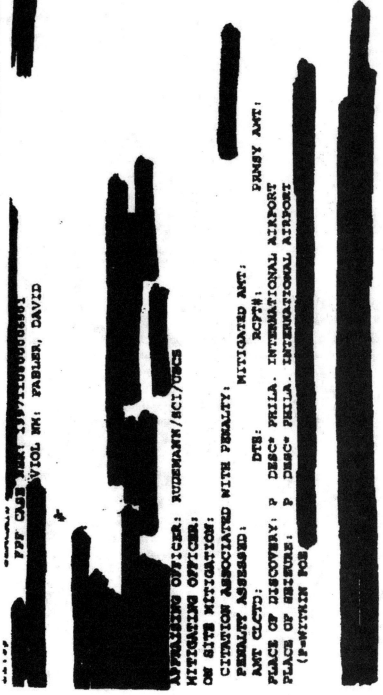

FPF CASE ... VIOL NM: FABLER, DAVID

APPRAISING OFFICER: RUDEMANN/SCI/USCS
MITIGATING OFFICER:
ON SITE MITIGATION:
CITATION ASSOCIATED WITH PENALTY:
PENALTY ASSESSED: MITIGATED AMT:
AMT CLCTD: DTE: RCPT#:   PNLSY AMT:
PLACE OF DISCOVERY: P DESC* PHILA. INTERNATIONAL AIRPORT
PLACE OF SEIZURE : P DESC* PHILA. INTERNATIONAL AIRPORT
(P=WITHIN FOR

The Deposition hearing took place in the U.S. Attorney's office in Philadelphia. A metal detector protected the entrance. It served as a security clearance... and was a security related requirement that was required prior to obtaining the visitor's badge... a peal off stick-em label that said 'VISITOR - U.S. Attorney.' It also stated the date, but that was left blank. This last security related requirement didn't seem so security related, but it was a requirement all the same.

At the initially scheduled Deposition hearing, Lars the Titon stoogie smoking Customs Helmsman agent g'man indicated his witnesses wouldn't be available until later in the day. But he insisted I go on in the early morning. He was upset that I was two hours late... due to an auto mechanical problem and traffic into the city. Always a problem! However, nothing was mentioned about his witnesses' unavailability... until after I arrived for the Deposition hearing.

The day before the initial Deposition hearing, I told the shark that I was very concerned about the government hearing my side (I was supposed to be deposed first). Then, taking my story and carving their web into my tale. It was something I wasn't putting past them... considering all the stuff they'd been toting along the **Road to Jurisprudence**. They had twisted, turned, converted, and contorted every little detail... to fit into their version of what they wanted to have taken place way back when. And way back when, back near the beginning, we even had that e-mail from them saying they'd do that. The one that said no one would believe us... because they were from Customs.

After I arrived at the initial Deposition hearing, Lars the Titon cigar Customs Helmsmen said he wanted to cancel the hearing... because I got there late. He argued there wouldn't be enough time between my Deposition and the government agents who were giving theirs. Time that was needed to carve out their web!

I told the shark that I questioned the lack of timing between the Depositions. Whether it was one minute or three hours shouldn't have mattered! Unless they wanted to weave a web into my tale! However, the shark's questions to Lars the Titon cigar Customs agent Helmsmen was premised around the lack of Depositions as His Honor, the judge, had ruled. The shark wanted to know if the government was going to honor Freeman Ruhle's ruling order.

The shark threatened to go back to His Honor, the judge, and inform him the government was violating his order. Finally, after going back and forth with each other, Lars the Titon g'men cigar man caved in. Another date was set... three weeks later. The date for that Deposition hearing was the 1st Tuesday after the turkey eating day holiday. And we told them that I couldn't do it sooner because our trip to Jamaica had already been planned, arranged... and paid!

The morning after the night we returned from Jamaica, I dressed in a Cohiba Libre *IT'S ONLY CIGARS* T-shirt. I wanted to wear the Cohiba Libre *IT'S ONLY CIGARS* T-shirt to the Deposition hearing because I thought it appropriate... considering the circumstances. The picture of a Fidel look-a-like stoking a Cohiba look-a-like was too appealing to pass up. Anything to enflame the fumes of passion! And, then when I'd turn around, to see the *IT'S ONLY CIGARS* on the top... I knew would put them over the top. I kept thinking the humidor thing could be redirected down another path... toward a door to humor.

Unfortunately, Lars Titon the smoke Helmsmen never got it. All he could do was zero in on the T-shirt... when all else failed. He described, in detail, the Cohiba Libre *IT'S ONLY CIGARS* T-shirt. Then, he kept asking questions about where the Cohiba Libre *IT'S ONLY CIGARS* T-shirt came from... and how I got it. He couldn't believe they were actually made in America. All the while, I kept thinking it was all quite humorless. After all, it was only a Cohiba Libre *IT'S ONLY CIGARS* T-shirt. What was all the fuss about? Besides, printed literature wasn't banned by the Regs! And the Cohiba Libre *IT'S ONLY CIGARS* T-shirts *ONLY* had print on it. Meanwhile, I wondered if the government could take the T-shirt... and, if so, would they have to give me the print back? As the Regulations stated had to happen! Then, as suddenly as it began, it was over. At least, for me!

The 1st witness for the government was special agent Almen Notruful. Who, as it turned out, seemed very truthful! At least, by our standards! By the shark's 3rd question, it was quite apparent he wasn't present during the night of April 18, 1997... as his Affidavit had indicated. When asked, he said Lars Titon the smoker stoogie agent asked him to write his Affidavit... and to *specifically* word it the way he did! He agreed it appeared to be misleading... and apologized for any misunderstanding or confusion created. He certainly wanted no part of that. But he was just following orders!

David Weisenthal

Lars Titon the Customs cigar man objected to most of our questions, but relented when pinned down on whether he was instructing his client to not answer our questions. As the questioning continued, he seemed more and more uncomfortable with the nature and direction our cross-examination was taking. His anxiety as well as jittery movements rose to unprecedented levels. His eyelids began twitching and the corners of his lips curled into contorted fixtures with each answer given... by his own witness. Getting caught in lies heightens anxiety! It doesn't matter who you are.

A reason Lars Titon the Customs cigar man probably didn't prolong the questioning past our cross-examination had to be to control the damage inflicted. But the damage had already been done by the time we were done questioning the truthful Notruful special agent Customs man. The most damage occurred when agent Notruful stated that the agent we thought was him was actually supervisor Rudemann... who was going to be the 3rd witness to testify for the government.

Up next for the government was agent Narco. He was a man who'd walk down liar's lane on his way through the questioning process. Agent Narco was a real government man... loyal to a fault, and for all the wrong reasons.

We questioned him about this and that, but he couldn't remember anything. Anything other than something about me stating that I didn't have anything to declare on that fateful night! However, at first, he didn't even know who I was... although he'd seen me the previous night! When I reminded him of who I was, the shark kicked me under the table. After more than too many contradictions and some forty-five minutes had passed, the questioning was done. Again, Lars the Titon cigar Helmsmen Customs agent man decided it better not to continue the questioning. I thought it might have been discretion being the better part of valor, but those guys didn't seem to have a brave bone in their bodies.

Finally, the last to testify was supervisor Rudemann... who was agent Narco's supervisor. Supervisor Rudemann seemed fairly honest and above board. He was the guy that I confused with special agent Notruful... based on the Affidavit we got from special agent Notruful. However, when the government finally got around to answering our Interrogatories, special agent Almen Notruful wasn't mentioned... and another agent was. Somehow, the shark and I got the feeling that supervisor Rudemann got the picture. His answers were more the truth of what had actually taken place. And, maybe, that was the reason his statement wasn't part of the government's original motion for forfeiture.

When the shark asked his 1st question to supervisor Rudemann, supervision Rudemann joked about my return through Customs... the night before. He said that with all things considered I hadn't been kept too long. He also said he remembered me having been detained a lot longer in the past. We all laughed at his comment. All except Lars Titon the cigar smoking Customs agent man. I could see he understood my position. However, he was still a government Customs agent supervisor man. And he'd have to do what he'd have to do when he was ordered to do it... by his supervisor(s). It was in his job description!

Supervisor Rudemann answered all the shark's questions to the *best* of his ability... as he saw the situation. However, how he saw the situation was probably why Lars Titon the cigar Customs g'man didn't use him to submit an Affidavit. The truth always hurts!

The truth was also probably a reason why special agent Notruful wasn't involved more than he was. When truth is confronted, it usually wins... unless the truth is disproportionately exaggerated. And that seemed to be what the government was doing... disproportionately exaggerating the truth!

Agent Narco didn't need an incentive to exaggerate the truth. He worked for Customs. That was reason enough! The only truth he was interested in was the end result... as the end justified the means. He had been taught that in his training.

Neither Narco nor that Lars Titon cigar puff-daddy Helmsman cared about the truth. Their pot of gold was the victory they so desperately craved. One... they'd lie to get! For truth wasn't the name of their game. Their lying lined the lanes on The Highway To Justice! And they had hoped it'd lead us down a one-lane dirt road to nowhere.

Before I knew it, the day had passed. The questioning was over. At the end of the Deposition, everyone got up and left... including Lars Titon the Customs cigar Helmsman. And then, we even had a civil conversation... about our mutual past. He said he went to a high school near the one I attended. It turned out we knew some of the same people… and reminisced about experiences from the old neighborhood during the good old days.

After walking out the door of the government building, Lars the Titon cigar Helmsman puff-daddy stated he was leaving the case at the end of the year. He said someone else would stand in his steed on the day of my day in court. I wondered if he had a conscience… after all. But knew it had to be something else. The shark and I just looked at him. However, he didn't say anything else! And, when I saw him leave the U.S. Attorney's office that day, I knew it'd be the last time I'd ever see him. I couldn't say I was sad for that, but I was sad for ever having met him… in the first place.

Two and One-Half Minutes of Fame

***

The last time I saw that son of a Buck reporter man was at the gala Cohiba Libre *IT'S ONLY CIGARS* Cubano Noche dinner feast fest. He talked the talk about getting together to do an interview for his TV news station. However, I wasn't going to hold my breath.

I knew anyone could talk the talk. The son of a Buck newsman said it was possible the national channel would pick it up… considering the nature of the topic. However, I wasn't going to hold my breath.

He said, if not, it'd still be aired. And, if nothing else, would help spread the word… which had been my objective all along. However, I wasn't going to hold my breath.

Rouldy the Buck newsman fulfilled his objective when he attended the Cohiba Libre *IT'S ONLY CIGARS* Cubano Noche dinner feast fest smoke out food orgy. He ate to his heart's content, drank himself to oblivion, and smoked a Cuban… which he'd never done before. But damn if he hadn't wanted to. And, while Rouldy the son of a Buck reporter may've been a virgin Cuban cigar puff-daddy, his job took him to the strangest places where he met the weirdest people who did everything anyone could think of. To which, he was able to tell tall tales about smoke-screened snow-jobs that were designed to pull the wool over someone else's eyes. Somehow though, his words seemed more like a prophecy than an omen when he said his job '*had its perks.*'

When we first met in that out of the way wayward saloon town-hall watering-hole bar, that son of a Rouldolph Buck mentioned his local TV station and my eyes lit up. Almost as bright as the nose on Rouldy's ruddy face. I had a hard time controlling my glee while he had a hard time containing his sobriety. But he wasn't out to drink then drive… so it didn't seem to matter. And it wasn't at Lady Grace's hostelry café that Rouldy was getting sloshed. So we didn't have to worry if he was driving!

While drinking our drinks, we talked the talk. By the time it came time for me to leave he thought I walked the walk… because I was willing to take on the Goliath beast of the modern Western world. It also didn't hurt my image when I told him my name was David. And, although I was

215

a storyteller by nature and a raconteur by habit, most of all I was a Fabler by birth!

I knew the time would come when I'd see if Bucky walked the walk of the talk he talked. It would depend on that local TV news interview he swore he wanted to do. I knew things had a way of happening. And I knew they also had a way of not happening. But I really knew they had a way of happening sooner with a poke here and a prod there. Just as long as the poke wasn't too long or the prod too deep!

On my travels down the **Highway To Justice**, I'd heard many tales about who was going to do what… and when. More often than not though, I'd find myself abandoned along the road somewhere between disheartened and disappointment… when what was going to happen turned into a dead-end road stop sign. It was at those times when my disillusionment would become disproportional because I'd be stuck somewhere between here and there with nowhere in sight. Only the concrete slabs that went off in a direction all their own were visible. And it wasn't like the thoroughfare had much traffic cruising along the fast lane. After awhile, I began to wonder if I'd missed my turn. Only I wasn't sure if I'd been keeping track of the time… or miles. However, when Buck bit the bait and my moment was about to shine… even if it would only be for a couple of clicks of shame filled tick-tock fame I knew my time had finally come.

Not two months had passed since the ***Smoke It, Don't Poke It*** article ran in the press and the ink was still freshly printed in my mind. The Deposition hearing had run its course and all the Interrogatories were sent and answered… although some questions still lingered. The New Year was rapidly nearing and the final count was quietly counting down. On the day after the day the last of the New Year celebrations were to be shouted, the case of the century would be heard… maybe, around the world. If nothing else, it'd be played out for all to see. That is, if anyone was interested! And I knew, at least, some were.

Between the time Bucky, the red-faced Rouldolph reporter, and I talked at the Cohiba Libre *IT'S ONLY CIGARS* Cubano Noche dinner feast fest and the New Year's arrival, he made several attempts to contact government officials. *Specifically* reaching out to that Lars Titon of a Customs cigar Helmsman! Rouldy wanted to discuss the pending case. However, it soon became apparent that no one wanted to discuss the case with him. Instead, they kept passing the buck! Having failed to achieve his goal, Bucky contacted some others in the government. And *ALL* he got for *ALL* his efforts was *ALL* the time he spent trying to contact *ALL* those people and getting his buck passed over.

E-mails continued as did the search for anything involving Cuban cigars of any brand. People passed through Lady Grace's 21ˢᵗ century café foodery in record levels! All wished the *best* in the upcoming battle. And, even if they all didn't agree with the concept of the battle at hand, they all voiced support that victory was preferred over defeat. Everyone loves an underdog! It's an American thing… going back to our revolution for independence!

The excitement was building at a feverish pitch. Electricity was flying through the air. It could've been cut with a knife! The time was at hand and, at last, the last of the last was near. It was the stretch drive, the final leg of the journey, the last stop along the trek. It was the irrefutable conclusion that would decide the direction that that road was heading toward.

Two days before the last popper got popped and the last drop of sipped bubbly slid down anyone's throat, I received a call from Bucky the Rouldolph reporter man. He said he wanted to meet and film me for a 'live at five' on the *BIG* screen. I knew it then that he walked the walk of the talk he talked… because he was one of the very select few who'd kept their word and did what he said he would.

The following day, four days before the great Cubano cigar caper case court day, Bucky arrived at Lady Gracie's 21ˢᵗ century café, with his cameraman, to discuss the story… in detail. We spoke for fifteen brief minutes and the cameraman rolled his reel the whole time. However, Rouldy the Buck reporter said the footage would be edited down to a few short brief minutes… at *best*. I figured seconds at most. But I also figured it'd be aired. So, to me, it was worth the price of the cost of the ticket paid for admission.

On the night of the day we met to talk and filmed the action, after the local TV news network aired the news of the day, our phone lines lit up. Everyone who was anyone called to say they saw me on the local TV news network. However, I missed the broadcast. A last minute meeting with the shark had been set in order to go over last minute details. I guess everyone just wanted me to know they knew to watch the nightly news broadcast of the news of the day.

The day before my day in court, I woke up to the latest headlines in the papers. Pres-man Bill, being the guy who played with Castro's cigars in the Oral Office, decided to ease the Regulations concerning 'THE embargo.' It was much to, either, the delight or dismay of those Cubano 'nationals' and others who were affected by 'THE embargo.' That would depend on the side they were on... status quo or revolution!

Suddenly, everyone in America was allowed to give every Cuban, living in Cuba, up to $1,000.00 (U.S.) every year. Airline flights were also expanded from only between Miami and Havana to New York and Havana... and other cities and Havana as well. There was a relaxation of other rules too. However, the ban on Cuban cigars remained in effect. But all I could think of was how those headlines could affect the outcome of the case.

I thought there'd have to be some recognition on that movement. The cigars were worth less than $100.00. However, ten times that could be transferred between people in both countries. I also thought whatever the big fuss was over those smokes would surely be reduced down to ashes after the new news. But I also knew, most of all - time would tell!

On the eve of the good fight day in court dogfight, I went to sleep with a good feeling. I knew the timing couldn't have been better. Every paper in the land ran the tale about Pres-man Bill and our new stance on Cuba. Every TV aired the narrative as well. Amid all the *to do* about the relaxation of rules, my case was hitting the heels of a major shift in governmental policy. I knew it couldn't hurt! I thanked G-d for small favors... for, it seemed, G-d was on my side.

I couldn't sleep that night! *'I was tossing and turning... all night long.'* At morning's first light, I saw the first snow of the season. When I saw the white-covered ground, I secretly hoped that that first snow of the year wouldn't blanket the eyes of the countryside. And while I did think it was somehow appropriate... I wasn't really sure what to think. I remember wondering whether the weather would affect the hearing. All I knew was the day had arrived when I'd have my day in court. I was prepared to duke it out with those titans of swag. This was the day I'd been waiting for... for over two years. Now it was here... and I was there!

The restaurant Hemmingway made famous.

David Weisenthal

The menu at La Bodeguita del Medio.

La B del M

Menu al ritmo criollo

White rice	1.25
Black bean soup	1.75
Roast pork roll	9.50
Fried pork chunks	10.90
Roast leg of pork	10.50
Roast chicken whith cacerole sauce	8.90
Beef hash a la habanera	7.50
Shredded jerked beef	8.20
Fried cow meat	9.40
Black bean whith rice	1.75
Fried bananas or fried sweet potatoes	1.25
Season salad	1.50
House desseert	1.25
Bread and butter	0.30
Creole coffee	1.50

An English version is also offered. The food is wonderful...in any language.

Havana Dave with the chef and the current owners of this famous haunt.

In action... behind the scenes. Serving up their most famous recipe... Picma de Puerco Asada en sujugo 'Roast Pork Leg.'

Simple beginnings make sumptuous meals.

A vintage press for cane syrup... a key ingredient in the famous "Mojito."

Majestic architecture in old Havana.

Regal old homes flanked by new construction... a sign of the times.

A walking view from the streets of Havana

The majesty of times long ago.

A new hotel in Havana... with support from Canadian funding.
The total restoration of a beautiful hacienda.

A view of an avenue in a neighborhood outside Havana.

Peacocks roam the landscape... at the Hotel Nacional.

The sun sets on Havana.

Chapter 3
Havana Dave's Day In Court

A Son of a Story Teller's Tale

***

The elevator doors opened. Lady Grace and I walked out into the corridor in search of a sign that would signal the courtroom the case **U.S. v. 100 Cuban Cigars** was in. The sign we sought was Courtroom 4-C! Below it - U.S. District Justice Freemen Ruhle! We found the brass mounted sign on one of the two twin mahogany doors that was the only entrance into the courtroom... other than the door that led directly into the judge's private chamber. We opened the door and entered a newly reconstructed room that was built to assure those hollowed walls of justice would maintain the legacy of our country's history with freedom. It was a freedom designed to frame fairness with equity and was surrounded with a certain amount of impartiality. And amid the archives of the country's history, the history of the country's jurisprudence was instantly felt upon entrance.

The room was void of life. We sat on one of the wooden benches that lined the room behind a swinging gate, then waited for anyone who was anyone to show. The gate served as the separation that divided the viewers from the participants. In time, the twin mahogany doors began to open and people started entering the room. Each person took a seat on the benches near where the Lady Grace and I sat. Eventually, only a few seats remained... but we didn't recognize anyone. Finally, some familiar faces showed up... however they weren't the friendly kind.

Four people accompanied agent Narco and supervisor Rudemann. They all walked through the swinging gate together. Narco and Rudemann sat down on a seat in a row of seats behind the desk where the government sharks were to sit. Neither Rudemann nor Narco acknowledged my presence. But that's how it was supposed to be. The four people accompanying the two G-men Customs agents were two men and two women! Narco and Rudemann were dressed in their official blue uniforms while the two men were clothed in coat and tie. The women wore neatly attired business suits and heels. And everyone's garments were designed to tell a tale long before their story had even been told.

One of the women was petite, natty, and demure. The other, although blond and wispy, displayed a depraved air of malice... the likes of which would've turned Jack the Ripper green with envy. Every time she'd glance over in my direction, her sweet and innocent Ms. Hyde demeanor was stripped away to reveal a true Dr. Jeckle personality. It was as if she had an ax to grind with an old boyfriend she saw with a new girlfriend. And it was obvious she harbored a real bitch of a mean streak that flowed through her veins! Supervisor Rudemann informed them all of my existence. Thereafter, one at a time, one after the other, turned their heads to get a better look at who they wanted to smoke. Kill, that is…not inhale!

The two unknown men portrayed a contrast in polarity. The union so unique their appearance together marked the opposition of its nature. While both were tall, the similarities ended there. One was heavy set with eyes set in deep sockets. His short, light-colored, neatly-combed hair was thin in spots. If he'd been on a mission, he truly would've passed for a government secret agent man. And, the truth was, he was on a mission. For it could be seen from his bearing that he'd like nothing better than to shoot me down in a hail of fire. Anything that'd put an end to my questioning his government's policy! A policy he took joy enforcing with all the plumb of a *Mafia* hit man.

Although my case was only to settle an absurd level of archaic antiquated enforcement of stupidity, the unknown man was all business. He expressed the look of a bulldog he thought he was. And it was evident the buck stopped with him. For although some might've taken his corporate demure to be just another pencil-pushing ass-kissing yes-man, he knew all too well that he was the badest dog of them all.

Bulldog man's suit strained to contain arms that bulged through the coarse material. It was a visual sign of daily workouts that inflated muscles past the size of the apparel. His clothing verified the time spent in a gym, building upper-arm strength he knew would help him ensure the strong-armed tactics he so relished.

The other man's frame was thin and frail with dark hair that contrasted the pale color of his skin. His suit looked more expensive than bulldog man's clothing… but hung on his body in an out of style fashion. Looking at the two men, one couldn't help wonder what force of nature came together to unite these two vastly different people.

Prior to His Honor, the judge, making an entrance, my shark raced through the entrance doors. He sat down behind a desk next to where the recalcitrant group had positioned themselves. The desks the g'men sat behind were arranged next to each other in front of a raised podium where His Honor, the judge, was to sit… high above the masses and contestants. A sign of relief crossed my mind when I saw my shark enter the room because he was the shark I trusted to feed on the carcasses of the corpses that the opposition forces had lined up. As my shark placed his attaché case down on the desk in front of him, I made my way through the swinging barrier that delineated the players from the crowd. And passing through the gated aisle not only had me becoming a player, but I had become… THE PLAYER!

Suddenly, a silent hush quieted the crowd. The other door to the courtroom opened. A tall regal man with long distinguished white-hair entered the assembly. His hair color contrasted the hue of his black robe. Everyone stood in respect and waited for the robed one to sit before returning to their seats. The wait didn't last long! In the hushed room, a bellowed voice filled the quiet.

The Court: "Good morning, everyone. We're here in the matter of **United States of America vs. 100 Cuban Cigars**… Civil Action Number 98-3728. And, our first order of business, I understand it, is that the government has a motion for me. How is everyone today? Happy New Year!"

The petite and natty woman rose from her seat behind the desk and spoke into the microphone. "Very well, Your Honor. Good Morning! I'm Wendy Knight from the U. S. Attorney's Office. I'm here to move for admission *pro hae vice* of two attorneys. The first is Imma Beeche. She's with the U.S. Customs service in New York and she's a Deputy Associate Chief Counsel who was admitted to the New York Bar in 1996 and the New Jersey Bar in 1991. I also move for admission of D. Pete Animen who's from the U.S. Customs service in Baltimore. Mr. Animen is Assistant Chief Counsel and he's been admitted to the Florida Bar since 1980."

The Court: "I'm pleased to grant the motion. I welcome both Ms. Bitch and Mr. Enema to our Court."

Ms. Beeche: (Not rising from her seat… she spoke), "Your Honor…it's Beeche"

The Court:	"Beach!? How do you spell that?"
Ms. Beeche:	B-E-E-C-H-E! Beeche… as in a tree.
The Court:	"**Oh**! Okay. Beeeeeeche… tree! Got it!"

Out of nowhere a voice shot out that made my bones curdle. It wasn't so much what was said, but the intonation of how it was said… and I knew a ringer who was a shark when I heard a ringer-shark speak. D. Pete Animen was a shark of a different color. He talked like he knew his stuff… even if he didn't know what he was talking about. But D. Pete Animen knew working for the government gave him free reign to go after anyone in opposition to any idea of what his concept of law enforcement was. And D. Pete Animen's concept of law enforcement was to libel and slander anyone who questioned his government's authority regardless the basis for questioning… or the manner questioned! Because, to D. Pete Animen, the very fact any question existed meant the beginning of the end of the system he so strongly supported. G-d forbid that! For that was only the works of left-winged commie-loving anti-governmental liberals who were destroying his country! They could all go to hell! If he had any say in it and with his help… they all would!

D. Pete Animen:	(Rising from his seat, he stood tall before the audience as he addressed the court), "Your Honor! Theee corrrreeect prooooonuunnnncciiiiiation of my name is ANIMEN! A-N-I-M-E-N! D **period** PETE ANIMEN!"
The Court:	"Animen!? Oh, okay! Animen!" Without another thought, His Honor, the judge, looked at the petite and natty woman and spoke to her. "Now you're welcome to stay, Ms. Knight. It's an interesting case, I think!"
Ms. Knight:	"Cigars?!"
The Court:	"**Cuban** cigars! But if you want to go back to your office, it's up to you."
Ms. Knight:	"Okay, Your Honor. I may stay for a bit."

The Court:	"Very good. Now Mr. Shark, how are you?"
Mr. Shark:	(Rising from his seat), "Very good, Your Honor. It's nice to see you."
The Court:	"You have a tan."
Mr. Shark:	"It's my blood pressure, Judge. I was in the CJC and ran down here. I didn't want to be late."
The Court:	"Hmmm… as I remember, it wouldn't be your first time. Anyhow, with respect to how we proceed here, our friend, Mr. Helmsman…"
Ms. Beeche:	(Not raising from her seat she spoke his entire name), "Lars Titen Helmsman,"
The Court:	"Yes… Lars Titon Helsman! Has he an uncle or cousin named Matt? Maybe a distant relative!? I used to know a Matthew Helm who was a P. I. and who had quite an eye for his craft… and the ladies. Oh… those ladies!"
D. Pete Animen:	"Actually, we **really** wouldn't know, Your Honor."
The Court:	"You say, Lars Titon? Isn't that a cigar?"
D. Pete Animen:	"Lars Titon, Your Honor! We really wouldn't know about that… that is, being a cigar!"
The Court:	"The Lars Titon cigar… but of course! Well, I don't smoke them! Anyhow, he was here when we had the Rule 16 Conference on October 1st and we talked about the possibility of cross motions for summary judgment. And I'm saying this for your benefit because you weren't there. But when it became apparent that there were some issues… not a lot, but some factual issues, and Mr. Shark I'm sure recalls this… it was agreed that rather than having cross motions

for summary judgment, which was his idea, we'd have a brief Evidentiary Hearing. And we'd have a trial on those few issues in dispute so we could possibly avoid an unnecessary trip to the Court of Appeals... as to whether something was a genuine issue of material fact. Now, in reading the parties submissions on the Summary Judgment Motion that Mr. Lars Titon Helmsman filed and the record should reflect, and I'm by no means criticizing him for this, but as I understand it, he's no longer working with the Customs service. Well, I'd have to say it's no wonder... based on what I read."

D., Pete Animen: "That's correct, judge."

The Court: "But is there a reason for that?"

D. Pete Animen: "Well, I think there were a number of reasons, but there's no need for us to go into that here!"

The Court: "So, he's not here for whatever reason. Then, perhaps it was a *valedictory* gesture to his former employer... the filing of this Motion for Summary Judgment. Now, the parties also submitted their Pretrial Stipulation in accordance with my Order of October 1st. And there are certain facts that have been stipulated to. I remain of the view that is contained in my October 1st order. That is that there are a few facts and I think rather than debating whether it's a genuine issue, we ought to just hear the testimony and I'll do my Findings of Fact and Conclusions of Law in the next day or so. It seems to me that we'll save time this way. Now, since it's stipulated that Mr. Fabler brought certain Cuban origin merchandise back into the country and didn't have a license from OFAC, it seems the government has shown probable cause for the seizure here on those facts alone. So, that means Mr. Shark goes first. The only significance of this is that Mr. Shark goes first. And, quite

	frankly, I don't think any decision here is going to be determined on the burden of proof."
Mr. Shark:	(Rising from his seat), "I agree, Your Honor."
The Court:	"You agree with that?"
Mr. Shark:	"I agree, Your Honor. Just note my objection to the bottom line premise... that it shifts the burden. I wouldn't stipulate to that."
The Court:	I didn't expect you to."
Mr. Shark:	"But I have no problem with going first."
The Court:	"Also, your witness list had a conspicuous omission... Mr. Fabler. At the risk of making an ass of both you and me, I assume you're going to call him."
Mr. Shark:	"Oh, absolutely!"
The Court:	"And the other thing not stipulated is one of the defenses here... the issue of the Fully Sponsored or Fully Hosted visit. One of your witnesses was Herr Dueling. Is it agreed by both parties or is it an issue that Herr Dueling took Mr. Fabler to Cuba? I think it was in March, and was the host of that trip. That's how Mr. Fabler got to Cuba. Does the Service dispute that?"
Ms. Beeche:	(Speaking from her seat), "Your Honor, with regard to the trip to Cuba..."
The Court:	"STAND! When you address the Court... please!"
Ms. Beeche:	(Quickly rising from her seat), "If I may address several issues at this time. With regard to the trip to Cuba... it's the government's contention

that regardless of whether or not Mr. Dueling sponsored a trip to Cuba…"

The Court: "I understand your legal position on that, but I was trying to get at the factual issue of whether the government disputes whether Herr Dueling took Mr. Fabler to Cuba in March of 97. And that it was through his good offices, apparently as a friend, as a birthday gesture."

Mr. Shark: "Exactly, Your Honor."

The Court: "And that he bought the cigars and other cigarillos and so forth in Cuba."

Ms. Beeche: (Still standing), "There are certain issues with regard to the statements Mr. Fabler has made as to what was paid for by Mr. Dueling and what wasn't paid for by Mr. Dueling that the government disputes. However, the fact of whether Mr. Dueling paid entirely for the trip or not legally wouldn't change the forfeiture issue."

The Court: **"I understand the government's position on that!** But I'm trying to save time, that's all, as to whether we need to hear testimony on that. Because, as I take it, it's conspicuous in the Stipulation of Facts that there is no stipulation as to when, for example, Mr. Fabler was in Cuba and when he left Cuba or how he got there… that sort of thing. I take it the Service doesn't dispute that Mr. Fabler was, in fact, in Cuba."

Ms. Beeche: "The government does NOT dispute that he was, in fact, in Cuba."

The Court: "Also, I looked at the passport, and of course it is a copy, but I didn't see a stamp from the government of Cuba… in his passport."

Mr. Shark:	"It is my understanding, Your Honor, they don't stamp."
The Court:	(Leaning forward), "**They don't stamp**... in Cuba?"
Mr. Shark:	"That's my understanding, but they have the plane tickets. The government confiscated the plane tickets that Mr. Fabler had."
The Court:	"Can we have a stipulation as to when Mr. Fabler arrived in Cuba and when he left Cuba?"
Ms. Beeche:	"The government would welcome a stipulation."
The Court:	"What would those dates be, Mr. Shark, because it's not in the stipulation you submitted to me... or in the one Mr. Lars Titon Helmsman submitted to me."
Mr. Shark:	"Judge, I know the government has possession of the plane ticket they confiscated from Mr. Fabler that shows the actual dates of transport back and forth."
The Court:	"It was in March of 97, right?"
Mr. Shark:	"Yes!"
The Court:	"That was for a weekend?"
Mr. Fabler:	"Yes, it was, Your Honor."
The Court:	"Do you want to check that, Mr. D. Pete Animen? Do you have it in the files?"
D. Pete Animen:	(Standing up), "The actual dates of transportation?"
The Court:	"Mr. Shark thinks you folks have the plane ticket."

D. Pete Animen:	"We looked in our Evidence Room… and we do not."
The Court:	"Shall we stipulate that for two days… you tell me, two or three days?"
Mr. Fabler:	(Speaking from his chair), "Three days and two nights!"
The Court:	"So it was three days and two nights in March, 1997 that Mr. Fabler was in Cuba. Can we have a stipulation of fact?"
Ms. Beeche:	(Still standing), "Yes, Your Honor."
The Court:	"So then, that will be stipulated… three days and two nights. In terms of background, is the Service prepared to stipulate he went there with Andreas Dueling?"
Ms. Beeche:	"The government will stipulate that Mr. Fabler was in Cuba with Andreas Dueling."
The Court:	"And that Andreas Dueling is said to be a citizen of Germany and a resident alien in Jamaica. **AND he is NOT a United States citizen.**"
Ms. Beeche:	"We will stipulate he's **NOT** a U. S. citizen and that he's a German citizen. *However*, his residency IS in question."
The Court:	"But the important part, for our purposes, is that Andreas Dueling is **NOT** a U.S. citizen."
Ms. Beeche:	"The government will stipulate Andreas Dueling is **NOT** a U.S. citizen."
The Court:	**"FINE! That's very helpful!** Now the only issue other than background, and I'll certainly give both sides some latitude here recognizing the

243

factual issues, if any, are narrow that divide the parties, are the legal issues that are a gulf that I'll decide. It seems to me there is definitely a factual issue as to what happened by way of declaration which is an alternative basis for the forfeiture... and I have a genuine issue of material fact there. So I'm going to hear from Mr. Fabler on that. I'm perfectly happy to give some latitude by way of background and so forth, but I would think we could do this... this morning."

Mr. Shark: "I'd welcome that, Your Honor."

The Court: "And, of course... THE Service! I will hear from the Customs inspectors for their version of that."

Ms. Beeche: "If I may, Your Honor. Again, as you noted, I'm unfamiliar with what happened during the conference, but I was aware of a Motion for Summary Judgment pending. In the interest of expediency before this Court, I ask...given the fact that there are three separate bases for forfeiture, two under 1595 (a) and one on 19 USC 1497 for failure to declare, given the fact that you've stated that you find that there are issues of fact to be decided with regard to the issue of failure to declare under 1497 which would also cover one of the two bases under 1595 (a)... I'm only addressing to you the issue of 'THE (Cuban) embargo' and the basis for forfeiture under 1595 (a)."

The Court: **"I know that! I UNDERSTAND THAT!** You see, the problem was, the government had two alternative theories for the forfeiture."

Ms. Beeche: "Yes! So?"

The Court: "My concern, and I agree with you that as far as 'THE embargo' issue is concerned, is that that does seem almost purely legal if not purely

244

legal. I'm just being conservative in that respect. But my concern was that it would go up to the circuit and the circuit would say well, no, that's not right... there was an issue of fact there. By the way, what about the alternative basis for forfeiture? I just want for *your sake*, I mean, **after all, this case ONLY involves less than a hundred dollars.** So, I'm rather mindful of the fact that we should only do this once, at least in this Court. And we can get everything before us so that whoever is unhappy with my ruling can take it to the Court of Appeals and the Court of Appeals would only have it **once** because they'll have a complete record. I'm just being intensely practical, which is what I said at the Rule 16 Conference... **okay?**"

Ms. Beeche: "Okay."

The Court: "And this is **ONLY** going to take this morning... that's all."

Ms. Beeche: "Then, what I would offer..."

The Court: "Unless you are just **abandoning** that basis?"

Ms. Beeche "We are **NOT abandoning** any basis. NO!"

Mr. Shark: "We thought they'd stipulate to that, Judge... since they feel so strongly about their first position."

Ms. Beeche: "We are **NOT abandoning** any bases for forfeiture! However, what we would offer because we do believe 'THE (Cuban) embargo' issue is purely legal, is that we have asked an attorney from the Office of Foreign Assets Control to be present. So we ask he be permitted to testify as to the Cuban Asset Control Regulations... and to show that it is a purely legal issue."

The Court:	**"I MEAN THE Regulations ARE IN the Code**, but we're delighted to have somebody from OFAC. BUT the Regulations **ARE IN** the <u>Code of Federal Regulations</u>. We read those. So, I MEAN we **DON'T NEED ANYONE** to authenticate them… if that's what you mean."
Ms. Beeche:	"Well, I believe the only affirmative defense…"
The Court:	**"PARDON?"**
Ms. Beeche:	"I believe the only affirmative defense with regard to this Iranian embargo issue is that the **<u>Know As You Go</u>** pamphlet can be considered an instruction."
The Court:	**"Iranian embargo issue? Did you say an Iranian embargo issue? I thought this was a Cuban embargo issue… not an Iranian embargo issue!"**
Ms. Beeche:	"Did I say Iranian? I mean Cuban! I'm sorry, Your Honor. It IS a Cuban embargo issue!"
The Court:	"Okay! Maybe, it WILL be helpful. But *IS* he a person who **IS** competent to testify about **THAT** pamphlet?"
Ms. Beeche:	"YES, he is!"
The Court:	**"Because THAT pamphlet IS a mystery**, I must say!"
Ms. Beeche:	"He has reviewed the pamphlet and he can discuss the pamphlet *in the context* of the Cuban Asset Regulations."
The Court:	**"For that limited purpose**, I'll be happy to hear from him."
Ms. Beeche:	"Thank you, Your Honor."

The Court:	"In fact… I'm glad he's here."
Ms. Beeche:	"Thank you."
The Court:	"Now… maybe, we can make some progress here. Mr. Shark."
Mr. Shark:	"Yes, Your Honor?"
The Court:	"Shall we proceed?"
Mr. Shark:	"Mr. Fabler, would you take the stand."
The Court:	(Looking at the court stenographer the robed one said), "And, maybe, it would be better for you, Mr. Dick Tashon, if the witness is examined from the lectern."
Mr. Shark:	"Absolutely, Your Honor."
The Court:	"Mr. Fabler!"

With a wave of the judge's arm I got up from my seat and began walking toward the stand where I'd be sworn in! As I approached the seat I'd call home for the next few hours something began to overcome me. I became transfixed in thought. In the back of my mind I traveled off to another place in another time that wasn't too far back in time… nor that far away. Suddenly, I was lost in another life that had long passed me by. It was a place that changed my life… and, at the time, it didn't seem for the better. But this was another place in another time. And I had to face my fear(s).

It'd be a duel with the demon denounced! Hopefully the ogre monster that had crept under my skin would be slain and I'd finally be able to put to rest my fright from the horror I lived in fear of. I kept telling myself this was a civil issue… not criminal! Chill! And as Winston Churchill said, '*The only thing to fear was fear itself.*'" But the person some had come to know as Havana Dave was slipping farther and farther away from the crusty old shell of a son of a story telling soul who was about to tell some sorry sordid storied saga. And who went by the name David Fabler.

247

David Weisenthal

THE Truth, THE Whole Truth... and Nothing But THE Truth

***

I sat down on the stand and tried to settle in as a witness to obtain a certain comfort zone. Whatever comfort can be obtained from sitting in a witness chair! The robed one leaned forward. He seemed interested in every word I had to say. Then, he spoke in the same bellowed voice that he'd spoken before. And, when he spoke it was as if E. F. Hutton was speaking.

The Court:	"Get close to the microphone... because we *ALL* want to hear you, Mr. Fabler. Please proceed, Mr. Shark."
Mr. Shark:	"Yes, Your Honor. Your Honor, can I assume for the purposes of my examination that I should primarily focus on the declaration issue?"
The Court:	"You can do whatever background you want. I'm going to give you some latitude... just for the background... to put the case in context.
Mr. Shark:	"Mr. Fabler, directing your attention..."
The Court:	(Suddenly, the robed one interrupted. He had a question of his owned he wanted to ask, but his question was directed to me.) "I **have** question. Where do you live?"
Mr. Fabler:	"In Pine Forge, Pennsylvania."
The Court:	"Where?"
Mr. Fabler:	"Pine Forge!"
The Court:	"Where is that?"
Mr. Fabler:	"Pottstown! It's just outside of Pottstown!"

248

The Court:	"Because on the declaration you had an address and the reason I'm asking is because in the Summary Judgment papers I saw an address on Rittenhouse Square... One Rittenhouse Square."
Mr. Shark:	"That was back in 95."
The Court:	"Since 95... you moved?"
Mr. Fabler:	"Yes."
The Court:	"You're a citizen of Pennsylvania?"
Mr. Fabler:	"At this time, yes, Your Honor."
The Court:	(Leaning back in his chair, he swiveled it around for a second or two). Then he said, "That's fine!" He seemed satisfied by the nswer given to his question.
Mr. Shark:	Your Honor, we would also like to make clear that his driver's license was registered to his sister's home in New Jersey. And he used that JUST, *primarily*, to establish, you know, a driving circumstance.
The Court:	"Are they assigned to insurance premiums?"
Mr. Shark:	"I don't think so, Your Honor. He doesn't have a car. If he had a car then I would say that... maybe, that might be an issue. But you're thinking like a government person... and that's good, Judge."
The Court:	"Yes."
Mr. Shark:	"Mr. Fabler, directing your attention to April 1997 and going backwards a little bit. Were you in Jamaica in March?"
Mr. Fabler:	"Yes, I was."

Mr. Shark:	"And you traveled to Cuba?"
Mr. Fabler:	"In March… yes, I did."
Mr. Shark:	"Can you tell His Honor briefly where you came from and when you went there approximately? You came from America?"
Mr. Fabler:	"I was in Jamaica."
Mr. Shark:	"And while you were in Jamaica, did you have occasion to go to Cuba?"
Mr. Fabler:	"Yes, I did."
Mr. Shark:	"Tell His Honor about that, briefly, in terms of Mr. Dueling and the whole circumstance of how you went there. How you traveled and what you did."
Mr. Fabler:	"I went down to Jamaica on March 6, 1997. My birthday is March 7th. I had a number of friends who were there and, in fact, they got together for my birthday. We were at a friend's house and I'd been witnessing during the previous year or so people going to Cuba… but I never went! However, I did witness American citizens coming and going. Andreas asked if I wanted to go. He said 'Well, let's go to Cuba.' I said I didn't know about it… that was, about my being able to go. And I mentioned 'THE embargo.' But he said, 'No, you can go! I'll take you as my guest.' So, I looked at my passport to see what rules there were, if any, about it… and that directed me to the pamphlet **Know Before You Go**. I was given a copy when I came back to America on a previous trip to Jamaica. I had the book because I'd taken a chess-set to Jamaica… and I was interested in bringing it back into the country. When I asked

a Customs agent about it, she gave me the **Know Before You Go** book."

Mr. Shark: "Let me just interrupt you for a minute. For purposes of the record or perhaps I can have this marked as C-1. May I approach the witness, Your Honor..."

The Court: "Yes."

Mr. Shark: "I would ask you to take a look at what has been marked as C-1. Would Your Honor like a copy?"

The Court: "**Yes!** And this is **which edition** of that?"

Mr. Shark: "This is the April, 94 version. And is this the document you're referring to, Mr. Fabler?"

Mr. Fabler: "Yes!"

Mr. Shark: "Can you take a look at it briefly to make sure?"

Mr. Fabler: "This isn't all in order... but, yes."

Mr. Shark: "Have you taken a look? Is this the document you were just referring to in your testimony?"

Mr. Fabler: "This is the April 94 version. And it **is** the book I was referring to!"

Mr. Shark: "OK! Please continue. You were looking at this document?"

Mr. Fabler: "Yes! A Customs agent gave it to me on a previous trip into America... when I asked about bringing a chess-set back into the country. That's when they gave me the book and said contact... there's a number in there or whatever. So I had this copy of that **Know Before You Go** book. Then, I started reading it."

Mr. Shark:	"Did you go to Cuba with Mr. Dueling on or about March 19th?"
Mr. Fabler:	"Yes!"
The Court:	"Wasn't it March 7th or around your birthday?"
Mr. Fabler:	"No! It was after my birthday. The conversation took place on my birthday. It was a couple of weeks later that we went."
The Court:	"Okay! March 7th and March 19th!"
Mr. Shark:	"Describe for His Honor the financial arrangements or the circumstances. In other words, how did you go? Did you pay for anything when you went there?"
Mr. Fabler:	"No!"
Mr. Shark:	"Who paid for everything?"
Mr. Fabler:	"Andreas!"
Mr. Shark:	"He paid for your plane fare?"
Mr. Fabler:	"The plane fare... yes! He paid for everything!"
Mr. Shark:	"How did you fly there? Did you fly... what airlines?"
Mr. Fabler:	"Cubano Air!"
Mr. Shark:	"You went there and Mr. Dueling paid for your accommodations and all your expenses?"
Mr. Fabler:	"Yes! He went to a travel agent... or I guess you call it a travel agent in Jamaica. They had a package... hotel, airline, transfers from the airport to the hotel and a tour around Havana. It

was all one price! He bought the package. He bought one for himself and one for me. And he bought one for one other person as well."

Mr. Shark

"Now, the items that were ultimately confiscated by Customs when you came through on your return to the United States, those items that were obtained in Cuba, who purchased those?"

Mr. Fabler:

"Andreas!"

Mr. Shark:

"All of them?"

Mr. Fabler:

"All of them!"

Mr. Shark:

"In your Affidavit that was filed previously, you indicated those items did not exceed one hundred dollars. Would that be your testimony?"

Mr. Fabler:

"Yes!"

The Court:

"Let's just say that's the amount paid in Havana for them."

Mr. Fabler:

"Yes, sir!"

Mr. Shark:

"Now, at the end of that weekend, what did you do? Where did you go?"

Mr. Fabler:

"We went back to Jamaica!"

Mr. Shark:

"So, you didn't fly directly to the United States?"

Mr. Fabler:

"No!"

Mr. Shark:

"You say you went back to Jamaica?"

Mr. Fabler:

"Right!"

Mr. Shark:

"And you were there for a period of time?"

Mr. Fabler:	"Until April 18th!"
Mr. Shark:	"Then you came to the United States, correct?"
Mr. Fabler:	"Correct! I came back on April 18th because it was my mother's birthday the next day, so I came back for her thirty-ninth twenty-ninth birthday."
The Court:	(Shaking his head, the robed one wasn't sure he heard what he just heard). He questioned, "Thirty-ninth?" Then he asked, Twenty-ninth?" Finally he inquired, "Your mother, you say?"
Mr. Fabler:	"Yes, Your Honor! Her thirty-ninth twenty-ninth birthday!"
Mr. Shark:	"And you traveled from Jamaica to Philadelphia correct?"
Mr. Fabler:	"Yes!"
Mr. Shark:	"Now, when you returned to the States, and this is the important part of the testimony that His Honor really wants to hear about, in terms of the declaration business, and you've been deposed, and without me leading you, tell His Honor exactly what happened…"
The Court:	**"When you got to the airport…"**
Mr. Shark:	"…when you got to the airport!"
The Court:	**"… The Philadelphia International Airport."**
Mr. Shark:	"This is the crucial part of what His Honor's early indications were… in terms of this declaration business. And I don't want to lead you, Mr. Fabler."
The Court:	"Just tell us what happened."

Mr. Fabler:	"I had a shoulder bag and an attaché case. The cigars were in the attaché case because when I went back to Jamaica from Cuba, they have a limit on them. Only two boxes at a time! The others are confiscated because it's over the limit or they're put into… they keep them until you leave the country. That way they don't actually enter the country! And they give you a slip, which I don't have any more. But you go and claim them when you're going to catch the plane and they go into their holding bin."
The Court:	*"A humidor, I hope."*
Mr. Fabler:	"No! But it's very humid down there anyhow. So… you go in there, and it's right in the airport, and you give them their form. After signing their book they release your package(s). And, I put the cigars in my attaché after I retrieved them from Jamaica Customs."
The Court:	**"How many boxes?** *"*
Mr. Fabler:	"There were four boxes total, but two were in Jamaican Customs!"
The Court:	"Four boxes, two boxes… okay."
Mr. Fabler:	"Twenty-five, per box. Later, I walked up the ramp and I went to get my bag… my regular bag."
Mr. Shark:	"This is when you were in Philadelphia?"
Mr. Fabler:	"In Philadelphia, yes! When I turned to leave there was a man standing there who took my declaration card. He asked if I had more than $10,000. If I had been on a personal vacation or business… I think they were the terms and so forth. Then, he asked if I had anything to declare.

255

	I told him, 'Alcohol and tobacco products and miscellaneous other goods that were within my limit.' He told me to '*go to the counter.*'"
Mr. Shark:	"He directed you someplace?"
Mr. Fabler:	"Yes, I was directed…"
Mr. Shark:	Did you ever learn the name of that Customs agent?"
Mr. Fabler:	"No!"
Mr. Shark:	"To your knowledge, did we attempt to determine from the government the name of that particular Customs agent?"
Mr. Fabler:	"I believe so, yes!"
Mr. Shark:	"In the Affidavit we filed, we mistakenly identified that agent as agent Notruful, correct?"
Mr. Fabler:	"No! We thought agent Morren was the agent agent Narco went to. That is… his supervisor! Because the Government submitted an Affidavit from agent Notruful that said agent Narco went to him that night…"
Mr. Shark:	"But, in any event, we were never able to determine or were we ever able to take the Deposition or determine the identity of that particular agent?"
The Court:	"The first agent?"
Mr. Fabler:	"The first agent. No! We were never able to determine who he was."
Mr. Shark:	"And that first agent directed you to this other site, correct?"

Mr. Fabler:	"Where the secondary counter, I guess you call it, was…"
Mr. Shark:	"He directed you someplace else. It's your testimony…"
Mr. Fabler:	"There was nothing to fill out. It was already filled out, what I felt I had to fill out. But I told him when he asked me…"
Mr. Shark:	"And you told him you had tobacco products and alcohol to declare?"
Mr. Fabler:	"Correct!"
Mr. Shark:	"Continue."
Mr. Fabler:	"Well, I went over to the counter where agent Narco was. Only I didn't know his name at the time."
Mr. Shark:	"Now, just for purposes of the record, do you see agent Narco here?"
Mr. Fabler:	"Yes, I do!"
Mr. Shark:	"Can you identify him?"
Mr. Fabler:	"That gentleman wearing the blue uniform with the gold badge to my right. Over there to the right of the tall thin man at the end with the coat and tie on."
The Court:	**Okay!**"
Mr. Shark:	"For purposes of the record, Your Honor, I didn't until this moment realize that all of the government witnesses were here. If they're going to be called, I would ask that they be sequestered at this time."

| The Court: | "**Sure!** It's only going to be the two agents, right?" |

Ms. Beeche: "Two inspectors."

The Court: "I mean as far as *this* issue is concerned. It's the only relevance of sequestration... the two agents. Polly Anna, could you take them to the Jury Room?"

Mr. Shark: "Judge, also for purposes of the record, I note my associate just came into the courtroom. Her name is Sue R. Hammerhead. And she's been involved with me... *in this case*."

The Court: "I saw her name in the Deposition."

Ms. Hammerhead: "Good morning, Judge."

The Court: "Welcome to our Court."

Mr. Shark: "She's a new member of the Bar and has been with me for a year or so!"

The Court: "Congratulations. We have two new members of the Bar in our Court right here right now."

Mr. Shark: "Now, Mr. Fabler, you went over to the secondary location where you saw agent Narco, correct?"

Mr. Fabler: "Correct!"

Mr. Shark: "Tell His Honor what happened from there."

Mr. Fabler: "He asked for my declaration card. I gave it to him and he put it down where I couldn't see what he was doing with it. He asked me how long I'd been out of the country and if my trip was personal or business. Then he asked if I had in excess of $10,000. In response to his questions I told him it was a vacation and when he asked if I had more than $10,000, I told him I didn't. Next, he asked if I'd been on a farm or if I had any dairy products, stuff like that… and I said no to those things. Then, he asked if I had anything to declare. I told him I *had 'alcohol, tobacco and miscellaneous other goods.'* But I also told him they were within my limit! Then, he told me to put my bags on the counter. First, he opened my attaché case and reached into it. He took out the four boxes of Cuban cigars. I asked him what he was doing and he said they were contraband. I asked him why they were contraband and he said they were against the law. I told him I read a book that said that is not so, at least to my understanding that it wasn't so… and he asked what book. I told him I started with my passport and that it directed me to the **Know Before You Go** book. I told him I had a copy and asked if I could get it out of my suitcase…so I could show it to him! But he pulled one out and asked me if it was that book."

Mr. Shark: "When you say, 'He pulled one out…' what do you mean? Pulled one out from where?"

Mr. Fabler: "He reached below the counter into a drawer or something! I don't know where."

Mr. Shark: "So he didn't take yours?"

Mr. Fabler: "No! He didn't take mine! I didn't have permission to go into my bag at that point, so I didn't go into it. He produced one of his own."

Mr. Shark: "So, he produced a copy of C-1?"

Mr. Fabler: "Yes! I mean I never really looked at it, but it seemed to be a current…"

Mr. Shark: "But it was similar?"

Mr. Fabler:	"Yes! It was the same color... and the same cover style!"
Mr. Shark:	"And, when he produced that book, did he say anything when he held it up? Did he hold up that book and show it to you?"
Mr. Fabler:	"Yes! He held it up and asked if it was 'This book.' And I said, 'Yes, that book.' Then, he asked me 'Where in this book does it say you can have these?' I told him that I didn't remember the page, but I told him that I thought it was page 6... under the heading, 'Cigars and Cigarettes.' He opened it up and began reading. Finally, he said, 'But, but, but these words don't mean this!' I told him I interpreted those words to mean what they said. And he said, 'No, these words don't mean this.' Then, he left to get the other agent who I thought was agent Notruful, but it was supervisor..."
Mr. Shark:	"Rudemann!?"
Mr. Fabler:	"Yes!" Supervisor Rudemann! He brought supervisor Rudemann back to the counter... and that's where I engaged supervisor Rudemann."
Mr. Shark:	"Tell us what happened next. After supervisor Rudemann came to the counter."
Mr. Fabler:	"He said... and I don't remember the exact wording, but something to the effect... 'You can't have these.' I said the same thing I said to agent Narco. Then, we basically had the same conversation... about the **Know before You Go** book. I said it said I could have them. And he said, 'No, you can't go by that book.' Then, he said, 'Look, the only way...' and he was very polite to me at first, but he said, 'Look, the only way you can have these cigars is if you went to Cuba!' Then, he asked if I went to Cuba.

Mr. Shark:	"He asked you that question? He asked if you went to Cuba?"
Mr. Fabler:	"Yes, but not right away! First, he said I couldn't have them and he said why he thought I couldn't have them. Then, after he said the only way I could have them was if I went to Cuba, he asked if I went to Cuba. When he asked that question, I said, 'Well, as a matter of fact, since you asked, Yes, I did!.' However, no one asked that question before. But when it was asked, I said, 'Yes, I did!' And he said, 'You're under arrest. Give me your passport.' So I gave him my passport. Then, he called or somebody called an Immigration officer. Meanwhile, while all this was going on agent Narco was going though my bags! While we were waiting for the Immigration officer, only I didn't know we were waiting for the Immigration officer, supervisor Rudemann opened my passport and was looking through it. Then, he said, 'Right here... it says you can't do this.' I asked, 'What and where?' He said, 'Right here where it says... what is it... merchandise!' Can I get my passport to show you what he was referring to?"
Mr. Shark:	"Now, I'm going to give you an exhibit..."
Mr. Fabler:	"That was when I told him it stated it was only 'generally' prohibited. I forget the exact terminology."
Mr. Shark:	"May I approach, Your Honor?"
The Court:	"Yes, you may."
Mr. Shark:	"I'm going to show you what's been marked as Exhibit C-2. Is this your passport?"
Mr. Fabler:	"Yes!"

261

Mr. Shark:	"Is this the passport supervisor Rudemann directed you to" Mr. Fabler: "He didn't direct me to anything. This was what he asked for."
Mr. Shark:	"And then what did he show you in there that said whatever he was trying to tell you? Do you see it there?"
Mr. Fabler:	"I'm having a hard time reading this, but it's under the Treasury."
The Court:	**"Under the Treasury? You have the original?"**
Mr. Shark:	"The second page?"
The Court:	**"Get the original."**
Mr. Fabler:	"It's not my original, it's the current one because I lost…"
Mr. Shark:	"Look at the second page, David."
The Court:	"Page 2? *You mean under "Important Information*?"
Mr. Shark:	"Yes, Your Honor! Mr. Fabler, is this what you're referring to?"
Mr. Fabler:	"Yes. Page 2 says, '*Customs Service… The pamphlet* **Know Before You Go** *gives you current information about Customs Regulations and how they apply to articles acquired abroad. Obtain a copy from your nearest Customs office…*' blah, blah, blah. And in the Treasury section on page 3, it says, '*Treasury… As of November 1963, the purchase or importation of Cuban… goods or services are generally prohibited, except for information materials and limited goods imported directly as accompanied baggage.*'"

Mr. Shark:	"That's the portion he directed you to?"
Mr. Fabler:	"Yes, that sentence. He said, 'Look, it says right here you can't do this.' And I said, 'No, it says they're **generally** *prohibited.*' Then, I asked what the word **generally** meant? And I said, 'It has a comma, and it gives the exemptions… *except for.*'"
Mr. Shark:	"This is a conversation you were having with him?"
Mr. Fabler:	"Yeah… actually, both, supervisor Rudemann and agent Narco!"
Mr. Shark:	"So the two of you got into a semantical debate at that point. Is that correct?"
Mr. Fabler:	"Oh, YES! It was semantical. But it involved all three of us… actually!"
Mr. Shark:	"Going beyond that, what happened after that?"
Mr. Fabler:	"The Immigration officer arrived! Supervisor Rudemann walked over to the agent. I heard the Immigration officer ask where the Cuban 'national' was."
Mr. Shark:	"You heard an agent say what?"
Mr. Fabler:	"The Immigration officer asked where the Cuban 'national' was."
Mr. Shark:	"Were those the words you heard, Cuban 'national' person?"
Mr. Fabler:	"Where's the Cuban 'national?'"
Mr. Shark:	"Okay. That was in reference to you, I assume?"

Mr. Fabler:	"One should never assume! But I thought it, most definitely, was about me!"
Mr. Shark:	"So then what happened?"
Mr. Fabler:	"Supervisor Rudemann said, 'There's no Cuban, just him. He went to Cuba.' Then, he handed the Immigration officer my passport. There were some words said back and forth between them that I didn't hear. However, afterward I heard the Immigration officer tell him to give me back my passport."
Mr. Shark:	"Who said that?"
Mr. Fabler:	"The Immigration officer."
Mr. Shark:	"Did you hear him say anything else?"
Mr. Fabler:	"Supervisor Rudemann asked why and said, 'But he went to Cuba.' However, the Immigration officer said, 'Yeah! So? I don't care. He didn't do anything wrong. Give him back his passport.'"
Mr. Shark:	"Then, what happened after that?"
Mr. Fabler:	"Supervisor Rudemann handed me back my passport."
Mr. Shark:	"And then what happened?"
Mr. Fabler:	"Agent Narco was going through my baggage and other things... the paperwork and other stuff I had. I was asked why I went to Cuba and how long I was there. And other questions involving...
Mr. Shark:	"Who asked you these questions?"

Mr. Fabler:	"Supervisor Rudemann… but it could've been agent Narco. I don't really remember who asked what."
Mr. Shark:	"And, basically, you told them what you told us earlier in terms of how you went and what you did?"
Mr. Fabler:	"Yes, I told them I was taken as a guest. Meanwhile, Andreas Dueling was over at the next counter."
The Court:	**"Andreas Dueling WAS HERE with you?"**
Mr. Fabler:	"Yes! He was here! Andreas was at the counter across the counter from where I was. They were going through his stuff… like they were going through mine. He had four boxes also. And they took them too, but Andreas was told he'd get them back when he left the country. Supervisor Rudemann was talking to Andreas. Then, he asked both of us if we knew each other? I said… we both said… 'Yes!' Then, he asked if we were traveling together"
Mr. Shark:	"Are you two traveling together? He asked you that? Who asked you that?"
Mr. Fabler:	"Supervisor Rudemann! And I said, 'He's the one who took me to Cuba.' Andreas confirmed that he took me to Cuba and that the cigars were a gift from him when I said that the cigars were a gift from him…"
The Court:	**"Hold on! Herr Dueling told the agents the trip AND the cigars were a gift from him?"**
Mr. Fabler:	"Yes!"

The Court:	**"What did they say, the agents, when Herr Dueling stated the cigars were a gift from him to you for your birthday?"**
Mr. Fabler:	"Supervisor Rudemann said, 'We don't care about that.' And they confiscated Andreas' cigars also."
Mr. Shark:	"Then, what happened? You say they confiscated his cigars?"
Mr. Fabler:	"Yes! They confiscated Andreas' cigars also."
Mr. Shark:	"And then, ultimately, what happened? To your knowledge, were those cigars returned to him?"
Mr. Fabler:	"Andreas was told he could have his cigars back when he left the country. They gave him a form! And I said, 'You should give him back my cigars too because he gave them to me.' But they told me that I had them... and they didn't care."
Mr. Shark:	"Now, in addition to the items seized in your baggage, did you have, you heard me state to His Honor that confiscated from you were evidence of your trip to Cuba... plane ticket, hotel bill, etc."
Mr. Fabler:	"There was a receipt for the airline ticket."
The Court:	"The **Cubano** ticket."
Mr. Fabler:	"Yes, that's correct!"
Mr. Shark:	"And the government took that?"
Mr. Fabler:	"Yes, they took that. I mean, I don't know exactly what they took, but when I left Customs I didn't have it anymore. I was going to keep it as a souvenir! And I had the receipt from the hotel... but they took that too. At least, I didn't

have it when I left... after they went through my stuff!"

Mr. Shark:
"My point is, were you trying to hide you were in Cuba?"

Mr. Fabler:
"No! If I had been, I wouldn't have had that stuff on me and I wouldn't have told them I went there before they found the receipts that I went there."

Mr. Shark:
"Now, following the luggage search, did there come a point in time when you were asked for a body search or anything of that nature?"

Mr. Fabler:
"Yes!"

Mr. Shark:
"Tell His Honor about that. Were you accused of smuggling drugs as well? What were you told? I don't want to lead you."

Mr. Fabler:
"When I came down the steps there was an agent with a dog. I walked by the dog and the dog just sat there and did whatever they do..."

The Court:
"I think I know what they do."

Mr. Fabler:
"I went to get my checked bag! Then, I went where I was directed to go. I had a conversation with an agent who told me to go over to the counter. After which I met agent Narco who found the things I told him I had and the rest is history. After I met supervisor Rudemann, agent Narco began going through my stuff. After Andreas left the area, agent Narco took an eyeglass case with my eyeglasses in it out of my bag. He turned to the agent with the dog and said, 'Go test this.' The agent took..."

The Court:
"The eyeglass case?"

Mr. Fabler:	"Yes! He took my eyeglass case out of my bag and removed the glasses from it and said, 'Go test this.' I looked at him like he was crazy. I mean, what could I possibly have had in my eyeglass case with my eyeglasses in it? The agent with the dog left. When he came back a few minutes later he dropped off the case and just walked by, but agent Narco asked him what were the results? The agent with the dog said, 'Beautiful bright pink.' There was no reaction from agent Narco so I turned to him and asked what 'beautiful bright pink' meant? Agent Narco said, 'Positive!' I asked, 'Positive for what?' Agent Narco said, 'Marijuana.' I looked at him like he was crazy and I said, 'Wait a minute! You better have more because this isn't true. This is cigars! Not drugs! I don't have marijuana. You better have more.' I started getting very upset. Well, not very upset, but I raised my voice a little bit…"
The Court:	"**I would think that's understandable**… under the circumstances."
Mr. Shark:	"Ultimately, did they ask you to submit to a body cavity search?"
Mr. Fabler:	"Ultimately, yes… but they never did the body cavity search."
Mr. Shark:	"But they did ask… and did you agree to do that?"
Mr. Fabler:	"I agreed to be X-rayed! But they never did it! And the only reason I agreed was because it seemed the only way I was going to get out of there."
Mr. Shark:	"And that also involved signing some sort of waiver?"

Mr. Fabler:	"Right! Agent Narco asked me if I would agree to be X-rayed. He also asked me a bunch of questions, when I was in the back... when they took me to the back room. One of them was 'what drugs' I'd done. I told him I didn't do any drugs, but he kept insisting I had. When he asked if I'd agree to be X-rayed, I told him I would if it would get me out of there sooner than I saw myself getting out of there. When he said it would, I agreed! But they never did X-ray me! Agent Narco said we'd have to go to a hospital to be X-rayed and that I would have to sign a form before anything would happen. Then, he wanted to know if I was sure that I wanted to sign the form. I told him, 'Let's just do it already.'"
Mr. Shark:	"My point is were you cooperating with them?"
Mr. Fabler:	"Yes! To the extent... I mean, the drug thing was out of control. I didn't have any drugs."
Mr. Shark:	"Now, you weren't arrested for drugs... and they didn't find any drugs?"
Mr. Fabler:	"Correct! There were no drugs... and I wasn't arrested for drugs."
Mr. Shark:	"Just going back for one..."
The Court:	"Then... you went on your way?"
Mr. Fabler:	"At the very end... yes! They gave me a form like the one they gave Andreas. And agent Narco told me he wanted me to sign it. It was a release, abandonment or something. I asked what it was and he said a receipt or something. When I said, 'No! I think I'm within my rights here.' He said, 'We want you to give them up' and I said no... again! I wasn't going to do that. Actually, at first I thought the form they gave me was the form I had to sign to get the X-ray because they said I

had to sign a form. And when I saw him filling out the form, I thought it was that form. Then, after he handed it to me he said, 'Here sign this.' That's when I asked what it was... and he said abandonment or something. And when I told him 'No!' I wasn't going to sign that. He said, 'Okay! Take your stuff and get out of here and don't let the door hit you in the butt on the way out.'"

Mr. Shark:

"There's been some business raised by the government concerning your failure to write a declaration as opposed to making an oral declaration. Tell His Honor briefly what your position is on that with respect to the book you read concerning C-1."

Mr. Fabler:

"Well, my interpretation was, and still is, that I could / can, make an oral stipulation as to what I had / have."

Mr. Shark:

"And then you didn't have to write anything down?"

Mr. Fabler:

"Not if I was within my limits. It said / says, write your name and stuff like that down in the identification part. But it said you can make an oral statement as to what you have..."

Mr. Shark:

"So, when you came through Customs and they asked you this question, do you have this or that, when you made your statement, I have tobacco and whatever, that was in your mind... the oral declaration?"

Mr. Fabler:

"Yes! It didn't say I have to say I had Cuban anything... only that I had this or that! And I had tobacco products and misc. other items. All totaling less than four hundred U.S. dollars."

Mr. Shark:	"And the reason why you didn't write it down was because of…"
D. Pete Animen:	"Objection, Your Honor! He's leading the witness quite a bit!"
The Court:	"**I know!** He's just trying to save time. *"*
Mr. Shark:	"**That's right!** Now, the reason you didn't write it down was because of what reason?"
Mr. Fabler:	"I could make an oral declaration!"
Mr. Shark:	"Because of the money limitation?"
Mr. Fabler:	"Ten thousand dollars? You mean the purchasing?"
Mr. Shark:	"Yes!"
Mr. Fabler:	"Four hundred dollars!"
The Court:	"And **your thought was** *that the value,* **the total value was less than four hundred**?"
Mr. Fabler:	"Yes, Your Honor… correct!"
The Court:	"**The value of the country of purchase**?"
Mr. Fabler:	"Well, what had been purchased, in Cuba… right!"
Mr. Shark:	"That's all I have, Your Honor! On this declaration issue… that is!"
The Court:	Thanks, well that's all we need now. Cross-examination, Ms. Beeche?"
Ms. Beeche:	"Yes, Your Honor!"

The Counter Offensive

***

Although bestowed with a pixy body, her bleached-out faded blonde hair that was knotted behind her head accentuated a witchy woman persona. It seemed to highlight a 'bad-to-the-bone' demeanor! Maybe, it was in her roots. Thin dark stringy strands that didn't disguise an appearance she'd hoped would show her to be something other than what she was. She probably saw it on TV. Blondes have more fun! However, her dark roots belied whether only she and her beautician knew if anything was used to enhance the color.

She hailed from a fat apple big inner city, but her manner manifested a self-styled fashion that told one and all she knew little from fashion. Her standards seemed stranded in a time long gone before it was fashionable back before the nineteen-nineties began. And when she opened her mouth, there was little doubt she was no southern belle. More rude than crude, her guise foretold a character that despite being careful with the choice of words, it was apparent her roots were from some seedy side of a different track.

She sat for several seconds before rising from her seat. It was the practiced art of her reputaire... designed to form fear and beads of nervousness across the brow of the intended. However, Havana Dave wasn't a fabler to be taken lightly. Being an experienced story telling weave warrior, he'd dealt with her kind in his past. Only, it wasn't Havana Dave she was preparing to battle, but some half-shelled armor that hid behind a mask. And she was too well versed to be deceived by any impersonation. For she had been taught the art of her craft by others who were trained in the art of impersonation! But, would that be enough?

Ms. Beeche: "Good morning, Mr. Fabler!"

Mr. Fabler: "Good morning!"

Ms. Beeche: "Would you agree with me that you're an experienced traveler?"

The Court:	"Excuse me, Ms. Dohingey, take your coat off and stay awhile."
Ms. Dohingey:	"I'm cold, Your Honor... thank you."
The Court:	"Cold!? That's a rare statement in this courtroom. Okay... go ahead!"
Ms. Beeche:	"Would you agree with me, Mr. Fabler, that you ARE an **experienced** *international* traveler."
Mr. Fabler:	"More so than some, but less so than others. However, to certain places, maybe, yes!"
Ms. Beeche:	"How many times have you traveled internationally in the last ten years?"
Mr. Fabler:	"I was asked that before, but I couldn't give that Lars Titon Helmsman an answer then. However, within the last ten years... you say? And this is 99! So from 89?"
Ms. Beeche:	"YES!"
Mr. Fabler:	"Well, I haven't done all that much traveling in the past ten years. Let's just say circumstances and all. Maybe, ten times or so... more or less."
Ms. Beeche:	"Would you agree with me that within the last thirty years you've traveled internationally in excess of thirty times."
Mr. Fabler:	"Probably yes, but that's only once a year on average. And I know many who have traveled much more... more often."
Ms. Beeche:	"Mr. Fabler we're not talking about others here... nor the frequency of their travels."
Mr. Fabler:	"That may be true, but everything is relative. So when you ask about being 'experienced,' I

analyze it in reference to others. I did it more or less than they did."

Ms. Beeche:

"Mr. Fabler, please confine your answers to the questions I'm asking. When you had the opportunity of traveling internationally you also filled out Customs declarations... on a regular basis?"

Mr. Fabler:

"I don't know how much of a basis your determination of regular is, but it becomes a perfunctionary thing after a while... for some people."

Ms. Beeche:

"And you had the opportunity during your thirty years of international travel to read Customs declarations?"

Mr. Fabler:

"Again, it becomes a perfunctionary thing. In other words was it vacation or business related! Was there in excess of $10,000... and so forth."

Ms. Beeche:

"And during your years of international travel since 1962, were you *generally* aware of 'THE (Cuban) embargo?'"

Mr. Fabler:

"There's that word *generally* again. I don't understand the basis of your use of 1962 as a basis for 'THE (Cuban) embargo,' because 'THE (Cuban) embargo' wasn't in force then. Was it?"

Ms. Beeche:

"Since the inception of 'THE (Cuban) embargo,' have you been *generally* aware of it?"

Mr. Fabler:

"*Generally?* I knew there was *generally* something. *Specifically*, **No!** It seems the government is big on making the word *generally* seem as if **it is** *specifically*. Why not ask if I *specifically* knew about it? But, maybe, you don't know the *specifics* either... especially, when you use terms like 1962 or Iran in association with 'THE (Cuban) embargo!'"

Ms. Beeche: "What was your *general* understanding of 'THE (Cuban) embargo?'"

Mr. Fabler: "I didn't have a *specific* understanding, but I knew there was *generally* something... only I didn't know what! That was why I looked at my passport to see what it *specifically* stated about 'THE embargo.' And it directed me to the **Know Before You Go** pamphlet for the *specifics*... or so it stated.

Ms. Beeche: "Let's talk about your passport which was previously marked C-2. Now, would you agree with me that when you entered the country on April 18, 1997... you read your passport prior to this trip. And it helped you in determining how to declare your goods or not declare your goods when you came into the country?"

Mr. Fabler: "Yes and no! Yes, I read my passport! To some extent it helped, but not to the extent you want to think it did. And no! It didn't *specifically* address the declaration of goods... in the manner you want to suggest it did."

Ms. Beeche: "And what portion of your passport did you read that helped you in deciding what to do when you arrived at Customs in April, 1997?"

Mr. Fabler: "As I said, nothing in my passport *specifically* explained anything other than to read the **Know Before You Go** pamphlet for *specific* instructions... which I did. However, in my passport I read, 'Treasury' and I read...

The Court: **"You mean the section headed 'Treasury?'"**

Mr. Fabler: "Correct! And I read 'Customs Service.'"

Ms. Beeche:	"Does anything in 'Treasury' or 'Customs Service' sections on pages 2 and 3 of your passport *explicitly* authorize you to enter goods of Cuban origin as you did on April 18, 1997?"
Mr. Fabler:	"*Explicitly*? **No**! However, does it *explicitly* **exclude** goods of Cuban origin? *Explicitly?* No! Did I take that to be sort of an explanation? Yes! And I want to emphasize that there was no *explicit* **excluding** of those products. Which I took to mean…"
Ms. Beeche:	"You testified that you read the part under Treasury, where it said, '*As of November, 1963, the purchase or importation of Cuban… goods or services are **generally** prohibited, except for… limited goods imported directly as accompanied baggage.*'"
Mr. Fabler:	"'**Generally** *prohibited…* comma… *except for… limited goods imported directly as accompanied baggage*!' Correct! What do the words '*except for limited goods imported directly as accompanied baggage*' mean? And it would be nice of you to let me finish answering your questions before moving on to others."
Ms. Beeche:	"Mr. Fabler, please confine your answers to ONLY answering my questions."
Mr. Fabler:	"I AM answering your questions. I can't help it if you don't like my answers."
Ms. Beeche:	"Your Honor, would you please instruct the witness to answer my questions?"
The Court:	**"I believe he's answering your questions. But if you insist… Mr. Fabler, please answer Ms. Beeeeeeche's questions**.*"* (Turning his head back toward Ms. Beech, he asked),**"Okay!?"**

Ms. Beeche:	"And you also read the portion which read, *'Transactions related to travel to Cuba are **generally** prohibited. For current restrictions and licensing information call or write the Office of Foreign Assets Control, U.S.Department of the Treasury, Second Floor Annex, Washington, DC 20220 or call (202) 622-2490.'"*
Mr. Fabler:	"Again, what does the word **generally** mean? But, yes... I read that!"
Ms. Beeche:	"Any time prior to April 18, 1997, did you call the Office of Foreign Assets Control in Washington, DC?"
Mr. Fabler:	"It didn't say I had to! And I didn't feel I had to!"
Ms. Beeche:	"That wasn't the question. Did you call..."
Mr. Fabler:	"No! I didn't!"
Ms. Beeche:	"Did you write to the Office of Foreign Assets Control?"
Mr. Fabler:	"Again, it didn't say I had to! And I didn't feel I had to!"
Ms. Beeche:	"That's not the question. Did you write..."
Mr. Fabler:	"No! I didn't!"
Ms. Beeche:	"You said you felt after reading page 2 of your passport, I believe was your testimony, that you could refer to the Customs **Know As You Go** manual for instructions regarding your trip... is that correct?"
Mr. Fabler:	"You mean the **Know Before You Go** pamphlet? I don't know any book called **Know As You Go!**

	My passport *specifically* directed me to that book. So, YES, that was the next place I went."
Ms. Beeche:	"Let's look at what has been marked as C-1. The April 1994 edition of the Customs Manual known as **Know As You Go**."
The Court:	"Turn to Page 6."
Mr. Fabler:	"Your Honor, its called **Know Before You Go**... not **Know As You Go!**"
The Court:	**"Yes! I think she IS talking about the SAME pamphlet here. We ARE talking about the SAME pamphlet... aren't we, Ms. Beeche?"**
Ms. Beeche:	"Your Honor, Mr. Fabler knows the title of the book we're *all* talking about. The name doesn't really matter. Now, Mr. Fabler, you testified earlier that you read this manual prior to April 1997, is that true?"
The Court:	**"But just for the record, so the record is correct, the book we're *ALL* talking about IS called Know Before You Go... and NOT Know As You Go. Isn't that correct, Ms. Beeeeche?"**
Ms. Beeche:	"Yes, Your Honor... it is! Now, Mr. Fabler, answer my question!"
Mr. Fabler:	"Yes! I looked at my passport... and it directed me to it. So I read it... correct. And, yes... I do know the name of that book. But apparently you do not because you keep referring to it by a name that it isn't! I'd think that if I were to do that you'd be all over me like flies on yesterday's tuna."
Ms. Beeche:	"I'd like to direct you to page 1 under the heading 'Your declaration.' Would you please read the

first paragraph, including the first two bulletin items."

Mr. Fabler:
"'You must declare all articles acquired abroad and in your possession at the time of your return. This includes articles that you purchased. Gifts presented to you while you were abroad, such as wedding or birthday presents.'"

Ms. Beeche:
"Now... you're alleging the tobacco items that were seized from you were birthday presents from Mr. Andreas Dueling?"

Mr. Fabler:
"Yes!"

Ms. Beeche:
"And was it your understanding after reading this section of **Know As You Go** that you'd have to declare all of the items that were seized from you?"

Mr. Fabler:
"I DID declare!"

Ms. Beeche:
"Was it your understanding that you had to?"

Mr. Fabler:
"Oh, I'm sorry... yes!"

Ms. Beeche:
"On the first page of **Know As You Go** there's a statement from George Weise, who was the Customs Commissioner at that time that said, '*Read it carefully*,' meaning this manual. And later, '*Don't hesitate to contact us if there is anything you would like clarified*'. Prior to April 18, 1997, did you ask for any clarification from anybody at Customs regarding bringing in any of the seized items?"

Mr. Fabler:
"Again, the pamphlet, **<u>Know Before You Go</u>**, didn't state I had to contact anyone. I didn't feel I needed clarification of anything. It was obvious what was written. I mean, it was written in English. And I speak English."

Ms. Beeche:	"At the airport, prior to the search of your luggage, did you ever request clarification from any Customs emloyee as to what you needed to declare or any clarification of any regulations regarding Customs or importation of these seized items?"
Mr. Fabler:	"Again... I didn't feel I needed any clarification! And I made an oral declaration... of everything I had!"
Ms. Beeche:	"That's NOT my question. Did you request clarification or instruction from a Customs employee prior to the search of your luggage about bringing in the seized items?"
Mr. Fabler:	"I DID answer your question! I didn't seek clarification because I wasn't confused. I can read the English language. I didn't feel I needed clarification. And I DID declare the articles I brought into the country. Which words don't you understand that I said?"
Ms. Beeche:	"Your Honor, again, would you please instruct the witness to answer my questions?"
The Court:	"Once again, counselor, **I believe he IS answering your questions. Just because his answers aren't to your liking isn't reason enough to instruct him to answer all your questions... to your liking.**"
Ms. Beeche:	"But Your Honor..."
The Court:	"Ms. Beeeeeeche... lets continue! Shall we!? I want to get this over with today... please!"
Ms. Beeche:	"Going back to page 1, the second paragraph from the bottom where you testified that you read the entire pamphlet. Did you read: '*The price*

actually paid for each article must be stated on your declaration in U.S. currency or its equivalent in the country of acquisition. If the article was not purchased, obtain an estimate of its fair retail value in the country in which it was acquired.' Did you read that section before?"

Mr. Fabler: "Yes! I mean, I imagine I did!"

Ms. Beeche: "I'd like to show an exhibit which has been previously marked as government Exhibit 1, which is a Customs declaration."

Ms. Beeche: "May I approach, Your Honor."

The Court: "Yes!"

Ms. Beeche: "Mr. Fabler, do you recognize this document?"

Mr. Fabler: "Pretty much so, yes!"

Ms. Beeche: "Is that your signature on the bottom?"

Mr. Fabler: It looks like it might be mine, yes."

Ms. Beeche: "Is this the Customs declaration which you submitted on returning to the United States from Jamaica on April 18, 1997?"

Mr. Fabler: "I would assume it is, yes. But then again I never assume because it makes an ass out of, both, you and me."

Ms. Beeche: "Your Honor, I would move government Exhibit 1 into evidence."

Mr. Shark: "No objection!"

The Court: "It will be admitted."

Ms. Beeche:	"Now, Mr. Fabler, in any place on this declaration, did you estimate the value of the seized items?"
Mr. Fabler:	"No! Not written… because as I've said on more than many occasions, I made an oral declaration. The total of what I had did NOT exceed the level where I had to make a written declaration. And as the pamphlet stated, the Customs agent could easily have instructed me to fill out the form for whatever reason… which he did not do."
Ms. Beeche:	"Did you estimate the value of the seized items at the time you were questioned by Customs on that date?"
Mr. Fabler:	"Before or afterwards?"
Ms. Beeche:	"Withdrawing that question. Is there any place in this declaration where you made a written list of the seized items?"
Mr. Fabler:	"No! I didn't feel I had to make a written list, if I was within the limits… per the instructions of the **Know Before You Go** book."
Ms. Beeche:	"Next to the item marked number 14 you placed a dash where it says U.S. Dollar Amount, isn't that true?"
Mr. Fabler:	"There's a line there… yes!"
Ms. Beeche:	"And when you handed this Customs declaration to the Customs agent you had filled out the entire first page portion, isn't that true? That's your handwriting, isn't it?"
Mr. Fabler:	"That's appears to be my handwriting… yes!"
Ms. Beeche:	"In the box marked number 9, entitled, Countries visited on this trip prior to U.S. Arrival, what did you write?"

Mr. Fabler: "Nothing!"

Ms. Beeche: "Why did you write nothing?"

Mr. Fabler: "Because I missed that... I just didn't see it."

Ms. Beeche: "You also failed to mention that you traveled to Jamaica on your trip, is that correct?"

Mr. Fabler: "Yes! It would appear so. As I said, I missed that question!"

Ms. Beeche: "And you failed to mention that you traveled to Cuba on your trip, is that correct?"

Mr. Fabler: "Yes. It would appear so... as I said, I missed that question. But I was on a plane that flew directly to Philadelphia from Jamaica, so it was obvious I'd been in Jamaica... and, as you just pointed out, I missed that also."

Ms. Beeche: "Was it obvious you had been to Cuba on the face of this document?"

Mr. Fabler: "It was obvious I'd been to Jamaica. And that's the point of your question"

Ms. Beeche: "That wasn't my question. Was it obvious on the face of this document that you traveled to Cuba?"

Mr. Fabler: "When they asked me, I told them I went there."

Ms. Beeche: "Again... that's not my question. Is it obvious from the face of the..."

Mr. Fabler: "You're absurd! No, it's not obvious!"

Ms. Beeche: "Isn't it true, Mr. Fabler, that you actually filled out every single portion of the face of the Customs declaration except for the items marked number 9 and number 3, your middle initial?"

Mr. Fabler:
"Number 3? What's your point? I filled it out as I thought I had to."

Ms. Beeche:
"Would you agree with me that you filled out everything except items marked number 3 and number 9?"

Mr. Fabler:
"On the front side?"

Ms. Beeche:
"On the front side!"

The Court:
"Well, it speaks for itself*!*"

Mr. Fabler:
"I agree, Your Honor… it speaks for itself!"

Ms. Beeche:
"On the item marked number 6, when you filled out the number of family members traveling with you, what did you put next to that?"

Mr. Fabler:
"A line!"

Ms. Beeche:
"What did that mean?"

Mr. Fabler:
"I didn't have any family members traveling with me."

Ms. Beeche:
"So… would it be safe to assume that in writing that line next to the item marked number 6 meaning nothing, that when you wrote the line next to the number marked 14 you mentioned that you had nothing of any value to declare?'

Mr. Fabler:
"I didn't have anything in excess of what the exemption limit was!"

The Court:
"Because it says here, "If you have nothing to declare, write O. So was it advertent. Was it

	a deliberate choice of yours not to put a zero under 14?*"*
Mr. Fabler:	Yes! There wasn't a trigger in my mind to, you know, that I needed a number because it was within…"
The Court:	**"The four hundred dollars!"**
Mr. Fabler:	"The limits… yes!"
Ms. Beeche:	"So, where do you believe that if it was under $400 you wouldn't have to put that amount in the box marked number 14? Where did that come from?"
Mr. Fabler:	"On page…"
The Court:	**"Where it says, 'The amount of duty to be paid.'"**
Mr. Fabler:	"On page 2."
The Court:	**"RIGHT! That's where you got the information about the duty-free exemption of $400!?"**
Mr. Fabler:	"I'm sorry?"
The Court:	**"That's where you got the information about the duty-free exemption of $400, on the back where it says *'The amount of duty to be paid will be determined by a Customs Officer. U.S. residents are normally entitled to a duty-free exemption of $400 on those items accompanying them.'* Correct!?"**
Mr. Fabler:	"Correct! That conformed to information in the book."
The Court:	**"RIGHT! But the question she's getting at, and I'm trying to get at, you knew that? I mean,**

	because you're an *experienced* international traveler you knew that, right?"
Mr. Fabler:	"That there was…"
The Court:	**"There *was a $400*…"**
Mr. Fabler:	"A threshold…"
The Court:	***"YES!"***
Mr. Fabler:	"Correct!"
The Court:	**"I think that's what she is getting at."**
Ms. Beeche:	"No! *No, it's NOT*! What I'm getting at is that he knew there was a $400 duty-free exemption, but he believed that… withdrawn! Well, you testified you knew of the $400 duty-free exemption. What led you to believe that even if you were carrying goods less than $400 you wouldn't have to declare the value in the box marked number 14?"
Mr. Fabler:	"When I came into the country I was asked if I had anything to declare. I made an oral declaration. I said… nothing in excess, not in excess of the amount…"
Ms. Beeche:	"Mr. Fabler, I'm not asking you what happened at the airport."
Mr. Fabler:	"Yes, you are! Only you're doing it in an indirect manner. When you asked, 'What led me to believe that even if I was carrying goods less than $400 I wouldn't have to declare the value in the box marked number 14? So, you are asking me about what happened at the airport.

Ms. Beeche:	"Your Honor, how many times do I have to ask the court to instruct Mr. Fabler to answer my questions, and my questions only?"
The Court:	*"And, Ms. Beeeeche, how many times does the court have to tell you that it thinks that he IS answering your questions."*
Ms. Beeche:	"**No, he isn't**! I'm asking him where he filled out this form?"
The Court:	"**Then, for God sakes, ask him where he filled out the form? And stop beating around the bush!**"
Ms. Beeche:	"Mr. Fabler, where did you fill out this form?"
Mr. Fabler:	"Probably on the plane!"
Ms. Beeche:	"And, on the plane, when you didn't include a value in the box marked number 14, why didn't you include a value…"
Mr. Fabler:	"How many times do I have to answer that question? I already answered it how many times? Just how would you like me to answer that?"
Ms. Beeche:	"… even though it was under $400?"
Mr. Fabler:	"Because…"
Mr. Shark:	"Your Honor, I think this has been asked and answered five times already."
The Court:	"**SUSTAINED! Objection to the extent there is an objection. IT IS SUSTAINED!**"
Ms. Beeche:	"Your Honor, what I'm trying to distinguish here is that there's nothing that states on the U.S. Customs declaration or in the **Know As You Go** manual that simply because you're under the

$400 exemption you don't have to state the value of the goods you're bringing into the country."

The Court:
"First of all, Ms. Beeeeche, the pamphlet we're ALL talking about is called <u>Know Before You Go</u>! If that's the name of the book you're referring to, call it by that name. Okay!? Now, on page 2 of the <u>Know Before You Go</u> book... it states, '*You may declare orally to the Customs inspector the articles you acquired abroad if the articles are accompanying you <u>AND</u> you have NOT exceeded the duty-free exemption allowed (see pages 5 though 8).' I mean, we're ALL talking about the same pamphlet... are we not!?"*

Ms. Beeche:
"I will address the oral declaration in my next line of questioning."

The Court:
"Then, get to your next line of questioning. The objection has been asked and answered because you've already asked this question FIVE times now... and it has been answered FIVE times now! So, let's go to your next question."

Ms. Beeche:
"At the time you filled out your Customs declaration, did you read the reverse side of the Customs declaration form?"

Mr. Fabler:
"I can't remember if I read it or not. It's more a perfunctionary thing... as I said."

Ms. Beeche:
"Isn't it true in your Deposition you said you didn't..."

Mr. Fabler:
"Pardon?"

Ms. Beeche:
"Isn't it true that during your Deposition you said that you didn't read the notice?"

Mr. Fabler:	"I may have read it and I may also not have read it. I don't remember."
Ms. Beeche:	"But right now you don't recall?"
The Court:	**"I think Mr. Fabler doesn't remember if he read it on *this trip*, right!?"**
Mr. Fabler:	"I'm sorry?"
The Court:	**"You don't remember if you read it... on *this trip*!?"**
Mr. Fabler:	"On that *specific* trip... no! Correct! I've read it, but I don't remember when. As I've said, it's a perfunctionary thing... just fill out the form. On the back is a list that you mark down. I remember there used to be two cards on separate things and it's changed over the years. Now, on the back there's a list there and you just... if you're over the limit... you fill it out."
The Court:	***"Right!"***
Ms. Beeche:	"But isn't it true that, during your Deposition, you stated you didn't read the reverse side of this declaration?"
Mr. Fabler:	"It's possible!"
Mr. Shark:	"Objection, Your Honor!"
The Court:	***"SUSTAINED!"***
Ms. Beeche:	"You signed under a line which read I have read the notice on the reverse and have made a truthful declaration. Do you stand by that statement?"
Mr. Fabler:	"You're required to sign the form. If it's not signed the agent gives you the form and says sign it. I signed it, yes! And I stand by what

I've continuously stated about signing the form. Yes!"

Ms. Beeche: "I'd like to return to the **Know Before You Go** manual marked C-1."

The Court: "He has it in front of him."

Ms. Beeche: "If I may just have one moment, Your Honor. Now, on page 2, it addresses the issue of oral declarations. Was it your understanding when you filled out your Customs declaration form that you'd be making a written declaration an oral declaration for your goods?"

Mr. Fabler: "Would you say it again?"

Ms. Beeche: "For the goods you were bringing into the United States in April, 1997, what was your intention when you were on the plane landing at Philadelphia International Airport as to how you could declare the goods you were bringing into the country?"

The Court: "That is, Mr. Fabler, if you had any intention at all!"

Mr. Fabler: "I was going to make an oral declaration... because nothing required me to make a written one. Unless I was asked to fill it out... which I wasn't!"

Ms. Beeche: "So you planned on making an oral declaration. How did you know about an oral declaration?"

Mr. Fabler: "Is there something wrong with your hearing? For the umpteenth time, I read it in the **Know Before You Go** book."

Ms. Beeche: "In the **Know Before You Go** book, on page 2, it states, '*You may declare orally to the Customs*

Inspector the articles you acquired abroad if the articles are accompanying you and you have not exceeded the duty-free exemption allowed. A Customer Officer may, however, ask you to prepare a written list if it is necessary.' It then states, *'A written declaration will be necessary when: More than one liter of alcoholic beverages, 200 cigarettes (1 carton) or 100 cigars are included. Isn't it true you brought in 209 cigarettes on April 18, 1997.'"*

Mr. Fabler: "I brought back…"

Mr. Shark: "Objection! I don't see the relevance of this, Judge."

The Court: **"I don't really either**! But the point is that he brought in some cigarillos, correct?"

Ms. Beeche: "Your Honor, the defendant admitted in his Deposition that he brought in 209 cigarettes… not cigarillos. I can show you that portion of the Deposition. And that is in excess of 200 cigarettes and therefore, requires a written declaration. I'd like to get that on the record that he brought in 209 cigarettes."

Mr. Fabler: "First of all, I didn't say that I brought in 209 cigarettes. I said I brought in a carton of cigarettes. However, it was not a complete carton! I wasn't asked if it was full or not. At the Deposition I was told by, both, my lawyer and Lars that Titon Helmsman to ONLY answer the questions asked and not to volunteer information. I did as I was instructed. And I was NEVER asked if the carton was full or not! So I didn't volunteer that information. I mean it could've been asked, but it wasn't! It's no different than today when you stated on more than several occasions for me to ONLY answer your questions. I ONLY did what

	I was told to do! Answer the question(s)… and that question wasn't asked!"
Ms. Beeche:	"May I refresh…"
The Court:	"Sure, go ahead. Let's clarify this. But the seizure was for 100 Cuban cigars, 9 Cuban cigarettes, which I now am told they are, well, cigarillos, 1 Cuban wood jewelry box, 5 Cuban key chains, 1 Cuban coin, and 15 Cuban mini-cigars."
The Shark:	"Exactly, Your Honor…"
Ms. Beeche:	"But, Your Honor, may I ask another question? Mr. Fabler, in addition…"
Mr. Shark:	"Objection, Your Honor. Your Honor is right on point. The carton of cigarettes, whether they're 100 or 200 or whatever, wasn't a subject of the seizure."
Ms. Beeche:	"But Your Honor, it's irrelevant whether they were subject to a seizure. Mr. Fabler, was carrying cigarettes in addition to the seized items when he entered the country on April 18, 1997!"
The Court:	"Okay, you can answer her question, Mr. Fabler!"
Mr. Fabler:	"What was the question?"
Ms. Beeche:	"Were you carrying…"
The Court:	"Were you carrying ordinary cigarettes?"
Ms. Beeche:	"… cigarettes that were not seized?"
Mr. Fabler:	"There was a *partial* box of cigarettes, YES! There was an **incomplete** box, YES! I was never asked if the carton was a complete box. It was missing 2 packs that were given away to a

friend when I was in Jamaica. He wanted some American cigarettes that were sold in Cuba... cigarettes that were illegal to be sold in Cuba because of 'THE embargo.' They were illegal because it was illegal for those cigarettes to be in Cuba in the first place and the Cuban Asset Control Regulations states as much. Both... because they were passed through Cuba and because they could easily be used in torture. So a friend of mine wanted some for souvenirs. Do you want to know who asked for and got them?"

Ms. Beeche: "May I have one moment, Your Honor?"

The Court: "Yes! Then, I'd like you to wrap this up! At least, this phase of it! Maybe this is a good time to take a break."

Ms. Beeche: "Thank you, Your Honor. I was just taking a look."

The Court: "We'll take a ten minute break."

The robed one stood and walked out of the courtroom. As a sign of respect, everyone rose from their seats when he got up from the bench... and remained standing until he left the room. I got up from the court's hot seat and approached the Lady Grace who was with my shark and his able-bodied assistant... Sue R. Hammerhead. I wanted to know how he felt it was going. Only I heard him say to not talk so much. Talk so much!? Hell, I thought I'd been focused on my answers. What did I know!? I knew I didn't know how it was going.

Then, I saw Ed Ditor in the crowd. He said he was there for moral support, but I knew he was probably just looking for a story to tell. Edit Ed said he felt I was doing pretty good and questioned the intelligence of those government people. However, the bulldog secret agent G-man loomed in the background. And I knew a shark who was a ringer when I saw a ringer shark.

I was too preoccupied with all the happenings that were happening to notice Marc Ken Tyme and that Buck of a Rouldolf were also present.

They both approached me to pay their respects. Being another kind of shark, Marc Ken Tyme was just marking time that day. With little to do in his life he took time to check out another whose time had come. And Rouldolf Buck, despite not having a camera crew by his side, was still very much the reporter he was.

His feature, only a few days before, whetted an appetite for the story he really wanted to tell. What better way to tell a tale then to tell it on TV!? Bucky wanted to be sure his narrative was the fable the world would see... first. And the first to tell the tale would have a scoop of a story on all those who'd profess to be a scoop snooper galore.

Suddenly, the Judge's chamber door opened. Everyone returned to their respective places. Lady Grace stood behind my sharks who were standing behind their desk. All the observers were at their seats, waiting for His Honor, the judge, to sit down before taking their seats. All the government people stood in wait for the robed one to enter the room before resuming the dissection of an enemy they knew as David Fabler. And Havana Dave returned back to the court's hot seat.

His Honor, the judge, entered the room and sat down. Without waiting for one second to pass, he asked the government female shark, "Did you find a reference in the Deposition?" She told him she had and he immediately asked, "What page... what line?"

Ms. Beeche: "Page 55, line 10, which reads: Answer: I brought in a carton of Marlboro cigarettes. Question: And you brought in what else? Answer: And I brought in 9 Cuban cigarillos."

The Court: "Okay!"

Ms. Beeche: "Mr. Fabler, in those statements in your Deposition did you not testify that you brought in one carton of cigarettes and 9 Cuban cigarettes?"

Mr. Fabler: "No! First of all they were cigarillos... not cigarettes. There's a big difference. However, more to the point is that a carton is merely a box... an outer containment with packages inside it. Yes. I brought in a carton of cigarettes, but it didn't have a full 10 packs inside…"

Ms. Beeche: "Isn't it true that you never mentioned in your Deposition that the carton was less than full?"

Mr. Fabler: "Yes… that's true! I didn't mention that! I've already stated that!"

Ms. Beeche: "And you never mentioned it before today, isn't that true?"

Mr. Fabler: "Once again, no one ever asked me if it was full or not. No one ever asked how many cigarettes were in the carton. So to answer your question for the third time… YES! I never mentioned it during the Deposition… because I wasn't asked. And I've been told on more than several occasions to ONLY answer what was asked… and I wasn't asked if the carton was full. We've already gone over this! Several times I think! However, one year ago last April, when my lawyer and I first met, I told him about that partial carton of Marlboro cigarettes… and he said it wouldn't be an issue! Apparently, he was wrong… because it seems to be an issue!"

Ms. Beeche: "Isn't it true in fact that your entire case is made up of legal arguments created after the fact to try to fit into the Cuban Assets Regulations?"

Mr. Fabler: "You're absurd. I questioned **Know Before You Go** when I was at Customs that night… not afterwards! I didn't know about the Cuban Regulations that night. If anyone's making anything up to fit into those Regulations… it's you. It seems you're the one trying to adapt all this to the Regulations, not me! I read the words and I questioned those words… immediately!"

Mr. Shark: "This is ALL objected to, Your Honor!"

The Court:	"**Yes! Sustained!** But he did answer the question. However, I would've sustained it."
Ms. Beeche:	"Isn't it true that…"
Mr. Shark:	"If we were before a jury, I would have objected sooner, Your Honor."
The Court:	"I understand that. I can attest from seeing you in action in other cases that you, for sure, would've objected to this whole line of questioning. And I must say you would've had good reason to object to it."
Mr. Shark:	"Knowing that you're a jury that will instruct yourself appropriately, Judge, I think you can disregard that comment."
The Court:	"I will so instruct myself!"
Mr. Shark:	"Thank you!"
Ms. Beeche:	"Isn't it true that at the airport you never mentioned to any Customs representative that you went to Cuba as a guest of Mr. Andreas Dueling?"
Mr. Fabler:	"Wrong! Before I was even asked, I told them everything was a gift. I didn't mention his name, but I said everything was a gift! Then, when I was asked, I told them. Later, **THAT SAME** night, I told them I was a guest of Andreas… and when they told Dueling that he could have his cigars back I questioned why Andreas couldn't have the cigars he gave me, in Cuba, back. What I think is true is how you change everything around to meet your position and disregard everything that doesn't go towards that end. In fact, Andreas also stated that he took me to Cuba as a gift and bought those items."

Ms. Beeche:	"Isn't it true that you never mentioned… well, didn't you say that, excuse me, didn't you say that when one of the agents had said to you, were you traveling with him, you said, yes?"
Mr. Fabler:	"Finally… you admit to something that was correct. Yes, correct!"
Ms. Beeche:	"However, isn't it true you never mentioned to the Customs agents that you traveled to Cuba as a fully sponsored gift from Mr. Dueling?"
Mr. Fabler:	"What is wrong with you? That is completely wrong! I said it was a gift. However, I didn't tell them that… because I didn't know about fully sponsored at that time. However, I did tell them Andreas took me to Cuba… several times! What difference does it make if I mentioned the words 'fully sponsored' or not. You people, Customs, know the meaning and definition of that term and of what fits into it. Saying that the trip was a gift fits into that category. And you people, Customs, know it."
The Court:	**"Mr Fabler, you didn't use that locution… however, did you?"**
Mr. Fabler:	"No, I didn't!"
The Court:	**"Because that's a legal term."**
Mr. Fabler:	"Right! I told them he took me! And I said I went with Andreas to Cuba and that he paid for my travel."
Ms. Beeche:	"Isn't it true that in fact Mr. Andreas Dueling didn't pay for everything on your trip, regarding your trip to Cuba?"
Mr. Fabler:	"What!? Now you've fabricated witnesses that were in Cuba and supposedly saw me

297

	pay for something? Get REAL! He paid for everything!"
Ms. Beeche:	"Isn't it true that you purchased that carton of cigarettes in Cuba with your own money?"
Mr. Fabler:	"No!"
Ms. Beeche:	"Isn't it true that you submitted an Affidavit in support of your petition for admission of forfeiture of the items that were seized?"
Mr. Fabler:	"Yes!"
Ms. Beeche:	"Isn't it true that in that Affidavit you stated, Customs agents wouldn't return any of the gifts that I brought from Cuba. Interestingly, the Customs agents did return a carton of Marlboro cigarettes which had been purchased in Havana."
Mr. Fabler:	"When that Affidavit was being done we were going back and forth, my attorney and I, with it. I wasn't with them at the time. So I went in and signed the form and gave them the information. At the time I went in I told them some of the stuff they wrote wasn't accurate. But Stephen said, 'Look just give…'"
Ms. Beeche:	"Mr. Fabler…"
Mr. Fabler:	"You asked me a question! Now please let me finish… thank you! So I signed the form, okay? And then I went through everything with Ms. Hammerhead and I left the signed form with her. Later, she finished filling out the form. And later when that Lars Titon Helmsman asked me about it I told him… no. That it wasn't correct!"
The Court:	"So **that part** of your Affidavit, you say, is incorrect."

Mr. Fabler: "That *specific* part, yes!"

The Court: **"Okay! Next question!"**

Ms. Beeche: "So you signed an Affidavit *that was false?*"

Mr. Fabler: "You're toooo much! I just said I pre-signed it! The Affidavit wasn't false! It wasn't like the one a Customs agent named Notruful signed which was completely false… implying he was there when he wasn't even in the building. And we didn't find that out until the Depositions… when he admitted as much."

Ms. Beeche: "You also stated other false statements in your Affidavit, isn't that true?"

Mr. Shark: "This is ALL objected to, Judge. This characterization of false statement! It was a simple mistake… on our part, not his! He testified to that at his Deposition. Let's be fair about this. I admitted the error was on my office's part. Now, if she wants to ask him about other inconsistencies…"

The Court: "She's getting at his credibility though… so go ahead! But let's try to bring this to an end **very soon**… okay?"

Ms. Beeche: "Didn't you sign an Affidavit, that same Affidavit, where you said that when agent Narco left you he spoke with agent Almen Notruful."

Mr. Fabler: "THIS IS TOOO MUCH! A government agent submits a misleading and false Affidavit that was signed by someone named Almen Notruful who purports to have been a Customs agent I interacted with that night and I am held at HIS word. Two g'men agents submitted Affidavits when I didn't know either of the names of the two agents I interacted with that night. I thought agent Notruful was one of the agents I interacted with because of **his** Affidavit. I believed agent Almen Notruful was supervisor Rudemann... at least that's the way I read it. Your agent misrepresented the situation and led me to believe something that wasn't. Now, you're trying to use his lie against me. You ARE way TOOO much!"

"Two Affidavits were submitted, one from Agent Narco and one from Almen Notruful who indicated he was supervisor Rudemann. On the night in question I interacted with two agents. Since one Affidavit was by agent Narco it seemed logical to assume the other was from the other agent who turned out to be supervisor Rudemann... only it was agent Almen Notruful!"

"Let me ask you a question! How come the government didn't have supervisor Rudemann submit an Affidavit? Why did agent Notruful state in his Affidavit that agent Narco came to him for advice when, in fact, agent Narco went to supervisor Rudemann? How come agent Notruful isn't here today... to testify? If anything it was a government agent who submitted an Affidavit that was false and misleading... and he did it on purpose and with intent! SOOOooo... Your Honor, since credibility is being examined here, maybe, the government's credibility should be taken into account *as well*. And if it isn't, I'd like to know why... under the circumstances!"

Ms. Beeche: "Did you ever in fact speak with agent Almen Notruful?"

Mr. Fabler: "He was never there!"

Ms. Beeche: "So, again, you made another false statement in your Affidavit?"

Mr. Shark:	"Objection!"
The Court:	**"SUSTAINED!** *SUSTAINED!"*
Ms. Beeche:	"Isn't it true that you were never placed under arrest?"
Mr. Fabler:	"When an officer of the U.S. government says you're under arrest... you've been placed under arrest... that's my interpretation. I didn't feel I was free to go and he demanded my passport! What would've happened had I not given it to him... or tried to leave the building? I believed, at the time, that I was under arrest... yes! Even though it's true I didn't have handcuffs put on me... but all the same I felt I had been placed under arrest."
The Court:	**"Because you didn't feel free to go!"**
Mr. Fabler:	**"Correct!** In my mind, I wasn't free to go! I'd been placed under arrest."
The Court:	**"Right!"**
Ms. Beeche:	"Who stated to you that you were under arrest?"
Mr. Fabler:	"Supervisor Rudemann... but on my Affidavit it's by agent Almen Notruful. I thought agent Almen Notruful was supervisor Rudemann. Supervisor Rudemann demanded my passport."
Ms. Beeche:	"Isn't it true you were never subjected to a body cavity search?"
Mr. Fabler:	"That's true... AND, I never said one was performed. However, I WAS asked to be X-rayed!"
Ms. Beeche:	"Isn't it true you've been making these allegations against the Customs agents because

you were previously arrested in a Customs related smuggling conspiracy and sentenced to 51 months?"

Mr. Fabler:

"I haven't made any false statements or allegations. I only stated what occurred. I never said a body cavity search was performed! Can't you hear? What words don't you understand? They asked me to be X-rayed! It was requested... not performed! And I wasn't arrested in a Customs smuggling conspiracy. You need to do your homework! I was arrested in a conspiracy to possess. It had NOTHING to do with Customs."

Mr. Shark:

"Objected to, Judge!"

The Court:

"SUSTAINED! Although he did answer! Msss. Beeecheee where are we going?"

Ms. Beeche:

"This goes to bias, Your Honor, as to the statements he's making against..."

The Court:

"Even if I were to believe he made misleading statements, which I don't, under Rule 403, its probative value is hugely outweighed by its unduly prejudicial effect."

Mr. Shark:

"Judge, if we could just correct the record. He was never arrested in a Customs situation. Mr. Fabler was convicted of a conspiracy involving marijuana that was in Mississippi..."

Mr. Fabler:

"Alabama!"

Mr. Shark:

"He wasn't trying to import it. And it has nothing to do with this... and they know it."

The Court:

"Look, as I said before... even to the extent it has any probative value, it's outweighed!"

Ms Beeche:	"As a final matter, isn't it true a journalist named Ed Ditor interviewed you with regard to this matter?"
Mr. Fabler:	"Did he? Is that the question? Did he?"
Ms. Beeche:	"Did he?"
Mr. Fabler:	"I was interviewed… yes!"
Mr. Shark:	"This is *objected* to, Judge!"
Ms. Beeche:	"Your Honor, I'd like to…"
The Court:	"I can't rule on an objection until I see what we're talking about."
Ms. Beeche:	"Your Honor, I'd like to…"
The Court:	"Let me see it first, Mr. Shark."
Ms. Beeche:	"Your Honor, I'd like to question the witness with what has been marked previously as government Exhibit 8."
The Court:	"G-8?"
Mr. Shark:	"It has nothing to do with the declaration issue!"
The Court:	"Let me just see what this is."
Mr. Shark:	"May I have a copy?"
The Court:	"Is this from a magazine of some kind?"
Mr. Fabler:	"Of some kind… but it's a weekly City Paper paper!"
The Court:	**"I'm asking her. She's offering it. What is this? What's it from?"**

Ms. Beeche:	"I'd have to ask the agents. Can I just have a moment to confer where it's from? I'd just like to…"
The Court:	**"You don't know? Well, Mr. Fabler, do you know? Please… we're just trying to save time here. Where's it from?"**
Mr. Fabler:	"I was interviewed by Mr. Ed Ditor. He's the editor of a paper called the City Paper paper… here in Philadelphia. He's here in this courtroom today… and I believe he's available to testify! Should anyone desire him to!"
The Court:	"This is from the city newspaper?"
Mr. Fabler:	"No… it's a paper called the City Paper paper. And this was an article that he did just about a year ago… I think last January 8th or something."
The Court:	"Okay then… go ahead!"
Ms. Beeche:	"Isn't it true that you told Ed Ditor, and he quotes you, in this article about a previous trip to Cuba: 'Havana was a pretty cool place. I was able to *sneak* home 25 fine Cuban cigars which I gave to an uncle.'"
Mr. Fabler:	"I **didn't** say that! I **can't** be held accountable for what others say or write. I think its called journalism! I have a witness who was there who can verify what I said and didn't say when I was interviewed. Why don't you call him up here to testify? He's HERE in this courtroom… now! And he's willing to testify…"
Ms. Beeche:	"Isn't it true you were fully and wholly aware of 'THE (Cuban) embargo?'"
Mr. Fabler:	"Didn't we already go over this? I knew there was something, but I didn't know what it was…

and I still don't! It changes all the time… like yesterday, when it changed again! Do **you** know what it *specifically* is? Once again, I looked at my passport and that referred me to the **Know Before You Go** book for clarification."

Ms. Beeche: "Isn't it true the **Know Before You Go** pamphlet refers, in many instances, to the prohibition against bringing in Cuban articles?"

Mr. Fabler: "I have quite a different interpretation of that pamphlet! "

Mr. Shark: "Objection."

The Court: **"Sustained! Sustained! It's argumentative! I'm getting TIRED of this…"**

Ms. Beeche: "Thank you, Your Honor. No further questions."

The Court: "ANY RE-direct?"

Mr. Shark: "Just briefly! In your Deposition, when you were asked about the discrepancy in your Affidavit in terms of that word… what answer did you give to that?"

Mr. Fabler: "Of what word?"

Mr. Shark: "The word concerning the purchase of the Marlboro cigarettes that should have read which were purchased in Havana as opposed to…"

Mr. Fabler: "Oh, Yes! It came up and I told…"

The Court: "What page?"

Mr. Shark: "Page 63, Your Honor."

Mr. Fabler: "I told that Lars Titon Helmsman it was an incorrect statement and he proceeded to…"

The Court:	**"I SEE IT!"**
Mr. Shark:	"And that basically was as a result that you were in Pottstown and we were faxing back and forth Affidavits… and we were trying to get this answer done in a timely manner, correct?"
Mr. Fabler:	"Right! Finally, I came into your office and you said to just sign the form… although it wasn't complete. Then, I sat down with Ms. Hammerhead and verbally finished it. Later, she signed it and filled it out… but it had already been signed by me prior to her finishing it."
Mr. Shark:	"Here's the bottom line, Mr. Fabler. You've testified here today that you orally declared to the first Customs agent who stopped you that you had items of alcohol and tobacco, correct?"
Mr. Fabler:	"Correct! I declared it to two agents, right! Actually all three agents…"
Mr. Shark:	"But, initially, you declared to that first agent and then he directed you to that secondary site…"
Mr. Fabler:	"Second agent! First agent! Correct!"
Mr. Shark:	"Where you went through this business… is there any doubt in you mind about that?"
Mr. Fabler:	"None! Zero!"
Mr. Shark:	"You've heard here today and you heard at the Deposition where they said you didn't declare and you were attempting to smuggle. Is that accurate?"
Mr. Fabler:	"**No**! I raised the issue of the **Know Before You Go** book then. I immediately raised it. I said it to both agents that night. **Both** agents! In fact,

agent Narco even held up the book and asked, 'This book? Where in this book does it say you can have Cuban cigars?' Then, he said, when he read it that those words didn't mean what they said! And I told him how I interpreted it! My raising the issue was **immediate**! If I didn't raise the issue that night then, maybe, I could understand their point. But I raised the issue that night…'"

Mr. Shark: "That's all I have, Judge!"

The Court: "Any Re-cross and *it's limited.*"

Ms. Beeche: "No, thank you, Your Honor."

The Court: "I think I understand the testimony. Thank you very much. Mr. Shark, I take it you're done?"

Mr. Shark: "That's all!"

The Court: "Now, Ms. Beeche, I assume you want to put on your agents?"

Ms. Beeche: "Yes, Your Honor."

The Court: "**Okay!** Mr. Fabler, thank you… you're done!"

Mr. Fabler: "Thank you, Your Honor."

With that, the soft inner core hidden by Havana Dave's hard outer shell got up from the witness stand and walked over to the bench where his shark sat. With each stride taken, the crusty outer shell became a softer than hard persona that turned back into David Fabler. And, maybe, it was David Fabler who'd been on that witness stand all along while Havana Dave just sat and watched the narrative of the fable that was the yarn of a tale that he had lived to tell. Time would tell!

The Court: The robed one turned to the government's Mako and asked, "Who do you want to start with?"

Ms. Beeche:	"Agent Buster Narco!"
Mr. Shark:	"Judge, I'd just move C-1 and C-2 into evidence."
The Court:	"They will be admitted."
Mr. Shark:	"I'd also object to the newspaper article."
The Court:	"It hasn't been moved. It was just for Cross-examination, I assume. "
Ms. Beeche:	"Your Honor, at this time I'd like to move government Exhibit number 8 into evidence."
Mr. Shark:	"Can I see it?"
The Court:	"I take it there is no stipulation as to this?"
Mr. Shark:	"No, Your Honor! I just object to its being admitted!"
Ms. Beeche:	"Your Honor, I believe the witness authenticated it as he knew it to be a publication in a publicly available article. I would ask the Court to take judicial notice."
The Court:	**"But for its purpose it wasn't an accurate record of what he said. He said it didn't... it wasn't accurate. And besides you can call Mr. Ed Ditor to the witness stand if you choose... I don't think they'd object. Isn't that correct, Mr. Shark?"**
Mr. Shark:	"Exactly, Your Honor."
The Court:	**"So, that's my problem. I mean you certainly tried to make your point, but he says it's not accurate. Besides YOU introduced it and couldn't even identify what it was or where it was from. And, if memory serves me well, I**

believe the witness, as you so identified him, only authenticated it... because I asked him to. Without him, the witness, you'd have no basis for submitting this. Now... MOVE ON! And agent Narco... stay close to the microphone as you testify, officer!"

Agent Narco: "Yes, Your Honor."

The Court: "**Proceed**, Mssss. Beeeche*!*"

A Tangled Web Is Weaved When The Practice Is To Deceive

***

He was a trained law enforcement officer, but what he was trained for was anyone's guess. Like those who went before him, he nervously sat on the court's hot seat. It came with the territory. Sitting on a witness stand, swearing to tell the truth, the whole truth, and nothing but truth, can do that to anyone... who's not going to do what they swear to do! There's a difference between catching a common criminal and testifying against the common citizen.

His hands shook and body twitched. It was obvious he wasn't comfortable sitting in the seat he occupied. But, maybe, if he was going to do what he swore he was going to do, then it might be different. However, now, it was his time to endure the heat of the seat. The tables were turned... and, although he'd been well briefed, nothing in his training prepared him for what he was about to face.

Ms. Beeche: "Inspector Narco, who's your employer?"

Agent Narco: "The United States Customs service!"

Ms. Beeche: "What is your position with the U.S. Customs service?"

Agent Narco: "I'm a Customs inspector."

Ms. Beeche: "Where are you assigned?"

Agent Narco: "I'm a part of the contraband enforcement team. And right now I'm assigned to the manifest review unit."

Ms. Beeche: "How long have you been a Customs inspector?"

Agent Narco: "Over three years."

The Court: "**Over** three years?"

Agent Narco:	"Yes!"
Ms. Beeche:	"What did you do prior to being a Customs inspector?"
Agent Narco:	"I was a Customs aide with the Customs service."
Ms. Beeche:	"For how long were you a Customs aide?"
Agent Narco:	"Approximately four years."
Ms. Beeche:	"What are your duties as a Customs inspector?"
Agent Narco:	"My **main** duty is to protect the revenue of the UnitedStates!"
The Court:	**"Your duty is to protect the revenue of the United States?"**
Agent Narco:	"Yes, Your Honor! That is my **main** duty!"
The Court:	**"Excuse me. But can anyone in this courtroom please tell me how much it's costing the United States to bring this action here today... over what is it - one hundred c*igars*?"**
D. Pete Animen:	"I object, Your Honor... that isn't the issue of this proceeding."
The Court:	**"Of course it isn't, but I just had to ask! Curious minds might want to know, you know!"**
Ms. Beeche:	"In April of 1997, where were you assigned?"
Agent Narco:	"Philadelphia International Airport, Terminal A, Arrivals building."
Ms. Beeche:	"On April 18, 1997, did you meet David Fabler?"

311

Agent Narco:	"Yes!"
Ms. Beeche:	"Can you please describe the circumstance(s)."
Agent Narco:	"Passenger Fabler presented himself and his luggage to me at my secondary counter."
Ms. Beeche:	"And he arrived from where?"
Agent Narco:	"From Jamaica!"
Ms. Beeche:	"What happened when he presented himself to you?"
Agent Narco:	"I asked for his declaration card and began to question him."
Ms. Beeche:	"Did he give you what's been previously marked as government Exhibit 1?" Turning to the bench she asked, 'May I approach the witness.'"
The Court:	"Yes."
Agent Narco:	"Yes!"
Ms. Beeche:	"Did you review his declaration?"
Agent Narco:	"Yes... I went over the declaration with the passenger."
Ms. Beeche:	"What did you ask him?"
Agent Narco:	"I *specifically* asked if he was on business or pleasure."
Ms. Beeche:	"What did he say?"
Agent Narco:	"He said... pleasure."
Ms. Beeche:	"Did you ask him anything else?"

Agent Narco:	"Yes! I went down the questions on the declaration… and asked if he had any fruits, meats, plants or if he was on a farm or ranch. He said, 'No!' Then, I asked if he was carrying over $10,000 in U.S. or foreign equivalent or if he had any stocks or bonds. He said, 'No!' Next, I asked if he had any commercial items that he was going to sell or use as samples. Once again, he said, 'No!' Finally, I asked if he had anything to declare… either gifts that were given to him or gifts that were given to him to give to someone else. And I asked if he had acquired anything! All of which he said 'No' to!"
Ms. Beeche:	"Then, what happened?"
Agent Narco:	"I began to examine his luggage."
Ms. Beeche:	"Did you find anything in his luggage?"
Agent Narco:	"I found four boxes of Cuban cigars and some key rings with Cuban little cigars. They were like cigars. They were made of metal or plastic that had Cuban identifiers on them. He also had a wooden box that had Cuban… Cuba… on it. He had a Cuban coin… and he had another little box that had, they were like, cigarettes inside."
Ms. Beeche:	"What, if anything, did Mr. Fabler say when you found the cigars?"
Agent Narco:	"Nothing much. He just asked what I was doing."
Ms. Beeche:	"Did he ever mention the **Know Before You Go** book?"
Agent Narco:	"No!"

The Court:	**"You're POSITIVE that, on that night, he never mentioned the <u>Know Before You Go</u> book?"**
Agent Narco:	"Yes, I'm positive! **He never mentioned it.** I would've remembered!"
Ms. Beeche:	"If I may approach the witness, Your Honor?"
The Court:	"Yes."
Ms. Beeche:	"I'd like to show you what's been previously marked as government Exhibit 5: Custody Receipt for Retained or Seized Property and a custody bag of the seized property. Would you describe the bag, please... the contents of the bag?"
The Court:	"Could we have a stipulation..."
Mr. Shark:	"Yes!"
The Court:	"...that what was in the bag are the seized items..."
Mr. Shark:	"Yes, Your Honor."
The Court:	"So... we will save time."
Ms. Beeche:	"And could we have a stipulation, as well, that all the goods are from Cuba that were contained in the seized bag?"
Mr. Shark:	"Yes."
The Court:	"So stipulated."
Agent Narco:	"Do I have to take anything out?"
The Court:	"Pardon me?"

Agent Narco:	"Do I have to take anything out?"
The Court:	"No! You don't have to take it out. We will just save a little bit of time, agent Narco."
Ms. Beech:	"And those are the goods that you took out of the defendant's suitcase?"
Agent Narco:	"There was one item in addition to that that wasn't in the suitcase."
Ms. Beech:	"And what was that?"
Agent Narco:	"They're Cuban mini-cigars."
Ms. Beeche:	"Where were they taken from?"
Agent Narco:	"After the examination… during the baggage examination… there was a green leafy substance that was found in an eyeglass case that was tested using one of our tests. It's for THC… it's usually for marijuana, hash or hash oil! And… it tested positive! At that point, I requested a pat down from my supervisor."
Ms. Beeche:	"And who was the supervisor?"
Agent Narco:	"Andy Rudemann!"
Ms. Beeche:	"And what happened with supervisor Rudemann?"
Agent Narco:	"Supervisor Rudemann approved the pat down. At which time, myself and another inspector escorted Mr. Fabler to one of our search rooms off to an area that's away from the public. And we… I… patted Mr. Fabler down. A bulge was found. At this point, I don't know if I actually removed it or the passenger removed it, but they were mini-cigars from Cuba."

Ms. Beeche:	"At any time prior to the pat down search, did Mr. Fabler present the mini-cigars from Cuba to you and declare them?"
Agent Narco:	"No!"
Ms. Beeche:	"I'd like to refer you to what's been marked as government Exhibit 5… a Custody Receipt for Retained or Seized Property. Did you write this document?"
Agent Narco:	"Most of the writing on it is mine. There is some writing in the block, number 13, that our Seizure Custodian, due to an inventory, made notes about the bag. They examined the bag because they had their inventory to do. Lines numbered 4 and 5 were written by, I think, supervisor Rudemann. And the final… I signed for all the contents at the bottom."
Ms. Beeche:	"Your Honor… at this time, I'd like to move the government exhibit, marked number 5, into evidence."
The Court:	"Could I have a copy? Admitted, the Custody Receipt."
Ms. Beeche:	"Could you explain why you wrote Items 1, 2, and 3 in block 20, supervisor Rudemann wrote 4 and 5, and then you wrote number 6?"
Agent Narco:	"Honestly, I don't remember! I don't know if, at that time, I was doing queries on the computer or if we were back in the pat down room."
Ms. Beeche:	"At any time, did you do a body cavity search or request a body cavity search from Mr. Fabler?"
Agent Narco:	"No!"

Ms. Beeche:	"At any time, did you place Mr. Fabler under arrest?"
Agent Narco:	"No!"
Ms. Beeche:	"No further questions, Your Honor."
The Court:	"Any Cross-examination?"
Mr. Shark:	"Yes, Your Honor."

THE Truth Can Never Be THE Truth When It IS A Lie

***

My shark rose from his seat and stood behind the desk looking down at some papers that lay on the table. He remained silent for several seconds. Just as the beech bitch before him... my shark hesitated with his questioning of the suspect. It was a hesitation designed to form fear and anxiety from the approaching conflict and could only be felt by the one who sat in the hot seated chair. I looked at the witness and saw he was nervously sitting in his box. His hands were shaking... a visual sign he was unsure of the consequence from the conflict confronting him. Even before the first question, agent Narco had been reduced to just another witness with a fear of the unknown overtaking the power of the position he held. And, the interesting thing was that, it was self-inflicted.

Mr. Shark:	"Agent, we took your Deposition some time last month or so, correct? Do you remember?"
Agent Narco:	"Yes, sir."
Mr. Shark:	"At that time, you didn't remember a whole lot about what you did that day. Do you recall?"
Agent Narco:	"There **were** some things that **were** still vague."
Mr. Shark:	"Were!? And are you clearer today about what transpired on that day?"
Agent Narco:	"Yes! My memory recalls **ALL** the events of that night... now!"
Mr. Shark:	"Good! Because you're going to need that memory today! Now, one of the things you didn't recall during the Deposition, in response to either my question or Ms. Hammerhead's question, was that when you were at the secondary site you didn't know if Mr. Fabler had been stopped by anybody or had any interaction with another Customs agent prior to your encounter with him, correct?"

Agent Narco:	"Yes, sir."
Mr. Shark:	"You didn't know if that happened or not, right?"
Agent Narco:	"I still do not know."
Mr. Shark:	"You didn't know or you didn't remember what you said that day when you were asked?"
Agent Narco:	"At the time of the Deposition that is true. I didn't know."
Mr. Shark:	"But today, you do remember and you do know, right!?"
Agent Narco:	"I have a much better recollection now, yes!"
Mr. Shark:	"And when you were at the secondary site and when Mr. Fabler presented himself to you, do you remember whether or not you accessed Mr. Fabler's information in the computer? You do remember saying you didn't remember if you did that or not?"
Agent Narco:	"Yes, sir."
Mr. Shark:	"Is that yes to the question that you remember or that you accessed Mr. Fabler's information in the computer that night? What are you saying 'yes' to?"
Agent Narco:	"Yes, I don't remember if I accessed Mr. Fabler's information in the computer that night. And I still don't remember!"
Mr. Shark:	"So you may have done that initially... before you conducted your search, correct?"
Agent Narco:	"No!"

Mr. Shark: "No?"

Agent Narco: "I don't understand what you're saying."

Mr. Shark: "I know! As obtuse as my question may be... I apologize. So let's try this. You don't remember here today whether or not, before you searched his bag, if you used your computer to find out anything about Mr. Fabler? You don't remember if you did that or not. You may have. And you may not have, right?"

Agent Narco: "You could say that, yes!"

The Court: "But you agree you just don't know?"

Agent Narco: "I don't recall."

Mr. Shark: "But, at some point, you did access the computer... right?"

Agent Narco: "About Mr. Fabler... **NO! I did not!**"

Mr. Shark: "But just a few minutes ago you stated that you may have... and your testimony was that you were doing queries on the computer. So what queries were you doing on the computer... if not about Mr. Fabler?"

Agent Narco: "**I didn't use a computer!** I think you're confused about what I said!"

Mr. Shark: "I'm **NOT** confused about what you said, agent! Your Honor... can we have the testimony read back, please?"

The Court: "**Yes! I thought he stated he did queries on a computer also. Please read back the testimony on that.**"

Stenographer:	"Question: Could you explain why you wrote items 1, 2, and 3 in block 20; supervisor Rudemann wrote 4 and 5; and then you wrote # 6? Answer: Honestly, I don't remember! I don't know if, at that time, I was doing queries on the computer…"
Mr. Shark:	"Soooo… you **WERE** on a computer! What queries were you doing?"
Agent Narco:	"I don't remember… ever being on the computer! I must have mis-spoke…"
Mr. Shark:	"But you were on a computer that night, right?"
Agent Narco:	"I honestly don't recall… if I was or not!"
Mr. Shark:	"And if you were on a computer that night… you'd have remembered, right?"
Agent Narco:	"Right! I would've remembered doing that! But I don't recall…"
Mr. Shark:	"You **DON'T** recall!? Okay! And in your business, so to speak, you don't search everybody's luggage, CORRECT?"
Agent Narco:	"Correct!"
Mr. Shark:	"It's at your discretion, correct?"
Agent Narco:	"Yes!"
Mr. Shark:	"In terms of your discretion, sometimes when you access the computer certain information that is secret that you're not allowed to tell any of us here causes you to then implement a search, correct?"
Agent Narco:	"Not necessarily!"

Mr. Shark:	"What's that answer mean, can you explain that?"
Agent Narco:	"I can't really answer to what I'm saying, dealing with the actual... anything with the computer."
Mr. Shark:	"And that's because... and you sort of gave the same answers before at the Deposition, as you are here today, to His Honor, when I asked you at what times do you use the computer terminal to check people's credentials. Your answer was due to the nature and sensitivity that you're not required or allowed to answer that question. Do you remember that answer?"
Ms. Beeche:	"Could I just have the site as to where you're reading?"
Mr. Shark:	"Page 16 of his Deposition."
Agent Narco:	"May I see what I said?"
Mr. Shark:	"Sure! May I approach, Your Honor?"
The Court:	"Yes, you may!"
Mr. Shark:	"Let the record reflect I'm showing the witness page 16 of his Deposition."
Mr. Shark:	"Did I read that right?"
Agent Narco:	"Yes! That's what I said in the Deposition."
Ms. Beeche:	"Your Honor, I object to this line of questioning, it's irrelevant. The inspector testified he doesn't recall whether or not he even did a search."
Mr. Shark:	"That's my very point, Judge."
The Court:	**"That is the point! Overruled! I understand the point! The objection is overruled!"**

Mr. Shark:	"Would it be fair to say that you do hundreds of searches in the course of your duties… correct?"
The Court:	**"You mean, per day?"**
Mr. Shark:	"In the course of your week's or month's activity?"
Agent Narco:	"Not at this present time. Not on my current job."
Mr. Shark:	"We're NOT talking about now, agent Narco. But back then?"
Agent Narco:	"I don't know if I'd say hundreds."
Mr. Shark:	"A lot?"
Agent Narco:	"When you say, it's was a lot…"
The Court:	**"Well, on April 18, 1997, could you give me an estimate as to how many passengers you interacted with that day? Was it more than one?"**
Agent Narco:	"Yes! It was more than one!"
The Court:	**"And was it less than a thousand?"**
Agent Narco:	"Yes, Your Honor!"
The Court:	**"So, where between those two numbers was it, 100, 200?"**
Agent Narco:	"Maybe about forty!"
The Court:	**"FORTY!? Okay!"**
Mr. Shark:	"Now, in light of the fact that you don't remember whether or not, on that particular day,

you accessed any information particular to Mr. Fabler, you don't remember what caused you to then engage in the search of his luggage, correct? Or do you?"

Agent Narco: "Can you repeat the question?"

Mr. Shark: "Okay. In light of your telling us that you don't remember whether or not you accessed any information... *specific* information... pertinent to Mr. Fabler, prior to the search, you don't remember why, in your discretion, you made a determination to search his luggage?"

Agent Narco: "That's up to the discretion of each inspector on each individual who comes through. It could be that that night Mr. Fabler was nervous."

Mr. Shark: "I don't want you to guess."

Agent Narco: "Mr. Fabler **WAS** nervous that night when he came up to my counter."

Mr. Shark: "Are you telling His Honor that?"

Agent Narco: "Yes!"

Mr. Shark: "You never said that before, correct? In your Deposition or anything! Is this something that you thought of between the time of the Deposition and today?"

Agent Narco: "No!"

Ms. Beeche: "Objection, Your Honor. It WASN'T asked at the Deposition."

The Court: **"OVERRULED! You want a *'what's wrong with this picture?'* You want to include Mr. Fabler's non-comment about the incomplete carton issue at the Deposition, but this**

isn't okay? Why would Mr. Shark have
questioned what he had no thought to ask
based on his answer(s) given? Next question!
OVERRULED!*"

Mr. Shark: "At the Deposition, do you remember being asked
a whole lot about the contact you had? And you
gave a whole lot of, I'm not really sure, I don't
remembers. You never told us that the reason, one
of the reasons, why you searched his luggage was
because Mr. Fabler appeared nervous, right?"

Agent Narco: "Your Honor, could I go a little further than a yes
or no answer?"

The Court: "You can say yes or no and then explain your
answer."

Agent Narco: "What I said was, first of all, under my discretion
as an inspector, I do **not** need any reason to search
a bag. If any passenger comes up and presents
themselves... they are presenting themselves
for examination. I don't need a reason or any
kind of reasonable suspicion or anything. If I felt
the person was nervous when he came up to be
examined, I'd examine his bag."

Mr. Shark: "I never asked that! Could you answer the
question here?"

The Court: **"Agent Narco, you're NOT answering the
question. I'm NOT asking for speeches. We're
asking you to answer questions. The question
that Mr. Shark asked was, is it true that you
haven't until this very moment mentioned in
either your Deposition or any place else that
the reason you searched Mr. Fabler's bags was
because he was acting nervous, YES or NO?"**

Agent Narco: "Yes, Your Honor."

The Court:	**"Fine!** Next question*!"*
Mr. Shark:	"Now, is there anything else that wasn't testified by you at your Deposition or not asked by me or Ms. Hammerhead that caused you to trigger your discretion to search Mr. Fabler? Is there anything else other than his nervousness?"
Agent Narco:	"On a flight from Jamaica I search when a person presents himself. I search the bags on an Air Jamaica flight."
Mr. Shark:	"Every person?"
Agent Narco:	"If they present themselves."
Mr. Shark:	"So, since Mr. Fabler was on a flight from Jamaica when he approached you, he didn't have to have been nervous for you to have searched his bag, correct!?"
Agent Narco: "	Mr. Fabler was nervous that night! That was why I searched his bag."
Mr. Shark:	"Please answer my question, agent Narco."
The Court:	**"Agent... answer the question(s) asked... please!"**
Agent Narco:	"No! He didn't have to be nervous, but he was... and that was why I searched his bag."
Mr. Shark:	"What you're telling us is that you didn't search every person that came though your location that evening or that day, correct?"
Agent Narco:	"If they came to my counter, yes, I did!"
Mr. Shark:	"So you searched every person's luggage, that's what you're telling us?"

Agent Narco:	"Most likely, yes!"
Mr. Shark:	"When you say 'most likely,' I'm not asking you to guess, sir!"
Agent Narco:	"I don't recall exactly how many people I examined that night."
Mr. Shark:	"I didn't ask how many people you examined that night. I'm asking if you remember searching every person's luggage that night when they came to you."
Agent Narco:	"I can't recall how many people came to me or whose baggage I searched that night."
Mr. Shark:	"But, just a few minutes ago, His Honor asked you how many people you interacted with on that night. Do you recall him asking you that question?"
Agent Narco:	"Yes!"
Mr. Shark:	"And you answered, forty! Do you recall saying that number?"
Agent Narco:	"I don't remember!"
Mr. Shark:	"You **DON'T** remember what you said... **ONLY** a few minutes ago!? Would you like us to read back your testimony? Would that help you remember what you said?"
Agent Narco:	"It may have been forty! And it may not have been forty!"
Mr. Shark:	"Now you don't know how many passengers you interacted with!?"
Agent Narco:	"I can't recall..."

Mr. Shark:	"Agent Narco… do we need to have the record read AGAIN! That is, as to your testimony here today?"
Agent Narco:	"NO! I don't need the record read. I just don't remember how many…"
The Court:	**"But the point is you searched everyone off that Air Jamaica flight?"**
Agent Narco:	"That came to my counter, yes."
Mr. Shark:	"And how long did that take?"
Agent Narco:	"I don't know. I might have seen five passengers that whole night."
Mr. Shark:	"Five? Now you're telling His Honor that it was only five. Didn't you just tell His Honor on the night in question that you saw forty passengers?"
The Court:	**"I thought that too!"**
Agent Narco:	"I really don't know how many passengers I saw that night… that is, how many came to my station."
Mr. Shark:	"Okay. So we are down to five passengers, right?"
Agent Narco:	"Yeah, five! Okay!"
Mr. Shark:	"Where was Mr. Fabler in that number of five?"
Agent Narco:	"I don't recall."
Mr. Shark:	"You're making all this up right now, today, aren't you… officer?"
Agent Narco:	**"NO!** No sir!"

Mr. Shark:	"Well, it sounds like that. Again, this isn't something you shared with us at the Deposition… that on this particular day you searched every passenger that was in your line that came off of that Air Jamaica flight? You never told us that… right? What else didn't you tell us?"
D. Pete Animen:	"Objection, Your Honor."
The Court:	"Sustained."
Mr. Shark:	"I'm sorry! Is there anything else that caused you… so that you're saying now… let me go back with it, that there was no discretion in searching Mr. Fabler. All five people that were on that flight… you searched their bags, is that what you're telling us?"
Agent Narco:	"It could've been more than five. I just use five as a general figure!"
Mr. Shark:	"Now… it may have been more than five!? How many more…"
Agent Narco:	"I don't know! I don't recall! I don't remember! What do you want me to tell you?"
The Court:	**"The TRUTH, agent!"**
Mr. Shark:	**"Yes… the TRUTH! Let's start with the truth agent Narco. Okay!?** So how long does it take to search a passenger when they come to your station?"
Agent Narco:	"Depends… everyone is different. There is no pre-set time limit or length."
Mr. Shark:	"And do you keep records of everyone that comes to your station?"

Agent Narco:	"There is a sheet that is marked with the name and a record of what occurred."
Mr. Shark:	"So you COULD go to that record and see where in those five passengers Mr. Fabler was in terms of coming to your station, correct?"
Agent Narco:	"Those records are filed away. I wouldn't know where to look for them."
Mr. Shark:	"Of course, you wouldn't! And I don't suppose you ever asked, either. But you COULD look it up where in those five, more or less, people Mr. Fabler was? If you knew where to look, right?"
Agent Narco:	"If I knew where to look! I suppose so!"
Mr. Shark:	**"You SUPPOSE so?** But everybody who came off that flight was searched?"
Agent Narco:	"If they came to my counter, yes."
Mr. Shark:	"Why was that?"
Agent Narco:	"Because they presented themselves to my counter."
Mr. Shark:	"And it was an Air Jamaica flight?"
Agent Narco:	"And my counter is a secondary counter."
Mr. Shark:	"Precisely, my point. Now that you shared that with us, and I appreciate that, the secondary counter is where people go who have something to declare, correct?"
Agent Narco:	"Not necessarily."
Mr. Shark:	**"Not necessarily? But usually, correct?"**

Agent Narco:	"**No!** People can come to the counter to ask questions."
Mr. Shark:	"Not necessarily, and not usually, what…"
The Court:	"**But, in fact, people who do have things to declare go to the secondary counter, correct?**"
Agent Narco:	"Not all the time, Your Honor."
Mr. Shark:	"This is absurd, Your Honor. **I'd love to see the results of a lie detector test!**"
D. Pete Animen:	"Objection, Your Honor!"
Mr. Shark:	"I only have a few more questions here, Your Honor." Supervisor Rudemann wasn't there, initially, when Mr. Fabler presented himself, correct?"
Agent Narco:	"I'm not sure where supervisor Rudemann was."
Mr. Shark:	"But he wasn't there, initially, when Mr. Fabler presented himself, correct?"
D. Pete Animen:	"I object, Your Honor! He said he didn't know where supervisor Rudemann was?"
Mr. Shark:	"Your Honor, agent Narco stated earlier that he had a much better recollection of the events on that night today. However, he doesn't remember what happened, who was where, or what was said. He doesn't remember how many people he saw or how long it took to see and search them. He doesn't remember where Mr. Fabler was in those five more or less people. And why any and all those people were searched. This is absurd! I have one last question, Your Honor. Agent Narco who did you go to for advice after confronting Mr. Fabler that night?"

Agent Narco:	"I went to my supervisor... supervisor Rudemann."
Mr. Shark:	"You went to your supervisor, supervisor Rudemann!? But a minute ago you just said you didn't know where supervisor Rudemann was that night. When did you find out where he was that night? That is... at what point, and by whom, did you find out where supervisor Rudemann was that night?"
D. Pete Animen:	"I object, Your Honor. He stated he didn't know where supervisor Rudemann was that night."
The Court:	**"Overruled! Agent Narco stated he didn't know where supervisor Rudemann was that night... but he went to him when he sought advice on the situation. How did he know where he was if he didn't know where he was? I want to hear this! Answer the question, agent Narco!"**
Agent Narco:	"I don't remember!
Mr. Shark:	"You're making this up now... aren't you agent Narco?!"
Agent Narco:	"No! I don't remember where supervisor Rudemann was or how I found him. That is, if anyone told me where to look or whatever."
D. Pete Animen:	"Objected, Your Honor. How many times does he have to state that he didn't remember where supervisor Rudemann was... that night?"
Mr. Shark:	"I didn't ask him if he knew where supervisor Rudemann was that night, only if he was there when Mr. Fabler initially presented himself to Agent Narco at his station.
The Court:	**"Overruled! Answer the question, officer!"**

Agent Narco:	"I don't remember where he was."
Mr. Shark:	"But you do remember going to supervisor Rudemann that night?"
Agent Narco:	"Yes!"
Mr. Shark:	"Why did you go to supervisor Rudemann... that night? Did you need him with any of the other 5 or whatever number of people you searched... that night? Why did you have to go to supervisor Rudemann when Mr. Fabler was with you... that night?"
Agent Narco:	"I don't remember why I went to supervisor Rudemann. I just did!"
Mr. Shark:	"And when you went to supervisor Rudemann, that night, what was your discussion about? What did you talk about?"
Agent Narco:	"I don't remember why I went to supervisor Rudemann. I just did."
Mr. Shark:	"Agent Narco... that wasn't my question. What did you talk about?"
Agent Narco:	"I don't remember!"
Mr. Shark:	"But you didn't talk about the **Know Before You Go** book, because if you did you would remember that conversation... correct?"
Agent Narco:	"Correct! I didn't discuss that book that night with anyone... because I would remember if I did."
Mr. Shark:	"And when you went to find supervisor Rudemann, you knew where to find him... correct?"

D. Pete Animen: "Objected, Your Honor. Ask… and answered!"

The Court: **"Mr. Shark… the witness has testified that supervisor Rudemann wasn't present when Mr. Fabler initially presented himself to his station. Let's leave it at that, shall we. I doubt that you're going to get any more from him… anyway."**

Mr. Shark: "Thank you, Your Honor. I have no other questions for this witness at this time. Besides, it wouldn't do me any good anyway! He's supposed to tell the truth up here on the stand, but…"

D. Pete Animen: "Objected, Your Honor!"

Mr. Shark: "That's all I have, Your Honor!"

The Court: "Any Re-direct?"

Ms. Beeche: "May I have one moment, Your Honor."

Mr. Shark: "Judge, maybe, also if we could get a stipulation. Agent… you didn't find any marijuana, correct, to your knowledge?"

Agent Narco: "There was a green leafy substance that tested positive for marijuana or THC."

The Court: **"That's NOT his question. His question was, DID YOU FIND ANY marijuana?"**

Agent Narco: "There was a green leafy substance that tested positive for marijuana or THC… which would be marijuana or THC."

The Court: **"IS THERE A STIPULATION FROM THE SERVICE? I THOUGHT WE HAD ALL AGREED TO THAT!"**

Mr. Shark:	"I thought there was too! And just how much of this supposed green leafy substance was there?"
Agent Narco:	"Enough to test positive for marijuana or THC!"
Mr. Shark:	"But not enough to arrest or to have as evidence…"
D. Pete Animen:	"Objection, Your Honor!"
The Court:	**"The record, it will say what it says. I think we did have a stipulation on that point."**
Mr. Shark:	"That's all, I have… for now, Your Honor!"
The Court:	"Any Re-direct? Make it brief!"
Ms. Beeche:	"Inspector Narco, did you fill out a narrative summary and a Customs Seizure Report with regard to the seizure after the seizure of the items from Mr. Fabler?"
Mr. Shark:	"Object, Judge."
The Court:	**"Sustained! It's beyond the scope of Cross."**
Ms. Beeche:	**"Why?** He's talking about what were the recollections in his direct examination of agent Narco regarding what happened at the time of the seizure. And the Seizure Report indicates, consistently, everything that inspector Narco just testified to."
The Court:	**"But the question(s) Mr. Shark asked, was whether the agent said them in his Deposition… and his answer was no! That's what it was directed *to*."**
Ms. Beeche:	"But there's an issue as to whether he was questioned about the specific questions in his Deposition. So it's really relevant. If he wasn't

	asked those questions in his Deposition, why isn't it relevant to…"
The Court:	**"That's a proper line of Re-direct, but that's not what you're asking now. He didn't ask whether there were any other reports."**
Ms. Beeche:	"Inspector Narco, could a passenger having come off an Air Jamaica flight that day, on April 18, 1997, have come to your secondary counter without talking… without having talked to anybody else?"
Agent Narco:	"Yes!"
Ms. Beeche:	"To your knowledge, did Mr. Fabler, talk to anybody else… prior to coming to your counter?"
Agent Narco:	"Not… I don't know."
Ms. Beeche:	"Are you sure that Mr. Fabler didn't declare any of the seized items, to you, prior to your inspecting his luggage?"
Agent Narco:	"No… I mean yes! I'm sure… because that's when I went over the declaration. And that would give the passenger a chance to admit or amend his declaration."
Ms. Beeche:	"Thank you! No further questions, Your Honor."
The Court:	"Any Re-cross?"
Mr. Shark:	"Yes, Your Honor. Agent… did you have a conversation with Mr. Fabler about the **<u>Know Before You Go</u>** book that night?"

D. Pete Animen:	"Object, Your Honor. The witness has testified that he didn't discuss that book with Mr. Fabler that night."
Mr. Shark:	"Actually, Your Honor, I think the witness testified that he didn't discuss that book with supervisor Rudemann… that night!"
The Court:	**"Go ahead, agent. Answer the question of whether you discussed that book with Mr. Fabler… that night."**
Agent Narco:	**"No!"**
Mr. Shark:	**"None!?** No conversation about that book… with anyone… that night?! "
Agent Narco:	**"No!"**
Mr. Shark:	**"You're absolutely positive!"**
Agent Narco:	**"Yes… I'm positive!"**
Mr. Shark:	"And if you had a conversation with him about that book, you'd have remembered that conversation, wouldn't you?"
D. Pete Animen:	"Objection, Your Honor. He's testified there was no conversation about that book… that night"
The Court:	**"Sustained!** I believe he has testified that there was no conversation with Mr. Fabler or with supervisor Rudemann or with anyone about that very mysterious book."
Mr. Shark:	"I'm done, Your Honor!"
The Court:	"You may step down, sir. I take it you're not going to call him again, are you?"
Mr. Shark:	"No, Your Honor."

The Court:	"You can stay in the courtroom, agent."
Agent Narco:	"Thank you."

With the questioning over, agent Narco got up from the hot seat and walked over to his place behind the government sharks. He seemed relieved to be finished with his ordeal... the fire having only seared his skin. And, maybe, it was a baptismal right of passage that every government agent goes through the first time they visit the hot seat. Or, maybe, it only seems that way... when the truth they tell isn't the whole truth and nothing but the truth. Then again... what A Tangled Web Is Weaved When The Practice Is To Deceive!

The Court:	"I assume you want supervisor Rudemann?"
Ms. Beeche:	"Yes... Your Honor."
The Court:	"Proceed, Ms. Beeche."

Supervisor Rudemann moved toward the box... where his testimony would be heard. The swaggered march he exhibited on that April 18th night was long gone... replaced with a staggered stroll! I didn't see the same forceful agent I saw when I first encountered him... although he was still in control of himself. The color of his blue uniform gave him that same self-filled confidence he had when I first saw him strut his stuff. And his hands didn't shake... not like the agent who preceded him. It was obvious he had little to tell and less to hide.

Ms. Beeche:	"Inspector Rudemann, who's your employer?"
Supervisor Rudemann:	"The U.S. Customs service."
Ms. Beeche:	"What is your current position with U.S. Customs?"
Supervisor Rudemann:	"I'm a Supervisory inspector."
Ms. Beeche:	"How long have you been a Supervisory inspector?"

Supervisor Rudemann: "Since 1986."

Ms. Beeche: "What did you do prior to that?"

Supervisor Rudemann: "I was a Customs warehouse officer and a Customs inspector."

Ms. Beeche: "Since when have you been working for the U.S. Customs service?"

Supervisor Rudemann: "November 1976."

Ms. Beeche: "What are your responsibilities as a supervisory Customs inspector?"

Supervisor Rudemann: "My responsibilities as a Customs supervisor are to lead, train, motivate, and provide guidance. I'm the authorizing officer on seizures, personal searches, and a variety of sorts for other administrative duties."

Ms. Beeche: "In April, 1997, where were you assigned?"

Supervisor Rudemann: "I was assigned to Terminal A, Philadelphia International Airport, passenger processing."

Ms. Beeche: "And were you the supervisor of agent Narco that day?"

Supervisor Rudemann: "Yes! I was!"

Ms. Beeche: "Did you have the opportunity to meet Mr. Fabler on that day?"

Supervisor Rudemann: "Yes! I did."

Ms. Beeche: "Please describe the circumstances of that meeting!"

Supervisor Rudemann: "That was during Air Jamaica's Flight 19. Inspector Narco came to me and advised me that he had a failure to declare and had intercepted Cuban articles, *specifically* four boxes of Cuban cigars from Mr. Fabler. I reviewed the declaration and pursued the remainder of the inspection."

Ms. Beeche: "What portion of the inspection occurred prior to you arriving at agent Narco's station?"

Supervisor Rudemann: "Agent Narco reviewed the declaration with Mr. Fabler. He had gone over it... and began his baggage inspection of the pieces of luggage that Mr. Fabler had with him. Then, he made a discovery of the..."

Mr. Shark: "This is ALL objected to. Unless... this good officer was present for that!?"

The Court: "Were you present?"

Supervisor Rudemann: "No! I wasn't present for everything."

The Court: "Only testify as to what you saw, sir."

Ms. Beeche: "When you arrived, what did agent Narco tell you?"

Supervisor Rudemann: "Agent Narco told me that Mr. Fabler didn't declared certain Cuban articles, *specifically* four boxes of cigars and other articles that were listed on the 6051."

Ms. Beeche: "What happened from that point on?"

Supervisor Rudemann: "From that point, agent Narco finished his inspection and requested a personal search be done on Mr. Fabler. He told me he found a small amount of a green leafy vegetable matter that he claimed field tested positive for marijuana."

Ms. Beeche: "Did you authorize a personal search?"

340

Supervisor Rudemann: "Based on what he said… yes! I did."

Ms. Beeche: "Were you present for the personal search?"

Supervisor Rudemann: "No."

Ms. Beeche: "What did the personal search consist of that you authorized?"

Supervisor Rudemann: "It was a pat-down search… conducted by agent Narco."

Ms. Beeche: "Did you authorize a body cavity search?"

Supervisor Rudemann: "Negative."

Ms. Beeche: "Did you arrest Mr. Fabler on April 18, 1997?"

Supervisor Rudemann: "No!"

Ms. Beeche: "Did you state to Mr. Fabler on April 18, 1997 that he was 'under arrest' at any time?"

Supervisor Rudemann: "I don't recall saying that, but a lot of things were said that night!"

Ms. Beeche: "Did you call an inspector or any employee of INS that came and discussed the issue of the claimant's travel to Cuba at any time. Or did anybody come over from INS to speak with Mr. Fabler or you and agent Narco about the circumstances of the seizure?"

Supervisor Rudemann: "Not that I recall!"

Ms. Beeche: "Did you authorize the seizure of the seized items?"

Supervisor Rudemann: "Yes! I did."

David Weisenthal

Ms. Beeche:	"What was the basis of your authorization for the seizure?"
Supervisor Rudemann:	"19 U.S.C. 1497, which is a failure to declare from 19 U.S.C. 1595(a) (c), which is the authorization of seized articles that are brought in contrary to other laws which are the OFAC Sanctions 31 CFR."
Ms. Beeche:	"What was the basis for you authorizing seizure for failing to declare?"
Supervisor Rudemann:	"In the review of the declaration and the examination conducted by agent Narco, agent Narco advised me that he had done a complete…"
Mr. Shark:	"Once again, Judge, I just have to object…"
The Court:	**"SUSTAINED!"**
Ms. Beeche:	"What's the basis…"
The Court:	"It's being offered for the truth."
Ms. Beeche:	"What's the basis of your authorization for the violation, the second violation you mentioned, with regard to 'THE (Cuban) embargo?'"
Supervisor Rudemann:	"Cuban articles imported from a third country aren't authorized."
Ms. Beeche:	"At any time, did the claimant tell you he'd been a guest, in Cuba, of a German 'national?'"
Supervisor Rudemann:	"He may have! But it didn't matter."
Ms. Beeche:	"I have no further questions, Your Honor."
The Court:	"Any Cross-examination, Mr. Shark?"

Busted

***

Mr. Shark:	"I just have a couple of questions, Your Honor. May I have the declaration page?"
The Court:	**"The declaration!? You want that!? That's G-1, I think!"**
Mr. Shark:	"May I show that?"
The Court:	"Sure!"
Mr. Shark:	"I'm sorry, your exact title was?"
Supervisor Rudemann:	"Supervisory…"
Mr. Shark:	"Supervisory-inspector?"
Supervisor Rudemann:	"Inspector is fine."
Mr. Shark:	"Inspector, taking a look at the government exhibit, marked number 1, you're familiar with that document… correct?"
Supervisor Rudemann:	"Yes."
Mr. Shark:	"We took your Deposition a month or so ago, myself and Ms. Hammerhead… correct?"
Supervisor Rudemann:	"Yes."
Mr. Shark:	"Briefly, there are Customs agents you supervise that are known as 'roving' agents… correct? In the facility where the planes come in… correct?"
Supervisor Rudemann:	"There are inspectors who are assigned to roving duties… yes."

Mr. Shark:	"And that's a title, I just didn't make that word up, right... roving?"
Supervisor Rudemann:	"It's not a title. It's a work assignment."
Mr. Shark:	"And on this particular day there were roving inspectors... correct?"
Supervisor Rudemann:	"Correct."
Mr. Shark:	"And it's correct to tell His Honor that roving inspectors encounter passengers and depending upon what's on the declaration or the interchange between the passenger and the roving inspector, they're directed to secondary sites where for instance in this case agent Narco was... right?"
Supervisor Rudemann:	"Correct."
Mr. Shark:	"Taking a look at the government exhibit, marked number 1, the item has a mark on the upper right-hand corner, correct?"
Supervisor Rudemann:	"Correct."
Mr. Shark:	"That would be put on that document, government Exhibit 1, by a roving inspector... correct?"
Supervisor Rudemann:	"Correct."
Mr. Shark:	"Correct! And there IS such an indication there. That that document was marked by a roving inspector... correct?"
Supervisor Rudemann:	"Correct."
Mr. Shark:	"At the time of the Deposition I asked if you were able to determine the identify of that roving inspector... correct?"
Supervisor Rudemann:	"You did ask... yes."

Mr. Shark: "At that time you were unable to… correct?"

Supervisor Rudemann: "That's correct."

Mr. Shark: "Subsequent to the Deposition, have you been able to determine who the roving inspector was?"

Supervisor Rudemann: "Negative."

Mr. Shark: "But, anyway, that mark tells us the individual who had this declaration encountered somebody before agent Narco… correct?"

Supervisor Rudemann: "In most circumstances… that's correct."

Mr. Shark: **"In most circumstances!? Who else would place that mark there?"**

Supervisor Rudemann: "No one!"

Mr. Shark: "So again, because by that marking there… that's what tells you that?"

The Court: **"Is that the T-1?"**

Mr. Shark: "That's correct, Judge. Isn't that right, agent?"

Supervisor Rudemann: "Yes."

Mr. Shark: "Once again, for purposes of clarification, when you got to where agent Narco was, the seizure or the discovery of the cigars had already taken place… correct?"

Supervisor Rudemann: "To the best of my recollection… yes."

Mr. Shark: "Yes?"

Supervisor Rudemann: "Yes!"

Mr. Shark:	"So, it's correct to tell His Honor that you don't know what the exchange was between Mr. Fabler and agent Narco... correct?"
Supervisor Rudemann:	"Just what was relayed to me by agent Narco."
Mr. Shark:	"Right!?"
Supervisor Rudemann:	"Yes."
Mr. Shark:	"By what he told you that night?"
Supervisor Rudemann:	"Right."
Mr. Shark:	"And again, from firsthand knowledge, you don't know who said what or whatever... correct?"
Supervisor Rudemann:	"Yes!"
Mr. Shark:	"And, again, it's fair to say that as a result of that T-1 there that Mr. Fabler had been encountered by someone other than agent Narco that caused him to go to the secondary location... correct?"
Supervisor Rudemann:	"Correct."
Mr. Shark:	"You weren't present for the search, but there were other agents or Customs agents who were present... correct?"
Supervisor Rudemann:	"There was one other inspector assigned. Pat-down searches are always conducted by two inspectors."
Mr. Shark:	"And that person isn't here today... right?"
Supervisor Rudemann:	"That's correct."
Mr. Shark:	"Is there a reason for his absence today?"

Supervisor Rudemann: "The attorney's didn't feel a need to call him…"

D. Pete Animen: "Objection… Your Honor."

Mr. Shark: "And you don't know *specifically* what was said by that person when the search was conducted… correct? And you don't know what was done or found either…"

Supervisor Rudemann: "Normal practice is…"

Mr. Shark: "I understand normal practice, but you don't know what was said?"

Supervisor Rudemann: "No! I don't! Correct!"

Mr. Shark: "And you don't know whether they said 'you're under arrest,' you know, 'You're a criminal, you're this, you're that…' you don't know anything about that?"

Supervisor Rudemann: "No! I don't… correct!"

Mr. Shark: "You don't know about someone saying, 'you're a traitor for having cigars.' You just don't know what was said… correct?"

Supervisor Rudemann: "Correct! I don't!"

Mr. Shark: "But you do know and you do recall Mr. Fabler and either you or agent Narco discussing what has been marked as C-1, the **Know Before You Go** pamphlet. You do recall that?"

Supervisor Rudemann: "Yes! I recall a conversation about the book… that night."

Mr. Shark: "Who did you have a conversation with about that book… that night?"

Supervisor Rudemann: "Mr. Fabler… and agent Narco!"

Mr. Shark:	"Agent Narco!? Why did you speak with agent Narco about *that* book?"
Supervisor Rudemann:	"Agent Narco approached me about that incident. He had the **Know Before You Go** book with him and said that Mr. Fabler referenced the section Cigars and Cigarettes. Agent Narco asked me to read what was written there and he said that Mr. Fabler interpreted the words to mean that he could introduce..."
D. Pete Animen:	**"Object... Your Honor."**
The Court:	**"Overruled! I want to hear this! You want to know why I want to hear this? It's simple! Agent Narco said there wasn't ANY conversation, be it with supervisor Rudemann or Mr. Fabler or anyone, about that book that night. However, this agent completely contradicts his testimony. And, THIS IS about credibility!"**
Mr. Shark:	"And this conversation with agent Narco occurred prior to your interaction with Mr. Fabler... correct!?"
Supervisor Rudemann:	"Correct!"
Mr. Shark:	"So based on your conversation with agent Narco prior to your interaction with Mr. Fabler would it be safe to say that you believed agent Narco had a conversation with Mr. Fabler about the **Know Before You Go** book?"
D. Pete Animen:	**"Object, Your Honor!"**
The Court:	**"Overruled! The agent said agent Narco said that Mr. Fabler interpreted the words to mean that he could introduce the articles in**

his possession into the country. I WANT TO HEAR THIS!"

Supervisor Rudemann: "I thought he had a conversation about that book... yes! I mean he stated as much!"

Mr. Shark: "And after your interaction with Mr. Fabler that night, would it be fair to say Mr. Fabler's belief was that his possession of these Cuban cigars and what-have-you, was that he was within his legal rights to have those?"

The Court: **"That was HIS contention."**

Mr. Shark: "Right! Not that you agree with that! But that was the subject of the discussion about that pamphlet?"

Supervisor Rudemann: "That's correct!"

Mr. Shark: "On that particular day, you don't know if agent Narco accessed information about Mr. Fabler prior to his search, or not, from the computer... correct? They have computers at the secondary site locations... correct?"

Supervisor Rudemann: "Correct... and correct!"

Mr. Shark: "You're able to take information from somebody to find out if they have a prior arrest record or if they have other traveling circumstances... correct?"

Supervisor Rudemann: "Correct. If there's a prior, yes, that's correct. If there's a prior Customs violation... yes!"

Mr. Shark: "Exactly! And that information is in the computer pretty much by just punching in the purpose of pertinent information, correct?"

Supervisor Rudemann: "That's correct."

Mr. Shark: "And, many times, it'd be fair to say that when you punch in some information, you know, if there's information in there about anything that an agent thinks is pertinent, that may trigger in that agent's discretion the ability to search that person... right?"

Supervisor Rudemann: "That's not the sole basis for any search."

Mr. Shark: "But it is one of the basis... correct?"

Supervisor Rudemann: "It's part of the total picture of the search... correct."

Mr. Shark: "Do you recall having any conversation with agent Narco as to why, in his discretion, or what, in his discretion, caused him to conduct that search of Mr. Fabler?"

Supervisor Rudemann: "You need to clarify what you mean by search. Search means, to me, a personal search! If you're talking about the inspection of Mr. Fabler's bags, I need to know which question you're asking about."

Mr. Shark: "Either! Take either one! Take either one! In either one, in either case, the search of his person... wait a minute! I think I know what you're saying. In other words, if you find something in the luggage that may trigger a personal search... like a body cavity search?"

Supervisor Rudemann: "That's correct."

Mr. Shark: "And, that's, you know, a fair assessment of my question, but let's assume the discretion that causes the agent to trigger the search of the luggage. Did agent Narco tell you what caused him to search Mr. Fabler's luggage?"

Supervisor Rudemann: "I don't recall him giving me any *specifics*... no!"

Mr. Shark: "You don't know whether it was a function of his accessing information from the computer. What it was... right? You just don't know?"

Supervisor Rudemann: "No! I don't."

Mr. Shark: "But you do recall having a conversation with agent Narco about the **Know Before You Go** book on the night of April 18, 1997... on the night Mr. Fabler came through Customs?"

Supervisor Rudemann: "Yes! I recall a conversation about that book that night."

Mr. Shark: "Could you give some *specifics*... what you recall about that conversation."

D. Pete Animen: **"Object, Your Honor!"**

The Court: **"Overruled! Answer the question, supervisor!"**

Supervisor Rudemann: "Agent Narco approached me about finding the Cuban products that we've already mentioned... and he had the **Know Before You Go** book. He asked me to look at it."

Mr. Shark: "He had the **Know Before You Go** book when he first approached you? And he asked you to look at it? What was he referring to? Why did he want you to look at the book?"

Supervisor Rudemann: "There was an issue with the Cigar and Cigarettes Section, that, apparently, Mr. Fabler had raised."

D. Pete Animen: "Objection, Your Honor! He wasn't present when that conversation occurred."

The Court:	**"He's YOUR witness! You're objecting to your OWN witness? OVERRULED! He's not asking about the conversation Mr. Fabler had with agent Narco, but what agent Narco had with THIS WITNESS about that book. I WANT TO HEAR THIS ALSO. You CAN answer!"**
Supervisor Rudemann:	"I don't remember it *specifically*, but there was some issue with the cigar and cigarettes wording. Agent Narco said Mr. Fabler based his importation on the wording and I told agent Narco that Mr. Fabler had misinterpreted the wording in the pamphlet. Then he asked me to intercede in the matter."
Mr. Shark:	"Which you did when you went to agent Narco's site and spoke with Mr. Fabler... right?"
Supervisor Rudemann:	"Correct!"
Mr. Shark:	"I appreciate your candid testimony. Thank you sir. That's all I have, Judge."
The Court:	"Any Re-direct?"
Ms. Beeche:	"Yes... Your Honor. Supervisor Rudemann, you had no opportunity to identify a roving inspector who, supposedly, examined Mr. Fabler that night... did you?"
Supervisor Rudemann:	"That's correct."
Ms. Beeche:	"To your knowledge, nobody at Customs was able to identify a roving inspector who spoke to the claimant that night... right?"
Supervisor Rudemann:	"Nobody was able to recall speaking to him directly... no."

Ms. Beeche: "Are you confident, as a supervisor, that based on your assessment of all the facts that you knew that night that Mr. Fabler hadn't made a declaration regarding the seized items?"

Mr. Shark: "That's objected to, Your Honor."

The Court: **"SUSTAINED!"**

Ms. Beeche: "What's the basis of the objection, Your Honor?"

Mr. Shark: "That's the ultimate conclusion."

The Court: **"It's the ultimate conclusion I'm supposed to decide."**

Mr. Shark: "He wasn't even involved with it."

Ms. Beeche: "I'm asking based on…"

The Court: **"HE WASN'T EVEN INVOLVED WITH IT! No foundation! Do you want a '*what's wrong with this picture?*' Ask your next question, will you?"**

Ms. Beeche: "Supervisor Rudemann, you weren't present for the conversation with Mr. Fabler and agent Narco were you? And you don't know what was said between them, do you… prior to your arrival at agent Narco's site."

Supervisor Rudemann: "No, I don't. I only know what I was told!"

Ms. Beeche: "No further questions, Your Honor."

The Court: "Any Re-cross?"

Mr. Shark: "Yes, Your Honor. Supervisor Rudemann… were you present when Mr. Dueling was searched?"

Supervisor Rudemann: "No!"

Mr. Shark: "Do you know who ordered Mr. Dueling's search?"

D. Pete Animen: **"Objection, Your Honor."**

The Court: **"Sustained! He said he wasn't present for the search..."**

D. Pete Animen: "Your Honor, we don't even know if Dueling was searched?"

Mr. Shark: "But there is a record of every search, Your Honor. Agent Narco stated as much. Of course, we have to take what agent Narco said with a grain of salt. And the record of the search could be found, if the government wanted to find it. That's only what I'm trying to determine Your Honor. Supervisor Rudemann has said that he was responsible for ordering Mr. Fabler's search... and it was the same night, the same place and the same time, so it's logical to assume he would also have ordered Dueling's search..."

The Court: "Sustained! I fail to see the relevance here, Mr. Shark."

Mr. Shark: "Then, I have no further questions, Your Honor."

The Court: **"Thank you, supervisor Rudemann. Now... we have the gentleman from OFAC who IS very KNOWLEDGEABLE about the <u>Know Before You Go</u> pamphlet, Ms. Beeche?"**

Ms. Beeche: "Yes, Your Honor."

The Court: "Is he your next witness?"

Ms. Beeche: "Yes, Your Honor."

The Court: "Sir, would you come forward."

The Man From OFAC

***

Behind the government advocators sat a tall pale rail thin dark-haired beanpole man. He stood and sauntered toward the witness stand's hot seat. And he strolled as if he had something stuck up deep inside his buttocks. I thought it was his underpants, but with a man like him it had to be his shit! His clothes draped off his body and showed that he'd never spent so much as one minute in a gym... except for when he was forced to attend that class. But he probably failed the course, anyway. Every movement his body made was a kind of spastic jerk that emitted an appearance of physically challenged... however, his handicap wasn't so much physical as it might have been mental.

It was obvious the man from OFAC's badge of courage was the badge he wore. Although he thought himself superior to all humanity, he was more than inferior when compared to the most common beast. I'd seen his kind before when I wore the clothes of a much younger man. And contrary to his opinion... his shit had a strangely rank odor!

The entire courtroom waited with baited breath for the man from OFAC to make known his knowledge of the literature that was known as **Know Before You Go**. The robed one was more than interested in what the man from OFAC had to say... to the extent that whatever he would say would clarify that **Know Before You Go** pamphlet. And while he was the man from OFAC I couldn't help but feel as if he was much more in tune with being the lad from glad... who I'd seen in all those commercials when I was a child. But what did I know!? I knew he wasn't what he wanted to appear like he was.

Then, the man from OFAC spoke... and everyone blinked. He was the man from OFAC? Not quite a lisp, but more than a slur. Every word that sprang from his mouth was as if his nose had been glued shut. He shot out each word in an arrogant tone. The likes of which hadn't been heard since Marie Antoinette told all those Frenchies to go eat cake. Holding his head high and cocked to one side, he displayed an air of haughtiness he felt would dominate the atmosphere surrounding his presence. However, it only served to heighten the actuality that he wasn't what he wanted to appear like he was. And everyone wanted to know not who he thought he was, but what hole he had climbed out of.

Ms. Beeche: "What is your name?"

The Man From OFAC: "Frank Lee Smallhead! F-r-a-n-k L-e-e S-m-a-l-l-h-e-a-d!"

Ms. Beeche: "Mr. Smallhead, what is your current position?"

The Man From OFAC: "I'm **the** Attorney-Advisor for the Office of Chief Counsel for Foreign Assets Control for the U.S. Dept. of the Treasury."

Ms. Beeche: "How long have you held that position?"

The Man From OFAC: "Since April... 1998," (And when he said that, everyone blinked and gasped... not sure they heard him correctly. For they were waiting for a top gun assassin villain... not some come-lately fly-by-night amateur hired hand!)

Ms. Beeche: "Are you knowledgeable about the Regulations involving 'THE (Cuban) embargo?'"

The Man From OFAC: "Yes, I am."

Ms. Beeche: "Where, *generally*, are they found?"

The Man From OFAC: "They're found in Volume 31 of the <u>Code of Federal Regulations</u>, Part 515."

Ms. Beeche: "Your Honor, if I may, just for reference in case anyone needs a copy of the CFR Regulations that were in effect at the time of the seizure."

The Court: **"WHAT? I mean we really can read the Regulations, honest. I thought he was going to tell us about this book."**

Mr. Shark: "That's what I thought too, Judge."

Ms. Beeche:	"He is! But he may be referencing the Regulations with regard to that. And so I'd ask to offer the reference… if anybody needs them."
The Court:	**"He can have them in front of him for that purpose. But that's the ONLY purpose of this that I'm going to allow. Excuse me sir, but did you say you've been an Attorney-Advisor for OFAC since… ONLY… 1998?"**
The Man From OFAC:	"Yes, since April… 1998."

The man from OFAC gave his answer to this question. Afterward, His Honor, the shark, and I as well as most of those in attendance looked around the room at one another in a state of astonishment. Everyone was confused by his answer. The government sharks had stated that he was on the stand ONLY to explain who, when and how the 1994 version of **Know Before You Go** got printed. But he had just testified that he hadn't begun working for OFAC until several years after the printing of that particular version. Something was amiss. What did everyone in that courtroom know? We knew the man from OFAC didn't know what the government wanted everyone to think what he knew.

Ms. Beeche:	"Now, Mr. Smallhead, did you have an opportunity to review the Customs manual, **Know Before You Go**?"
The Man From OFAC:	"Yes… I did!"
Ms. Beeche:	"In your opinion is there any…"
Mr. Shark:	"Could we just identify which one he's familiar with?"
The Court:	**"Yes! What edition?"**
Ms. Beeche:	"The 1994 version… which is the *current* edition."
The Court:	**"The April 1994 edition. Have you had a chance to review that?"**

Mr. Shark:	"Judge, for the record, we should note that the April 1994 edition **isn't** the *current* edition."
The Court:	**"I know! I know it isn't. At least, I understand from the papers it isn't. But that's the one we're talking about."**
Ms. Beeche:	"If I said that, it was in error."
Mr. Shark:	"She says a lot of things that are in error, Your Honor. I thought she said that was the *current* edition."
The Court:	**"She *did* say that!"**
Ms. Beeche:	"I'm sorry if I said that. I meant... I mean the April 1994 version."
Mr. Shark:	"Yes! She did say the 1994 version, but the 1994 version **isn't** the *current* version."
Ms. Beeche:	"Your Honor, we're talking about the 1994 version. I'm sorry if I said it was the *current* version. I stand corrected on that!"
The Man From OFAC:	"Yes, I've had... I've reviewed the April 1994 edition of the **Know Before You Go** manual."
Ms. Beeche:	"Is there anything in the **Know Before You Go** manual which would authorize... withdrawn. Are you familiar with the circumstances regarding the seizure issue?"
The Man From OFAC:	"Yes... I am."
Ms. Beeche:	"Is there anything in the **Know Before You Go** manual dated April 1994 that would have authorized Mr. Fabler to have imported those goods pursuant to the Customs Regulations that were pursuant to the OFAC Regulations?"

Mr. Shark: "Judge, just note my objection! I think the Court and myself were of the understanding this gentleman had some involvement in the production of the Customs publication..."

The Court: **"Yes! I agree! But let's do this because I'm anxious to hear from somebody from OFAC so that we can reconcile page 6 and the Regulations."**

Mr. Shark: "Judge... just note my objection."

The Court: "It is noted... **AND**, it is preserved."

Mr. Shark: "Thank you, Your Honor."

Clearly the robed one was troubled. He was having a hard time hiding his contempt for those who were attempting to abuse his court. And in an instant of a moment he made a decision to take control of his court. He said, **"Since I'm the Finder of Fact here**, I'm going to ask the questions. Open to Page 6!"**

The Man From OFAC: "May I have a copy of the April 1994 version of the **Know Before You Go** manual?"

The Court: **"Turn to page 6 of the April 1994 version... right!? You've got that?"**

The Man From OFAC: "Yes."

The Court: **"In the upper left under Cigars and Cigarettes it says, '*Not more than 100 cigars and 200 cigarettes (one carton) may be included in your exemption. Products of Cuban tobacco may be included if purchased in Cuba, see page 20.*' Now, would you turn to page 20 for me. Could you tell me what that is referring on page 20?"**

The Man From OFAC: "I believe it's a reference to the section called Prohibited and Restricted Articles... a section of this manual."

The Court: **"You believe... or you know?"**

The Man From OFAC: "Well, I didn't write the book! But common sense tells me it is a reference to the section..."

The Court: **"On page 20? What common sense?"**

Mr. Shark: "Your Honor, the **Know Before You Go** book, April 1994 version, doesn't have a section titled Prohibited and Restricted Articles. There is a section titled that in the 1997 version, but not the 1994 version. I thought you were referencing the 1994 version."

The Court: **"You're correct! I am talking about the 1994 version. Well, Mr. Smallhead..."**

The Man From OFAC: "Well, Your Honor, page 20 is just one page in a section. There's nothing..."

The Court: **"There's nothing in it about Cuba, though... wouldn't you agree with me!?"**

The Man From OFAC: "On page 20, no! But in the section... yes."

The Court: **"But it's citing page 20. I want to know what page 20 has to do with '*Products of Cuban Tobacco*.'"**

The Man From OFAC: "Well, I... if I, in my own personal opinion... if I were directed to this page, and it was a part of a section, for example, that I was directed to the first page of a section, I'd probably read the whole section."

The Court: **"But the reader is directed... here is the mystery to me, sir, and I'm glad you're here to** help me with this because it's my job to make sense out of this, okay?"

The Man From OFAC: "Yes."

The Court: "It directs the reader to page 20! But if the reader does as I did, go to page 20, all the reader gets is confused, isn't that right? Because it doesn't illuminate in any way, shape or form what it's cited for... which is '*Products of Cuban Tobacco may be included if purchased in Cuba.*' But on page 20, it says nothing about that, correct?"

The Man From OFAC: On Page 20, itself, it says nothing about *products of Cuban origin.*"

The Court: "So, therefore, you would agree with me that it is a meaningless citation?"

The Man From OFAC: "No! I'd disagree with you on that."

The Court: "Why do you disagree with me that it's meaningless?"

The Man From OFAC: "Because, in my opinion, when I'm referred to a certain page for information to be on there, I'd usually look around that page and..."

The Court: "So even though it says page 20... you, as a reasonable reader, would think that means some page other than page 20. Is that your testimony, sir?"

The Man From OFAC: "No! My testimony is..."

The Court: "I think that's what you just said to me, isn't it?"

The Man From OFAC: "No! I don't believe so."

361

David Weisenthal

The Court:	**"But there's nothing on page 20 about the subject, are we agreed? Look at page 20. The..."**
Ms. Beeche:	"Your Honor..."
The Court:	**"BE VERY CAREFUL!"**
Ms. Beeche:	(In an attempt to try and cut her losses), "Your Honor, the government will stipulate on page 20 itself..."
The Court:	(Anticipating what she was about to say, she was quickly cut off at the pass when she was interrupted), **"That it's a meaningless citation, will you stipulate to that too?"**
Ms. Beeche:	**"No!** *I can't stipulate to that."*
The Court:	**"Then, what does it mean if it cites something that IS irrelevant?"**
Ms. Beeche:	"Your Honor, we're looking at the pamphlet as a whole."
The Court:	**"No! No we're not! I'm looking at page 20! You folks wrote this! And it means nothing! Page 20 does NOT illuminate! It's a citation the way we do it in the law... correct? It's a citation or it's a cross-reference! But it doesn't illuminate it in any way, shape or form... does it?"**
Ms. Beeche:	"Your Honor, I gave you the stipulation with regard to page 20. Our argument is that page 20 is part of a section... and it mentions that..."
The Court:	**"Wait a minute..."**
Ms. Beeche:	"But I believe that would be..."

362

The Court:	**"Wait! Wait! No, counsel! Let's look at page 20…"**
Ms. Beeche:	"I stipulated to page 20! And I understand what you're saying about page 20 itself, but…"
The Court:	**"Because we ARE in agreement that we're talking about the English language… and the ordinary meaning of the English language… correct?"**
Ms. Beeche:	"Yes, Your Honor."
The Court:	**"As opposed to a technical meaning."**
Ms. Beeche:	"Your Honor, I believe this whole argument with regard to page 20 goes to whether Mr. Fabler intended to bring in embargoed items or not. But because he didn't…"
The Court:	**"It's NOT intent…"**
Ms. Beeche:	"Because he didn't say anything, it has nothing to do with intent. The issue is…"
The Court:	**"Of course not.***"*
Mr. Shark:	"Your Honor, the argument is that Mr. Fabler DID say something about the book… and it has been confirmed by supervisor Rudemann that Mr. Fabler did mention the book. So intent has to be considered here."
Ms. Beeche:	**"Your Honor, the issue here is the Regulations and what are the Regulations? Nothing else matters!"**
The Court:	**"But the citizen is using your document that you prepared. And he's trying to conform his conduct to what is stated in your document. And your document says '*Products of Cuban***

tobacco may be included if purchased in Cuba, see page 20.' Implying that something on page 20 will qualify or explain the prior sentence! But there's nothing on page 20 that has anything whatever to do with it. Wouldn't you agree with me that this is a mistake in the document?"

Ms. Beeche: **"No, Your Honor! What I would agree is that..."**

The Court: **"Can I see the *current* form of this? Does the *current* form of this have the *same* mistake?"**

Mr. Shark: **"No, Judge! They changed it. And, Your Honor, it was changed less than one month after Mr. Fabler went through Customs and questioned the language..."**

The Court: **"OH! So it was changed after this. Are you familiar, sir, were you involved in the amendment of this document?"**

The Man From OFAC: "I wasn't involved in the production of either of these documents."

The Court: **"So... let's just take a look at the *current* page 6."**

Ms. Beeche: "Your Honor, what I believe the witness' testimony would be relevant towards is that there's a *current* section, and there was an applicable section of 'THE (Cuban) embargo' Regulations which would explicitly..."

The Court: **"I know what the CFR says!"**

Ms. Beeche: "prohibit..."

The Court: **"I KNOW! But the CFR doesn't..."**

Ms. Beeche: "interpretations…"

The Court: **"I'M TALKING! HAVEN'T YOU LEARNED BY NOW THAT YOU DON'T INTERRUPT THE COURT WHEN IT'S TALKING?"**

Ms. Beeche: "Excuse me, Your Honor."

The Court: **"DON'T DO THAT AGAIN!** You do that a lot, you know, **STOP IT! Will YOU STOP IT?"**

Ms. Beeche: "Excuse me, Your Honor."

The Court: **"The fact of the matter is… the traveler isn't given the <u>Code of Federal Regulations</u>. The traveler is given the pamphlet <u>Know Before You Go</u>… correct? Correct!?"**

Ms. Beeche: "I'll stipulate the traveler may request information from either the Customs Service or the Office of Foreign Assets Control…"

The Court: **"That wasn't my question!"**

Ms. Beeche: "No, Your Honor! The traveler wasn't given the CFR…"

The Court: **"And in the…"**

Ms. Beeche: "… regarding his importation."

The Court: **"But the passport, the United States Passport *Specifically* references the document <u>Know Before You Go</u>. Are we agreed on that?"**

Ms. Beeche: "We agree on that."

The Court: **"Correct!? And in either version of the Customs pamphlet <u>Know Before You Go</u>, either in its 1994 or…"**

David Weisenthal

The Man From OFAC: "1997."

The Court: **"...May of 1997 edition, which is in my hand now, it doesn't purport to be a quotation from the <u>Code of Federal Regulations</u>..."**

Ms. Beeche: "No, it doesn't."

The Court: **"...Part 31, correct?"**

Ms. Beeche: "No, it doesn't, Your Honor!   It would be impossible to..."

The Court: **"Of course it would be!   Of course, it would be."**

Ms. Beeche: "directly reference the pamphlet..."

The Court: **"I don't disagree with you on that.**"

Ms Beeche: "...all of the laws Customs enforces."

The Court: **"I agree with you..."**

Mr. Shark: "That just isn't so, Your Honor!"

Ms. Beeche: **"I object, Your Honor."**

Mr. Shark: "Your Honor, if I may interject here.   Customs publishes Customs Publication Number 506.   It's a Customs declaration statement card in brief and it states, and I quote '*This handout is only a brief overview of Customs requirements.   If you want additional information, contact your local Customs office.   You may also call U.S. Customs directly under the Treasury Department listing.*' And this is the part I would emphasize, '*We will be happy to send you a copy of our brochure* **<u>Know Before You Go</u>**, *which describes* **in detail everything** *that you should... know before you go.*'"

366

Ms. Beeche:	**"I object, Your Honor."**
The Court:	"Oh! So there's other literature that supports this ambiguity? Let me see it*!"*
Ms. Beeche:	**"Your Honor...** *I object***! This has nothing to do with this issue!"**
The Shark:	"Your Honor... the whole issue is the government saying the literature doesn't mean what it says. They say the literature isn't the Regulations and the Regulations can't cover everything. However, they tell the citizen the literature IS to be obeyed... because the literature is the **complete** rules and Regulations. And the literature reflects the *current* rules and Regulations... when, in actuality, it doesn't! So what is the traveler to do? Follow what he has been told to follow and believe what he has been told to believe... or follow the rules and Regulations that he doesn't know anything about?"
The Court:	**"Yes... I understand, Mr. Shark. But my question to Mr. Smallhead is... may I infer, if you can answer this... may I infer that the fact there is no longer a reference to a meaningless page 20 suggests that this was reviewed and changed because of an inadequacy of the prior iteration of this? You have any knowledge of that?"**
The Man From OFAC:	"I don't really have any knowledge of the production of this pamphlet."
The Court:	**"Then, what do we need this witness for?"**
Ms. Beeche:	"Your Honor, because I believe he can testify..."
The Court:	***"I CAN READ..."***

Ms. Beeche: "that the OFAC Regulations *specifically* prohibit…"

The Court: **"I KNOW WHAT THEY PROHIBIT!"**

Ms. Beeche: "the giving…"

The Court: **"I don't need this gentleman to read the Code of Federal Regulations. I don't need it! It's NOT foreign law. We don't need an expert. It's U.S. Law. So… I don't need him for that. What I'd have loved is if he'd been knowledgeable in how this thing got prepared, but apparently he's just told me he doesn't."**

As the robed one talked, the man from OFAC started to raise his hand to say something. But, then, he thought better of it. He was afraid to interrupt the court… even if the government's tigress, Ms. Beeche, wasn't. Or, maybe, she just didn't understand that the court should NEVER be interrupted when it's talking. Instead, he lowered his hand and just sat quietly while the judge continued.

Ms. Beeche: "I believe that…"

The Court: **"So… what's his testimony probative of?"**

Ms. Beeche: "Well, I believe we agreed, when he was going to testify, that he'd testify regarding the **Know Before You Go** manual. And to my mind that included whether the pamphlet would be considered according to OFAC's Regulations… as an instruction."

The Court: **"That's a purely legal issue that I'll decide. It's purely a legal issue. As far as its drafting, I mean I'd have loved to have heard from somebody who would have told me about that because I still don't understand it. And you certainly haven't helped me understand this reference to page 20. Nor has the witness…**

because the witness tells me page 20 means some page or pages other than page 20."

Ms. Beeche:

"The government has put forth that the Customs manual **Know Before You Go** references 'THE (Cuban) embargo' in many instances. And whether there's a typo regarding page 20 or not, the reference to 'THE (Cuban) embargo' is listed many times. It's clear if there was a question... further authorization or information should have been sought. And the claimant never sought that information."

The Court:

"**Okay! But I don't need this gentleman to tell me that. Right? Because I can read the Know Before You Go and I can read the Code of Federal Regulations... Part 31 thereof!**"

Ms. Beeche:

"Well, Your Honor, at this point, you're interpreting the claimant's argument to be an argument of, basically, what I believe to be an *estoppel* argument, because the government erroneously published..."

The Court:

"**No! That's not his argument. His legal argument is that it's an instruction within the meaning of Part 31.**"

Ms. Beeche:

"Well, then, I believe the witness could testify..."

The Court:

"**And, that's purely, whether it's an instruction or not...**"

Ms. Beeche:

"As to what..."

The Court:

"**...that's a legal issue.**"

Ms. Beeche:

"...as to what's an instruction *generally* in OFAC. From the OFAC representative, what's an instruction?"

The Court:
"**Well, no! The problem is OFAC and Mr. Smallhead told us this several times. OFAC doesn't prepare this document. Correct?**"

Mr. Shark:
"Object, Your Honor! The witness only stated he wasn't familiar with the production of this document. Not that it wasn't published by OFAC! In fact, he wasn't even with OFAC when either of these documents were published."

Ms. Beeche:
"That's correct, Your Honor."

The Court:
"Mr. Smallhead?"

The Man From OFAC:
"I believe that my office, which is the Chief Counsel's Office, doesn't prepare... and I don't know if anyone in the Office of Foreign Assets Control, my client's office, is involved in the preparation of this document."

The Court:
"**Because this is a Custom's document... correct, sir?**"

The Man From OFAC:
"That's what's stated on it."

The Court:
"I mean, I assume OFAC has its own publications to the public?"

The Man From OFAC:
"Yes! There are publications OFAC offers for the public."

The Court:
"**And I assume they deal with 'THE (Cuban) embargo?'**"

The Man From OFAC:
"Yes! *Specific* ones deal with 'THE (Cuban) embargo.'"

The Court:
"**You have them with you?**"

Ms. Beeche:
"No! We don't... Your Honor!"

370

The Court:	**"So, if, for example, a citizen like Mr. Fabler wanted to get information from OFAC about how to comply with Part 31, he'd go to, I assume, this lay language document?** *"*
The Man From OFAC:	**"Yes!** The documents are available on the *Internet*! And they're available on a fax by demand service and by OFAC online."
The Court:	**"Oh, don't worry about that!** Could you give us the web site? **We'll just look it up on the** *Internet.* *"*
The Man From OFAC:	"Your Honor, the web site is in the revised document."
The Court:	**"Of <u>Know Before You Go</u>?"**
The Man From OFAC:	**"Yes! It's in the May 1997 version."**
The Court:	**"Right!"**
Mr. Shark:	"Your Honor, page 7 directs the citizen to the web site. So, perhaps the court should mark this document and make it a part of the record."
The Court:	**"Mr. Smallhead, is this the web site for the document you're referring to?"**
The Man From OFAC:	"Well, actually… no! Actually, it's been changed since then… because we've redone the web site."
The Court:	**"EXCUSE ME? Then, why don't you just give us THE** *current* **web site… www.ustreas. com, then what?"**
The Man From OFAC:	"Well, ER, ah… I really don't know what it is, but I believe its www.ofac.com at this point in time. However, I'm not sure… that is, I'm not a

371

hundred percent sure on this. I think that perhaps the fax sheets **they** *have* can give the proper number of it! It was recently changed... within the past... few... months."

The Court: **"Changed within the past... few... months... you say? And just how many months ago was it changed exactly? Do you know how long ago it was changed?"**

The Man From OFAC: "Yes!"

The Court: **"Well?"**

The Man From OFAC: "About six to eight months ago... or, maybe, a little longer."

The Court: **"But the web site you just mentioned, the OFAC web site as opposed to the Treasury, I realize OFAC is part of the Treasury. And, didn't you just say it was just changed within the past... few... months? You call six to eight months, and maybe longer, a few? *Just how many more months than eight are we talking about here?"***

The Man From OFAC: "Well, that was an old OFAC web site."

The Court: **"Answer my question please, sir. I asked how many more months than eight are we talking about here?"**

The Man From OFAC: "Well, Your Honor, it could be a few more months than eight."

The Court: **"Sir, I'm asking you again, how many more?"**

The Man From OFAC: "Well, it could be another three to four or more."

The Court:	"Sooo, let me see if I have this right. Your definition of a few months is actually a year or more, right?"
The Man From OFAC:	"Well, Your Honor, to be sure, I'm not sure exactly when it was changed. I'm sorry…"
The Court:	*"And this old web site would have told a citizen or any interested person, but it's of interest to us here, a U.S. citizen, in lay language about 'THE (Cuban) embargo?'"*
The Man From OFAC:	"Well… yes!? And no!"
The Court:	"Yes! AND *NO?* How do you mean yes and no?"
The Man From OFAC:	"Yes it's in plain language. However, it's in a text script. Which means you'd have to be able to decipher the script in the computer! If the computer can read it, it's of plain language. Yes!"
Mr. Shark:	"Your Honor… this is exactly what we're talking about. They double-talk. EVERYTHING they say is yes AND no! It's here, but it's not here. It's there, but it's not there. You can read it, but you can't read it. They give a web site they say can be checked out, but when it's asked for… suddenly, it's a different web site. And they're not even sure what and where the web site is! Or how to find it! How much more are we going to put up with this?"
Ms. Beeche:	"Your Honor, if we could go to the first page of the document?"
The Court:	"C-3 is the May 1997 iteration?"
Mr. Shark:	"Yes, Your Honor… it is! And I'd asked that we would move that into evidence."

The Court: "Yes! That will be admitted. And what did you just hand me? Is this the web site, Ms. Beeche?"

Ms. Beeche: "Yes... I believe it is... Your Honor! It was available in April 1997... regarding what was necessary to be known about 'THE (Cuban) embargo.' And that was referenced in both... the **Know Before You Go** manual... and the passport!"

Mr. Shark: **"I object, Your Honor! There they go again! The May 1997 edition was NOT available in April 1997... by its date that edition wasn't available until the following month from when this all took place..."**

The Court: **"Yes, I know, Mr. Shark! It seems Ms. Beeche has misspoken ONCE again. So what's the phone number of the fax on demand?"**

The Man From OFAC: "I don't know... off the top of my head, that is."

The Court: *"Is it 410-962-4141?"*

The Man From OFAC: **"No!"**

The Court: **"You know that it's not the number, but you don't know what the number is!? So I guess this number is where it's going to!?"**

The Man From OFAC: "Yeah... I would guess so! That's where it lists faxes were sent. I believe this may have been a copy of one that I faxed too."

The Court: **"But, you said, there's a fax on demand number... is that correct, sir?"**

The Man From OFAC: **"Oh yes! At least there was... at that time.** This is also, this is the same document as one of the ones available on the web site and these are constantly updated."

Mr. Shark: "I object, Your Honor! There WERE NO faxes on demand AT THAT TIME, EITHER! Once again, this is ALL poppycock! The government is sending out misleading information. They're double-talking ALL the time! I know the fax number, but I don't know it. It's a copy of something that the man from OFAC faxed, but he doesn't know what number he faxed it from... although he knows it's NOT the number. They don't want to give out the information YOU'RE asking them to give you. And if they won't give it to you, you CAN imagine the difficulty the average U.S. citizen has, will have... and has had."

The Court: "Yes, I'm aware of that. Okay, you say these are constantly updated?"

The Man From OFAC: "Yes!"

The Court: "So, for example, the Executive Branch yesterday made an announcement about some changes. And that those changes went after compliance with the Administrative Procedure Act! When they become effective, they will go immediately onto your fax on demand at the web site?"

The Man From OFAC: "We're currently trying to put that together. It's virtually immediate... once we publish Regulations. However, they're available to be picked up at the Federal Register Meeting Room. They usually immediately put them online as well."

The Court: "But MY POINT IS, after the comment period they become final and all that stuff, once they're final and therefore legally effective,

they will INSTANTLY be updated on both your web site and your fax on demand site?"

The Man From OFAC: "I don't know how fast they put it up. I don't know if it's instantly! Certainly, we try to do it as quickly as possible. Also, as you may know, we've been recently putting out the actual Regulations. However, this fax sheet and other fax sheets like this are installations of the Regulations and **aren't** meant to be legally binding. They're just explanations of what the Regulations say."

The Court: **"But if you put out the ACTUAL Regulations, then the citizen wouldn't need any explanations... would they? I mean the Regulations are THE Regulations! Aren't they? And do you tell the citizen that what you're putting out isn't legally binding?"**

The Man From OFAC: "Well...yes. And, no... Your Honor! I mean... the Regulations are being placed on the site as they happen. And publications of explanations of the Regulations are also placed on the web site as they occur. But they're not meant to be legally binding. They are just explanations! And I'm not sure what disclaimers are placed on the publications!"

The Court: **"I SEEEEEEeeeee! Okay... thank you sir."**

Ms. Beeche: "The government would move Exhibit 12 into evidence."

The Court: "Yeah, sure... G-12 is admitted."

Mr. Shark: "Judge..."

The Court: **"G-12 is THE *CURRENT* iteration of the fax on demand?"**

Ms. Beeche: **"Yes... it is, Your Honor.**

Mr. Shark:	"Your Honor, with respect to Exhibit 12, counsel for the government has indicated that this was in existence in April, 1997. And, I just note that although there's some indication here that they say it is so please note that in accordance with an announcement made by President Clinton on March 20th, the Regulations have been amended. I don't think that the statement that the Assistant..."
The Court:	"On its face it couldn't have been..."
Mr. Shark:	"Because what I see here is the third from the last page of the exhibit... dated May 13th."
The Man From OFAC:	"If I may, Your Honor..."
The Court:	**"What page? Yes!** The letter, on the letterhead of the Department of the Treasury, signed by R. Richard Newcomb, Director of the Office of Foreign Assets Control."
Mr. Shark:	**"So... it would seem that this was when this was actually published... and again the government has been caught in another lie!"**
The Court:	**"On May 13, 1998."**
Mr. Shark:	**"Which, once again, is AFTER the travel here."**
Ms. Beeche:	**"Your Honor, the witness has testified that this type of publication was available in April of 1997."**
The Court:	**"Yes, I'm aware that was his testimony... wasn't it Mr. Smallhead?"**
The Man From OFAC:	"That was my testimony. I think I may have mis-spoke before!"

377

The Court:	**"Then, Mr. Shark, it will be admitted for illustrative purposes… only. Okay? Fair enough?"**
Mr. Shark:	"Fair enough, Judge. But please note all this misspeaking the government does. And they ONLY acknowledge their error(s)… when they are caught in their lies!"
Ms. Beeche:	"I object, Your Honor! Would… given the absence of the definition of the word instruction in the Regulations themselves… would you permit the witness to testify as to OFAC's understanding of what an instruction is?"
The Court:	**"Is he qualified to testify as to that?"**
The Man From OFAC:	"If I may, I am…"
Mr. Shark:	"I certainly don't think so, Your Honor. Since it's not a definition of…"
The Court:	**"The word instruction in Part 31… this is legal argument, I think, anyway. The word instruction within Part 31 is not defined… are we agreed on that?"**
Ms. Beeche:	"Yes, Your Honor."
The Court:	**"There is no separate definition in the Definition Section… correct?"**
The Man From OFAC:	"For an instruction… no."
The Court:	**"And the fact that this gentleman didn't write Part 31, is there a…"**
The Man From OFAC:	"I'm sorry, Your Honor…"

The Court:	**"Is there an informational release or anything of an explanatory nature that OFAC has published that would illuminate this?"**
The Man From OFAC:	"There's a section of the Regulations themselves that would illuminate this."
The Court:	**"That's legal argument! So, he doesn't have to testify! It's NOT foreign law. He's NOT competent!"**
Ms. Beeche:	"Then, in the event that's the case, I'd just ask if we could be able to write final briefs… in this case."
The Court:	**"We're going to have a little oral argument and then I'm going to decide this case. Any Cross-examination?"**
Mr. Shark:	"Yes, Your Honor. Mr. Smallhead, when did you first become associated with OFAC?"
The Man From OFAC:	"April… 1998."
Mr. Shark:	"April, 1998!? And that was **AFTER** 1994?"
The Man From OFAC:	"Yes."
Mr. Shark:	"And that was **AFTER** April 1997?"
The Man From OFAC:	"Yes."
Mr. Shark:	**"Sooooo…….. YOU REALLY DON"T HAVE ANY KNOWLEDGE ABOUT THE 1994 VERSION of the <u>Know Before You Go</u> manual, do you?"**
The Man From OFAC:	"Well, I've read it."

Mr. Shark:	**"But, as far as how or who published it or the wording of it... you have NO *specific* knowledge of it?"**
The Man From OFAC:	"Again, I've read it!"
Mr. Shark:	**"You're NOT answering my question! You have NO direct or indirect knowledge as to the printing, wording or publishing of the 1994 version of the manual... do you?"**
The Man From OFAC:	"No! But, as I've said... I read it!"
The Shark:	**"And you have NO direct or indirect knowledge about the May 1997 version either... do you?"**
The Man From OFAC:	"Well, I've read that one also."
The Shark:	**"Once again... you're NOT answering my question! You have NO direct or indirect knowledge about the publishing of the May 1997 version, either... do you?"**
The Man From OFAC:	"No! But as I've said... I read it!"
The Shark:	"Yes... and Mr. Fabler read it also! His Honor has read it too... and I've read it. But none of us have any direct or indirect knowledge about who and / or how it got published. And we're talking about the 1994 version here... as well as the 1997 version. You know, Your Honor, this whole thing with this witness is one big fat joke. They don't want anyone to know anything about this. Not you, not me, and certainly... not Mr. Fabler! I have no further questions."
The Court:	"Thank you, Mr. Smallhead. It's lunchtime. We have to take a luncheon recess. I'd like to have brief closing arguments from everyone because

I want to try and decide this... this week, okay? Thanks."

Ms. Beeche: "Your Honor? May I Re-Cross the witness?

The Court: **"No!   I said its lunch-time!   Don't YOU listen?"**

Mr. Shark: "What time?"

The Court: "Two o'clock."

David Weisenthal

Mano a Mano y Shark to Shark...

***

Five minutes before noon the court recessed for lunch. In two hours and five minutes, 'THE case' would reconvene. Both my sharks declined Lady Grace's offer to eat with us and another shark we knew. His name was Fillmor Cupps. Fillmor was a caffeine junkie who drank coffee like there was no tomorrow. But only the high-test kind! The higher the kick, the mellower he became. And he had no use for the no-lead stuff. Besides being dead in the water, there were issues with the chemicals used to strip the beans of their strength and potency. Before his cup would run dry, he'd fill it up to the brim again with more.

Fillmor came to witness the proceedings first hand. His business involved swimming with a school of sharks who entertained people whose business was entertaining the masses. Fillmor fancied seeing history happen... hence a one-day absence from a life filled with boring daily functions.

Fillmor suggested the three of us eat at a greasy spoon diner near the courthouse. Walking out the courtroom door, I saw the g'ment lady-shark leaving the building accompanied by the government's three witnesses... the two Customs agents and the man from OFAC. Conspicuously absent from the group was that D. Pete Animen ringer shark whose presence was to make the buck stop with him.

Out of the corner of my eye something caught my attention. I turned and saw the bulldog shark disappear though the door that led into His Honor's, the judge's, private chamber. I thought how odd. I also thought that was illegal. But I didn't think it meant anything other than what it was. However, little is as it is... at least, when it comes to dealing with the government. I've never believed in coincidence... and, maybe, if I had followed my instincts I wouldn't have been where I was at that time in my life. And, maybe, I was exactly where I was.

All though lunch I kept thinking about how that Animen ringer shark had faded into nothingness as His Honor's, the judge's, chamber door closed behind him. I wondered what their conversation concerned. But being a guest in the big city of brotherly love from some small town of a weird bird he probably was just looking for a name of a good place to eat. Maybe, he

382

needed advice on a case he'd been working on that had no bearing on the case he was working on. Then again, maybe, I had it all wrong. Maybe, His Honor, the judge was headed out of town, somewhere down south... and he just wanted to know how to get to where he wanted to go. Maybe, where he wanted to go was an Oriole nest. Who knew? I knew I didn't. And only those two would ever know.

Sometime during lunch Lady Grace asked Fillmor when he thought His Honor, the judge, would be handing back those depressed deprived Cubanos. She thought it obvious a ruling would be forthcoming in our favor... and she hoped it would be quick. Kind of like a TKO in the 2nd round! Fillmor said His Honor, the judge, would first have to make a ruling. But he didn't think the ruling he'd make would be until sometime within the following few days. He based that on what Freeman Rhule had ruled at the beginning of court. And he said that even if I won, the government would most definitely appeal the ruling. He also felt those poor defenseless Cubanos wouldn't be free until long after any ruling came... if ever. We finished lunch by the time the time had run. Then, it was time to run back to court.

We walked into the courtroom and saw we were the last to arrive. The last that is, except for His Honor, the judge. No sooner did we take our seats when Freeman Ruhle's private lounge door opened... and everyone immediately stood. And I just wanted to know if His Honor, the judge, had a hidden camera in the courtroom somewhere. I mean, how did he know we had just arrived?

I looked over at the government side and saw the look on the face of that D. Pete Animen land shark and I saw the look of a man who knew he couldn't lose... or, maybe, wouldn't lose. I knew he knew something I didn't... and wondered whether his knowledge took place during the lunch he never ate. Then, I looked at His Honor, the judge, as he sat down... and I saw the look in his eyes as he looked at that bulldog D. Pete Animen ringer-shark. And I didn't like the look I saw. For it was the look of guilt... or conspiracy. It seemed to be just another peak at a long line of government conspiracies.

The Court: "Be seated everyone! Am I correct that the government is done with its witnesses?"

Ms. Beeche: "Yes, Your Honor."

The Court:	"And there is no other witness you want to call?"

Ms. Beeche: "No… there is not, Your Honor."

The Court: "Then, is there a rebuttal?"

Mr. Shark: "No, Your Honor."

The Court: "In that case I will hear a brief closing argument. Mr. Shark, come to the lectern! Won't you do that?"

Mr. Shark: "Yes, Judge! The first issue I'd like to address is the declaration issue we took testimony on. Frankly, I think once we get beyond that, the more substantive issue is the one underneath that. The declaration issue as I see it is very simple. My client has testified, and you had the opportunity to observe him, and I really think it comes down to credibility. It's credibility that you have to make as the jury… so to speak."

The Court: "Yes!"

Mr. Shark: "Therefore, what I ask you to do, in support of one version versus the other, is to look at the documentary evidence. And the key documentary evidence, from my viewpoint, is the declaration page and that little notation on the upper right-hand corner that corresponds exactly to what my client testified to. That is… that he was stopped by a Customs agent who directed him toward the secondary site! Add in the contradictory statements about discussing the **Know Before You Go** book that night by the two Customs agents… and, I think, you have to believe what Mr. Fabler says happened that night."

The Court: "That he said he had alcohol and tobacco products to declare."

Mr. Shark:	"Exactly! So, as far as we're concerned, my client is concerned, that declaration issue, and you've heard his position in terms of the oral declaration versus the written declaration, and I know the government doesn't want to hear that, but I really think it comes down to a credibility issue. Agent Rudemann candidly testified that marking was put on there by a roving agent. We established the roving agent was never identified, even though we attempted to identify him. And that then caused him to go to the secondary person. In terms of the secondary person, you had the opportunity to observe both witnesses."
The Court:	"Didn't inspector Rudemann tell us that if there is a pat down, there is somebody else there?"
Mr. Shark:	"Yes."
The Court:	"And we have not identified either him or her, have we?"
Mr. Shark:	"No... Your Honor! We haven't! I don't think they have identified him either. I think somebody mentioned the name of an agent named Notmi. We just found that out by somebody recently."
The Court:	"But in any event, I haven't heard from that person."
Mr. Shark:	"Right! You haven't heard from that person. Now, what I submit, Your Honor, is that beyond that, if you just look at the fact that he was at a secondary location... well, what was he really doing there? I mean, what he was doing there was, as the agent candidly testified at some point, was that everybody there was subject to having declared something. So, I think we're beyond that issue... without even having to consider his testimony. I don't think you have to find that

David Weisenthal

agent Narco was either remiss or not accurate in his testimony either, because I think that once that declaration is made to…"

The Court: "The roving agent."

Mr. Shark: "Yes… the roving agent! And the declaration issue in terms of the oral versus the written… although you might have some difficulty with the oral versus written. But beyond that I don't know what else there is. So I'd leave that determination for The Court. I feel what Mr. Fabler's intention was has clearly been demonstrated as well as what he was operating under. I think the more significant issue here, Your Honor, is this book **Know Before You Go**."

The Court: **"Right."**

Mr. Shark: "Right! And I don't think I could've cross-examined that individual from Washington, the OFAC person, any better than you did in terms of that… because I really wanted to find out too. In our Discovery, I asked that Lars Titon Helmsman, and many other people from the inception of this case… when my client first came to me and he brought me this book and asked, 'What do you think?' And I said, 'It looks to me like your right.' Then, we did some research and went beyond that… and, frankly, I think they're stuck with this. However, the problem I have is that the government is saying Customs is different than Treasury and Treasury is different than OFAC. Although, I'm an expert from OFAC… and OFAC says you can't do this and you can't do that."

The Court: "Aren't both a part of the Treasury? However, one is OFAC and the other is Customs."

386

Mr. Shark:	"That **is** correct. I guess the problem I have is that the government hasn't produced anyone who can explain the page 20 error! And if you just look at a fair reading of where it says…"
The Court:	**"I think it certainly bears the reading Mr. Fabler gave it. I agree with you!"**
Mr. Shark:	"Yes, but I think it even goes beyond that."
The Court:	**"Yes… I understand. But does that do the trick?"**
Mr. Shark:	"I think it goes beyond that… yes! It says '*Products of Cuban tobacco may be included, if purchased in Cuba.*' I mean that, to me, actually says you can do it. And I think that beyond whether or not he should've done anything more or whether he should've done this or he should've done that, I think if you just look at that, I think it tells the average person that this is what you're allowed to do."
The Court:	"Let's assume I agree with you. My question to you is, does that get you over the goal line?"
Mr. Shark:	"I think it can get us over the goal line… yes! I think that…"
The Court:	"Because I think 31 CFR does not say that."
Mr. Shark:	"Well, I can argue that."
The Court:	"Because your client didn't have a license from OFAC to bring goods back from Cuba, we are all agreed on that."
Mr. Shark:	"Well, I think two things. The first argument we made… deals with instructions, and that, therefore, this then becomes…"

The Court:	"But that's the instruction contemplated in 31 CFR. That's your legal argument?"
Mr. Shark:	"Exactly. I think, and I am no expert on Constitutional Law or statutory interpretation, but I remember a couple of things. First, if it's not in the definitions, the word has the normal meaning and instructions are instructions. And this, to me, is an instruction. So I think the argument, although the government pooh-poohs it and says, 'Oh no, there's no way this could be an instruction,' I think it could be... clearly. And going beyond that in 560, I think... it deals with this fully hosted business which, again, is **not** *specifically* defined. I think that is where, under the statute, my client is on ALL fours and totally appropriate. The government has stipulated that Mr. Dueling paid for his expenses and all of that. So that, again, isn't in dispute. And that GAVE him a license... implied, maybe. But a license all the same."
The Court:	"But Mr. Shark, if this were, I mean you and I have met before in criminal cases."
Mr. Shark:	"Yes, Your Honor."
The Court:	"Now, were this a criminal case where we'd have a *mens rea* requirement, your argument would be completely persuasive. But this isn't a criminal case... correct?"
Mr. Shark:	"No!"
The Court:	"So, therefore, it would seem that in reading 31 CFR there is no *mens rea* required. You either have a license or you don't."
Mr. Shark:	"But I think that the 560 G, is it?"

The Court:

"Do you not agree with me, that given the nature of this proceeding and the law we're operating under, it's after all as agent Narco said, it's a revenue producing part, it's the U.S. Treasury. And in this aspect it would appear to me that there is no *mens rea* required. Either you comply or you don't comply. I certainly am sympathetic… and I think your position and Mr. Fabler's position has a lot going for it in terms of what more could've been done without having a law degree? Because I think, as I perhaps suggested in my questions of counsel from OFAC, I think the 1994 version certainly bears the reading Mr. Fabler gave it. But my question, and I haven't decided the issue, is does that do the trick in this statutory regime? A very technical question."

Mr. Shark:

"It is! And I just, for the purposes of the position I take, have to disagree with that."

The Court:

"I understand. Your position is that that constitutes the instructions."

Mr. Shark:

"Absolutely."

The Court:

"Within the meaning of 31 CFR."

Mr. Shark:

"And therefore, obviating any license, and then that in conjunction with the fully hosted aspect of the statute… Judge… nowhere…"

The Court:

"Does it matter?"

Mr. Shark:

"Nowhere in the statute is there one of these big X's that says you can't do this."

The Court:

"No… I agree with you! It says *generally* and then et cetera."

Mr. Shark:

"And I think that is part of the problem. Although, they corrected it a little bit in their revised pamphlet, I don't think enough. I think what really needs to be done is for the government to take a whole new look at this. I mean when you think back, when I was in the third or fourth grade, my understanding of why we wouldn't, or couldn't, deal with Castro was because of Communism and all that. And I guess the bottom line on this is that..."

The Court: "So you were in the third or fourth grade when 'THE embargo' came about?"

Mr. Shark: "Yes."

The Court: "You make me sick."

Mr. Shark: "I guess my point is that this really changes all the time... depending upon what President we have."

The Court: "As recently as yesterday."

Mr. Shark: "Right! And when the Pope can go to Cuba, and he's allowed to go there, and get Cuban cigars and when companies like Nike or Coke or Philip Morris are allowed to employ slave labor and things like that... what are we doing with all this? This is ridiculous! These people in Cuba are, you know, this is a craft... rolling cigars and things of that nature. It's crazy because what they do is turn the whole thing around and say we can't support Castro, but those poor people have the ability to overtake Castro... if they really wanted to. And if Castro isn't there, then maybe this thing wouldn't happen, but it's just all backwards!"

The Court: "If I were a legislator or..."

Mr. Shark: "Judge, you just hurt my jury nullification argument."

The Court:	"Juries may be able to do that. I'm not sure I can because of something called the U.S. Court of Appeals that can nullify what I do, right?"
Mr. Shark:	"Understood!"
The Court:	"It's a very interesting point you've made. And it is one that is worthy of careful consideration. Let me hear from our friend from New York!"
Mr. Shark:	"Thank you."
The Court:	"Or our friend from Baltimore."
D. Pete Animen:	"If it may please the Court, Judge, I wasn't in the third grade when 'THE embargo' was placed into effect…"
The Court:	"What grade were you in?"
D. Pete Animen:	"Let's see, it was 1959… so, I was thirteen!"
The Court:	"Pardon me?"
D. Pete Animen:	"Thirteen."
The Court:	"That's better."
Mr. Shark:	"Your Honor!? 'THE embargo' wasn't enacted until 1963… not 1959. In 1959, Fidel Castro took power from Batista, but 'THE embargo, didn't begin then."
D. Pete Animen:	"Judge, what difference does the date 'THE embargo' started make? The point here is that the U.S. alleges three basis for forfeiture. The first two counts are pretty much tied together with whether the merchandise was declared or not. I believe the evidence you've heard today from agent Narco was that the claimant arrived at his station with a written declaration.

391

He testified he went through each and every one of those questions to which the claimant responded he didn't have anything to declare. Then, agent Narco conducted his search of Mr. Fabler's luggage and found the cigars in his bags. Subsequently, he found on his person additional merchandise. And it seems to go all directly counter to the argument of the claimant that he declared all the merchandise if he found…"

The Court: **"But didn't he say he declared it to somebody who never testified. I mean, apparently through everyone's good efforts we still haven't found the roving agent."**

D. Pete Animen: "Correct, Judge. I understand, but…"

The Court: **"So, he did speak to somebody before he spoke to agent Narco… correct?"**

D. Pete Animen: "That's correct, Judge, he probably did. Obviously what happened in that conversation we don't know, but that fact that…"

The Court: **"Excuse me! So, therefore, his testimony about saying he had alcohol and tobacco products to declare is un-rebutted."**

D. Pete Animen: "You're right, Your Honor! However, when he came to the station and spoke to agent Narco, assuming he told agent Narco he had these tobacco products, there wouldn't have been any need for agent Narco to take him back for a pat down and ultimately find, as was testified, these cigarillos on his person. They presumably would've been undeclared… otherwise, he would've said yes. I have these and pulled them out like a reasonable interpretation of what the testimony said happened."

The Court:	"But didn't agent Narco say no conversation occurred with Mr. Faber about the <u>Know Before You Go</u> pamphlet? And didn't we hear supervisor Rudemann say that a conversation DID occur between agent Narco and Mr. Fabler about that book?"
D. Pete Animen:	"No, not exactly, Your Honor. However, it's irrelevant anyhow! The testimony was cigarillos or whatever were found on his person AND there would've been no need to search his luggage or person IF he'd readily admitted them freely… as has been the testimony!"
The Court:	"Excuse me, sir… but it IS relevant! See! This IS a credibility contest… isn't it?"
D. Pete Animen:	"Yes, Judge… it is."
The Court:	"So, I have to take everything into account. And if agent Narco was NOT candid about his testimony of what occurred that night with Mr. Fabler, then I have to take that into consideration. Besides, agent Narco said the reason for the search of his person was because he found some substance that tested positive for THC in his eyeglass case. Whether he said this or that or didn't say this or that made no difference. So, I think I've heard everything I need to on credibility. Why don't you address the issues I was just talking to Mr. Shark about."
D. Pete Animen:	"Very good, Judge."
The Court:	"Because the thing that's most troubling about that, it seems to me, is that, at least, the 1994 version, as written, was, at least, to some extent gibberish… was it not? Because it made a reference to a page that added nothing, but confusion."

393

D. Pete Animen:

"I have to disagree with you on that, Your Honor."

The Court:

"And do you disagree with me also that that document, which after all every U.S. traveler is directed to that document whenever he or she opens their passport, is *specifically* referenced in everybody's passport... right?"

D. Pete Animen:

"Yes, it does... Judge."

The Court:

"So, therefore, the U.S. State Department who issues the passport assisted the Customs Service in highlighting the importance of this document to the American traveler. Now, what I find troubling here is that this document, as it existed at the time Mr. Fabler used it, certainly bears the reading by itself, within its four corners, bears the reading that Mr. Fabler gave it... wouldn't you agree?"

D. Pete Animen:

"I disagree, Your Honor!"

The Court:

"But it says, and I'm quoting the book now, it says, '*Not more than one hundred cigars or 200 cigarettes (one carton) may be included in your duty-free exemption. Products of Cuban tobacco may be included in your exemption, if purchased in Cuba. See page 20.*' Now can we agree that the words, at least, say what they say?"

D. Pete Animen:

"No, Your Honor, we can't!"

The Court:

"We can't? Then, please read the section titled 'Cigars and Cigarettes' on page 6 in the <u>Know Before You Go</u> pamphlet... of the 1994 version, sir."

D. Pete Animen: *"'Not more than one hundred cigars or 200 cigarettes (one carton) may be included in your duty-free exemption. Products of Cuban tobacco may be included in your exemption, if purchased in Cuba. See page 20.'"*

The Court: **"Now, sir, can we agree that the words, at least, say what the words say?"**

D. Pete Animen: "No, Your Honor... we can't!"

The Court: **"We can't? But you just read for yourself the words in the book that..."**

D. Pete Animen: "I know, Your Honor! But those words do NOT mean what they say!"

The Court: **"That wasn't the question, sir. I'll decide what those words mean! What I want from you is whether you can, at least, agree that those words say what those words say."**

D. Pete Animen: "I'd agree to the point that... where it says that... as far as the pamphlet says, that tobacco products from Cuba may be declared, see this page. Now, admittedly..."

The Court: **"As an English sentence that sounds like giving permission. And that's why I wanted to go to page 20 to see how that would limit it. But, of course, page 20 did NOT help at all."**

D. Pete Animen: "I think your take on this is the whole problem with this. First of all, if you look at the cover of the **Know Before You Go** book, it says *specifically* 'Customs hints for returning residents.'"

The Court: "Right!?"

D. Pete Animen: "Then, if you go to the inside cover, as we heard the testimony, the Commissioner of Customs at the time, George Weise says, '*I hope this booklet will help you understand our mission is to protect your interests. Please read it carefully and don't hesitate to contact us if there is anything you would like clarified.*'"

The Court:

"I know! But, look, let's be practical here. This book, would you agree with me, is intended for the lay reader?"

D. Pete Animen:

"Yes, Judge, it is."

The Court:

"The declaration form, one of which I filled out myself this past September, okay, is handed to you when you come into U.S. airspace. At least, that's when British Airways gives it to you and you get it and read it... and you do your best to fill it out. But again, most people who get this don't have lawyers sitting beside them and AREN'T themselves lawyers, and certainly they AREN'T tax lawyers or people skilled in this area... as our friend from OFAC and you are. And they have to make sense out of this document. They're sitting in an airplane and they don't have counsel... so they fill it out. Now, literally speaking, what Mr. Fabler put in his answer to number 14 is NOT incorrect in that the form says if you have nothing to declare, write zero... and he did NOT write a zero there. My whole problem with the line of questioning Ms. Beeche was getting into with Mr. Fabler was that it was as though she felt that Mr. Fabler was supposed to be a tax lawyer reading this. That's asking too much of the average American traveler... is it not?"

D. Pete Animen:

"Well, I think you may be overstating it a bit because as an experienced traveler, and he's testified he's an experienced traveler, and that he's filled out these things a lot. He's also able to read... and where it says to put a zero, a line was put there. And as it was brought out in the testimony where he didn't identify something else as a middle initial or something else at the top of the form of the line in front of him, the line meant nothing. The indication being that when he drew the line through at the bottom, even though it's not a zero, it indicated being consistent with what's up there."

The Court:

"Except, I mean, reading it literally in favor of the traveler, he didn't misrepresent himself there... because had he written a zero, the Service would be correct. But he did NOT write a zero! He just put an ambiguous line, whatever that means... which is nothing more than the ambiguous statements made in the Know Before You Go pamphlet. You want us to accept those ambiguous statements, but you don't want us to accept his ambiguous statement. That seems, at least, to me, to be trying to have it both ways... sir. Besides the form DOES say right on its face on the back, '*U.S. residents are normally entitled to a duty-free exemption of $400 on these items accompanying them.*' His understanding was, and I don't think it's disputed that, at least, in Havana the products were worth less than one hundred dollars. So a lay person reading that, it seems to me, thinks perhaps the right thing to put there is a line. Remember, he didn't know the exact amount because he didn't buy them... Herr Dueling did! And so maybe the only answer is to put a line there, isn't it, for a lay person?"

D. Pete Animen:

"Well, I guess if you read that, I'd have to go back again, to where it said what's the value of what you have... you've got to put that in. But he didn't put anything in there. If it's a zero... put a zero. He had merchandise on his person which had value. He testified that."

The Court:	**"But he didn't know what the amount was because he didn't buy it. They were gifts. See, that's the point. When I filled this out, coming back from London, I knew what things cost because I paid for them and I duly listed, you know, shirt, what have you. And I made the exchange rate calculation. But, you know, I'm a bit better trained to read these things than a lay person."**
D. Pete Animen:	"Well, if I may, Judge, it would seem then…"
The Court:	**"And I figured I couldn't get in trouble with your service if I listed on the second page there… if I was too inclusive. I knew I couldn't get in trouble, if I was too inclusive. But, my goodness, I've been in the legal profession a long time. So, I'm used to reading things like this. But this is meant for ordinary unskilled, non-legally skilled people to read… correct?"**
D. Pete Animen:	"That's correct, Judge."
The Court:	**"Just as <u>Know Before You Go</u> is intended for such individuals. Every American citizen's passport tells them to get this… correct?"**
D. Pete Animen:	"That's correct, Judge."
The Court:	**"The question then is, let's assume and I may be willing to assume that you're right and Mr. Fabler is wrong, does his state of mind make any difference? And isn't your argument that that doesn't make any difference?"**
D. Pete Animen:	"That's correct! It doesn't make any difference at all!"
The Court:	**"Because this isn't a m*ens rea* statute."**

D. Pete Animen:	"That's correct."
The Court:	**"But what about Mr. Shark's argument, and let me at the risk of putting words into his mouth do this. Say that the word instructions in the Regulations is proper to be construed as to include <u>Know Before You Go</u> as an instruction because in the ordinary meaning of the word and *generally* speaking, that's a good rule of construction that you use words in their ordinary meaning. Do I fairly characterize your argument, Mr. Shark?"**
Mr. Shark:	"Absolutely, Judge, Yes, it does. At least, one of my arguments… anyway."
The Court:	"What's your response to that?"
D. Pete Animen:	"My response to that, Judge, is it's a legal response. And I'm going to address that."
The Court:	**"I know it's a legal inquiry. But what's your response to as if it were the statutory construction even though it's not…"**
D. Pete Animen:	"The statutory…"
The Court:	**"Statutory… A regulatory, the regulatory construction by saying this instruction should read in its common ordinary meaning, and that <u>Know Before You Go</u> is such an instruction?"**
D. Pete Animen:	"Assuming arguendo that this is an instruction of some sort, the Office of Foreign Assets Control Regulations at 31 CFR 515.502…"
The Court:	**"Right!"**
D. Pete Animen:	"Talks very *specifically* in Subparagraph (b), '*No regulation, ruling, instruction, or license authorizes a transaction prohibited under this*

part unless the regulation, ruling, instruction, or
license is issued by the Treasury Department,'
and well, agreed, it is."

The Court: **"This IS issued by the United States Department of the Treasury!"**

D. Pete Animen: "That's right."

The Court: **"And not by OFAC!?"**

D. Pete Animen: "But it is the next part of that that says, and *specifically* refers to this part. AND **nowhere** in that document does it *specifically* refer to the Cuban Assets Control Regulations. Therefore, by the control regulation itself, even if you were to determine or find that this is an instruction, it doesn't give license to bring the stuff in."

The Court: **"Well, that's one reading of it! However, my problem is, I thought you were going to say that it's not an instruction because it wasn't issued by OFAC."**

D. Pete Animen: "I was saying arguendo, Judge."

The Court: **"I mean, you'd agree that this wasn't issued by OFAC. We were told by a gentleman who ought to know it wasn't issued by OFAC. It was issued by U.S. Customs Service, which like OFAC happens to be a part of the Department of the Treasury."**

D. Pete Animen: "No, I didn't say this doesn't rise to the level, at all, of an instruction. As it says by the cover..."

The Court: "What were the instructions then?"

D. Pete Animen: "We don't give instructions of Customs."

The Court: "Are there any instructions anywhere?"

D. Pete Animen: "I'm told by OFAC that they haven't issued anything which they *specifically* call an instruction."

The Court: "So, therefore, that's surplusage in the Regulations?"

D. Pete Animen: "My understanding is that it's boilerplate to include anything that they might issue."

The Court: **"Is there such a thing as boilerplate in the Regulations?"**

D. Pete Animen: "I'm not making legal argument, Judge. I was just saying that when it was drafted I have no personal knowledge as to how the Regulations were enacted."

The Court: **"They have boilerplate in contracts, but as far as I know there is NO boilerplate in statutes and Regulations. Every word has to be given effect."**

D. Pete Animen: "Judge, I'm not making legal argument. I'm making a factual argument. That was, I just heard that. But I think that if they issued anything which was *specificcally* a Regulation and very clearly we've done that, or a ruling, opinions that come out…"

The Court: **"Have there been any rulings construing what are instructions, as our friend from OFAC answered in the negative?"**

D. Pete Animen: "My understanding is there's not. I checked to see what I could find, and I couldn't find anything. Nothing was said and talked about an instruction coming from OFAC."

The Court:	"Because in the Customs area, I assume there are such things as in the OFAC area. I assume there are rulings that one can get as one does from the other branch of the U.S. Treasury!?"
D. Pete Animen:	"I'd assume so, but I don't know that for a fact."
The Court:	"Okay… anything else?"
D. Pete Animen:	"Yes, Judge. I think also going back to the pamphlet, just briefly, as the pamphlet says, *'If you need clarification, you can contact the Customs Service.'* You were confused…"
The Court:	**"How do you do that from an airplane?"**
D. Pete Animen:	"Well, he testified he had this book long before he took his trip to Cuba. He got it on a previous trip. Presumably at some point, and he's testified that he read the thing, I mean if he had any questions at all, he could've called or he could have simply not have brought in the merchandise."
Mr. Fabler:	"Your Honor, I wasn't confused in any way, shape, form or manner what-so-ever. The words meant what I read them to mean! I mean, I can read the English language!"
The Court:	"Mr. Fabler, please, Mr. D. Pete Animen has the floor."
Mr. Fabler:	"I'm sorry Your Honor. But I resent his misrepresenting my testimony."
The Court:	**"Now, crediting Mr. Fabler's testimony as I think we must, certainly at this point, when he went to Jamaica he had no intention of going to Cuba… it was Herr Dueling's suggestion on the occasion of his birthday. So, why would he even inquire as to an issue that would NOT have crossed his mind when he was on**

U.S. soil? Is it your position that what he should've done, when Dueling suggested his going to Havana, is to have said, Ah great idea, but I've got to make a call to area code 202 or whatever that number was on the passport? Is that a practical suggestion at a point like that? I mean this is a serendipity here of what occurred to Mr. Fabler."

D. Pete Animen: "It would seem to me to be reasonable, Judge, if he has the pamphlet, which he said he had, and he comes to this ambiguity, if he's not in a position to call Customs, it would seem very reasonable that he would…"

The Court: **"Well, here's my problem. And this gets us back to this G-d-awful 1994 version… because he didn't think there was any ambiguity! I mean he's testified to that and just reiterated it for us all to hear! And, to be honest with you, to the extent that there was an ambiguity, it was totally the creation of its authors. And we know this for sure, because Mr. Fabler did NOT write that. YOU ALL DID! And you made a citation to a page that makes no sense. Not to me, certainly NOT to Mr. Fabler… and, I might add, nor to Mr. Shark either. In fact, sir, the ONLY people who seem to think that it makes ANY sense are those WHO ARE responsible for the wording.**

D. Pete Animen: "Correct, Judge! But I object that we are the ONLY ones who seem to think it makes sense. I mean, no one else thought what Mr. Fabler thought. So that must mean… "

The Court: **"Hold on here, sir! Mr. Fabler ISN'T the ONLY one who thought what he thought about that wording. So, why should he bear the burden of that? Or to paraphrase Tina Turner, 'What's fairness got to do with it?'"**

D. Pete Animen: "Well, Your Honor, no one else ever questioned that wording before as you yourself have so stated. So it seems to me that fairness is in the sense of what would a reasonable person have done? You're a reasonable person, and you were confused..."

The Court: **"Mr. Fabler was NOT confused! How many times does he have to say that? Why don't you hear he was NOT confused? No one was confused when they read your words. Your words say what they said!"**

D. Pete Animen: "Your Honor, I'm getting tired of this."

The Court: **"Excuse me? You're getting tired? Of what? How many times does Mr. Fabler have to say that he wasn't confused! I certainly heard him say that. Why do you insist he was confused... when he says he wasn't confused?"**

D. Pete Animen: "I'm going to say it again. The pamphlet says, in essence, on the inside cover, that if you're confused, call Customs and they'll try to clarify it. Or he, alternatively, he could have, when he came up to see inspector Narco, he could have said that I'm confused by this, do I have to declare this? However, it was ONLY after the things were found that he said it. So there was ample opportunity for him to, at least, get a clarification once he arrived at the counter."

The Court: "But... it would not have done him any good... at that point."

D. Pete Animen: "Of course not... at that point anyway, you're correct... it would NOT have. Most of the arguments we're discussing here about whether he's confused still does NOT get over the point of getting a license."

The Court:	**"So, the only thing he could've done is to have applied for a license from OFAC! That's your position, right?"**
D. Pete Animen:	"That's correct, Judge."
The Court:	**"How many licenses does OFAC grant per year?"**
D. Pete Animen:	"I have no idea."
The Court:	**"Do you know, Mr. Smallhead?"**
Mr. Smallhead:	"Hundreds!"
The Court:	**"Pardon me?"**
Mr. Smallhead:	"Well… over a hundred."
The Court:	**"Over a hundred per year, any to individual citizens?"**
Mr. Smallhead:	"Oh, yes… many."
D. Pete Animen:	"So, he could've lied and OFAC may have granted him a license. We have no way of knowing. He didn't do that."
Mr. Fabler:	"Your Honor, OFAC **ONLY** grants licenses to Cuban 'nationals.' **Not** to U.S. born citizens! And wouldn't that seem to be a violation of the 5th Amendment for equal protection under the law? Also why should I have to lie to get a license?"
D. Pete Animen:	"Your Honor, could you have Mr. Fabler remain quiet here?"
The Court:	**"But isn't this his case, Mr. D. Pete Animen? I can understand his angst when you people keep misrepresenting his testimony!"**

D. Pete Animen:	"Yes, it is… Your Honor. But he does have an attorney present who can speak up if we're misrepresenting his testimony."
The Court:	**"But, both, he and his attorney have spoken up, sir! Only you people keep misrepresenting his testimony… anyway. Oh well, if you insist… Mr. Shark, would you please have your client listen to the testimony?"**
D. Pete Animen:	**"Thank you, Your Honor."**
The Court:	**"Mr. Smallhead, who do you grant these licenses to?"**
Mr. Smallhead:	"I have no idea, Your Honor. I'm not involved in that area. I don't know who the licenses are granted to. But I do know licenses are granted. Lots of licenses!"
The Court:	"Okay… anything else?"
D. Pete Animen:	"One last thing only… and I will make it brief. I heard opposing counsel talk about the fact that Customs is stuck with this pamphlet and it sounds like, at least, to some degree they're making an *equitable estoppel* argument. To that end, I'd merely reference U.S. v. Asmar and say the opposing party of the claim, in this case, doesn't meet the four tests that were set out for that! That being… a misrepresentation, reliance on that misrepresentation, reliance to the claims detriment, and the last one, which is really the big one, the affirmative misconduct by the government."
The Court:	*"And what?"*
D. Pete Animen:	"The affirmative misconduct by the government. There's no allegation and there certainly has

been no proof there was any sort of affirmative misconduct by the government with regard to this pamphlet with regard to this *specific* claimant. Therefore, Judge, we would state the stipulated facts are that he arrived with merchandise of Cuban origin, did not have a license to bring it in... and therefore is subject to the forfeiture."

The Court: "Any rebuttal, Mr. Shark?"

Mr. Shark: "Yes, Your Honor... just briefly. I don't know if you have your Code of Federal Regulations."

The Court: "I was given it, the courtesy of our friend from OFAC."

Mr. Shark: "So was I, and I appreciated that. If you could turn, Judge, to 515.544."

D. Pete Animen: "We need just to have a moment to get a copy of it, Your Honor."

Mr. Shark: "It seems to me..."

The Court: "544?"

Mr. Shark: "Yes, sir."

The Court: "Gifts of Cuban Origin Goods."

Mr. Shark: "It seems to me that if you do not find in our favor on the merits or the factual issue here that you could then still be in a position, under 544(b) that seems to indicate, and maybe we have an expert here that might be able to help us with that as well that, '*Specific licenses are issued for the importation directly from Cuba of goods which are imported...*'"

David Weisenthal

The Court: **"Does equity mean the license? I think equity here means that done which ought to have been done and it's ought to have been done?"**

Mr. Shark: "That's what it seems to be saying to me, Judge. And in this particular case this might be... that is if you don't rule in our favor, which we would ask you to do. But, as a hollow victory so to speak, I think you could be empowered or you could direct the government to give them back to us under this particular section... because it seems clearly less than $100 was spent in U.S. money."

The Court: **"That would be the small value it is referencing?"**

Mr. Shark: "Exactly. It would seem we were in compliance with that."

The Court: "Yes, but what about (ii)? Isn't this a 'direct or indirect financial or commercial benefit to Cuba?'

Mr. Shark: "Well, in that regard..."

The Court: **"In other words, wouldn't this be a situation where... and let's take your example. Let's say when his Holiness was in Cuba, an American priest was with him and a Cuban priest gave him something of Cuban origin, and the American priest brought it back. Now, that would not, it would seem to me, benefit Cuba because that was an act of generosity by a Cuban priest to him. Isn't that one meaning of this?"**

Mr. Shark: "Exactly, Your Honor. But I would also offer something which is not of evidence. If you would allow me to open the case that those cigars, Mr. Fabler believes, were acquired on the black

408

	market… so that it did not directly benefit Cuba. And he would testify to that."
The Court:	**"I'm shocked to hear that there's a black market there."**
Mr. Shark:	"And it's an form of art… for these cigars."
The Court:	**"There is, I guess."**
Mr. Shark: "	So that would be, and again…"
The Court:	**"This is an interesting argument. And because it's a new argument, I'm going to allow our friends from Customs to respond."**
D. Pete Animen:	"Thank you, Judge. I was going to discuss the issue of the Cuban gifts in my closing, but just decided it wasn't that important. However, as you pointed out…"
The Court:	**"It just became important."**
D. Pete Animen:	"It just became important is right. As you pointed out the second part of that which said 15, I'm sorry, it was 31 CFR 515.544. It does talk about no reason to believe that there's any direct benefit financial or commercial to Cuba or 'nationals' thereof. If it was bought on the black market or it was bought in Cuba or bought from a Cuba 'national,' it therefore was of benefit to a Cuban 'national.' Moreover, I would draw your attention, and unfortunately my book is a little bit out of date, to the July 1, 1997 edition of 31 CFR. I have been told this particular section, I'm going to cite, has been moved a little bit. But it's in this book. Its subject is Section 515.801. It's the licensing section, the whole Subpart H - Procedures. And Subparagraph (a) of that section talks about General Licenses! And it says…"

David Weisenthal

The Court:	"I have it."
D. Pete Animen:	"You have it, okay. It says that General Licenses have been issued authorizing…"
The Court:	**"Page and line?"**
D. Pete Animen:	"That's what I'm saying, Judge. My book, and this is the older one, has been re-codified. I'm not exactly sure what the section is, but I understand the language is almost identical. It's just the procedure."
The Court:	**"You say, it is almost identical? Would you call this in with a parallel cite?"**
D. Pete Animen:	"Yes, Judge, I will."
The Court:	**"Then, read it to us again."**
D. Pete Animen:	"The cite I have in this book is 31 CFR 515.801."
Mr. Shark:	"It should be in the pamphlet then, Your Honor."
D. Pete Animen:	"OH… it is!"
Mr. Shark:	"It would seem to be…"
The Court:	**"Wait a minute! 515 what?"**
D. Pete Animen:	"801, Judge. This is the issue I have. It's the second to the last statement on the page."
The Court:	**"Do you know what Sub part?"**
D. Pete Animen:	"Subpart (a) talks about General Licenses."
The Court:	"Yes!"

D. Pete Animen:	"It says they're all set forth in Subpart (e) of these Regulations. Then it goes to *Specific* Licenses, which Subparagraph (b) says, '*Transactions subject to the prohibitions contained in Subpart B which are NOT authorized by a **general** license may be effected **ONLY** under a Specific License*'. That's what they talk about, a *Specific* License under 515.544. However, there **IS** a procedure that a person **MUST** go through and it's laid out there... where it says, '***General*** Course of Procedure. And it lays out what the person **MUST** do."
The Court:	**"So, you're saying, that Mr. Fabler should, because of this unusual problem he should have asked for a license from the Director of OFAC to get these back?"**
D. Pete Animen:	"At this point, Judge, what we're saying is that the property is subject to forfeiture. But that was what he should have done... yes!"
The Court:	***"But my question is... that's what he should have done."***
D. Pete Animen:	"Yes, sir."
The Court:	**"When? Before he went to Cuba or after he came back. Because he couldn't have possibly applied prior to going to Cuba because he didn't know he was going to receive a gift before he went to Cuba... so he couldn't have applied before he went. Could he have? And after he came back, isn't that what this case is about? I mean no one told him, no one from Customs told him to apply for a license... did they?"**
D. Pete Animen:	"No, Your Honor... no one did! I admit he couldn't have applied prior to going to Cuba, but he should have after he returned. But

now, it's TOO late. Those items are subject to forfeiture."

The Court: **"Thank you."**

D. Pete Animen: "Your welcome, Your Honor."

Mr. Shark: "Judge, could I just make one last comment?"

The Court: "Okay, sure."

Mr. Shark: "Your Honor... the point is those cigars were a gift... and the government says a license is required for the gift. They also argue there can't be a gift because it benefited Cuba or a Cuban 'national.' The person who gave Mr. Fabler the gift received **NO** benefit from Mr. Fabler... and he **WASN'T** even a Cuban 'national' anyhow. If the government is arguing that it doesn't matter who receives the benefit, then I'd argue there's no such thing... as a gift. With the argument that a license is required for the gift... they never offered that, that avenue of relief, prior to this hearing. They never provided Mr. Fabler with any avenue to obtain such a license. And when this whole thing came down, it seems to me, they should've said 'well you need a license because it was a gift and here is how you apply.' But instead *all* they did when it, the seizure was contested, was to deny the contesting of the seizure... and say the **ONLY** avenue for recourse was to sue. **Now,** we're here and they're saying the **ONLY** avenue for relief was to apply for a license... after the fact. They keep changing their position... to meet the situation. And didn't the man from OFAC state that he didn't know who received a license from OFAC... or under what conditions those licenses were issued?"

"Finally, Your Honor... one last comment. You asked if there were any other cases like this and

I just want to comment on that. Our research discloses there are **NO** other such cases like this. I believe the reason for that is because when a case like this gets to this posture, what usually happens is the government is in the untenable position of trying to prove the tobacco, the products, in particular these alleged Cuban cigars, are in fact Cuban cigars. And that is something they can never prove. So, consequently, in more cases than not, my research has disclosed that they either give them back with a promise of, like, you know, just…"

The Court: *"Don't do it again!"*

Mr. Shark: "Exactly! That type of thing. Or people just don't follow through with it in the pursuit of the remedy. But that's what our research has disclosed. So, that's why we never saw a case like this."

The Court: "Well… I haven't found one either."

Mr. Shark: "Exactly, Your Honor! So I believe that's what we believe takes place. I mean we could have perhaps come in here and said that we're going to hold the government to their proof and have said for them to prove these are Cuban cigars, and I think they may have had some difficulty doing that… because our research shows they can NEVER prove that. But anyway thank you, Judge. I mean it was NEVER Mr. Fabler's intent to lie… about anything, including whether the cigars were Cuban or if his trip was a gift and that he, in fact, went to Cuba. So, the inference that he should have lied to get a license is completely beyond the scope of this case. I believe you HAVE to take the issue(s) of this case on the face of the facts that have been presented here… and the fact that Mr. Fabler could have lied about the origin of the cigars was NEVER in his mind. NOT here, NOT while he was in Customs... NOT ever."

The Court: "What we will do is this... and I've thought a great deal about this. I would hope to get something out to you... by fax. I will need everyone's fax numbers, and I'll get something to you tomorrow or the next day, okay? And I'm grateful to all of you for this. **This is certainly an INTERESTING matter**. And, by the way, what's going to happen to these cigars?"

D. Pete Animen: "At the risk of being flip, maybe, we will smuggle them out, Judge. But really they'll just be disposed of."

Mr. Shark: "Your Honor, PLEASE. I object to the inference here... Mr. Fabler NEVER intended to smuggle anything."

The Court: "Well... I think, in the least, you should give a few of them to the claimant! I mean, seriously, what does happen to them?"

Ms. Beeche: "Your Honor, there are several..."

The Court: "I mean I can't believe I'm going to see an ad in the New York Times."

Ms. Beeche: "Oh NO, Your Honor. We wouldn't do that."

The Court: "Of course not! I know you wouldn't put them up for auction."

Ms. Beeche: "At the point they're forfeited, they would be destroyed."

The Court: "They would be destroyed?"

Ms. Beeche: "Prior to that, there were options which were offered to the claimant... and we offered

414

exportation. However, they can't enter the territory of the United States. Since he DOES spend extraordinary amounts of time out of the United States, he could've re-exported them to another location and enjoyed them. Prohibition is them coming into the United States. Before... he did NOT accept our offer. And since he did NOT choose to re-export them... upon forfeiture, they will be destroyed."

Mr. Shark:

"Your Honor, the government ONLY tendered their offer to re-export the cigars... last month. BUT, by that point, Mr. Fabler felt they had to do that in the least... so he felt the issue should be pursued. I mean he had already spent all the time AND money he HAD to spend. But I believe if the government had made that offer, that option, in the first place then, maybe, his decision would have been different. However, they didn't... and he didn't."

Mr. Fabler:

"Your Honor? May I say one thing?"

The Court:

"Mr. Fabler, your attorney has represented you... and I think very adequately, sir."

Mr. Fabler:

"Yes, Your Honor, he has. But there's something I'd like to say. Besides, as you yourself have said... this is my case!"

The Court:

"Okay, but make it short. Okay?"

D. Pete Animen:

"I have to object, Your Honor."

The Court:

"Object, object! Is that ALL everyone here does? Overruled... but it is noted!"

Mr. Fabler:

"Thank you, Your Honor. I originally read my passport to see what it said about going to Cuba because I knew the rules changed over time. Nothing in my, then, *current* passport said

David Weisenthal

I couldn't go or import the articles that were imported. In fact, the passport said ONLY two things pertaining to 'THE (Cuban) embargo.' On page 3 in the Treasury section was, '*As of November 1963, the purchase or importation of Cuban... goods or services... are **generally** prohibited, except for informational materials and limited goods imported directly as accompanied baggage.*' Also, '*Transactions related to travel in or to Cuba... are **generally** prohibited.*' The ONLY other thing was the first sentence in the Customs Service section on page 2 that said, '*The pamphlet **Know Before You Go** gives you **current** information about Customs requirements and how they apply to articles acquired abroad. Obtain a copy from your nearest Customs Office or from the U.S. Customs service'*. And they listed an address."

"My passport instructed me to read the **Know Before You Go** pamphlet for further information... and a **more detailed description** because it stated the rules as listed *ONLY **generally** prohibit* the importation of merchandise. They also listed the exceptions, '*except for goods imported directly as accompanied baggage.*' It's my belief that what I brought back were in the exception of articles imported directly as accompanied baggage classification... as stated."

"Regarding travel to Cuba... my passport stated, '*Transactions related to travel in or to Cuba were (**ONLY**) monitored by OFAC.*' I believe travel related transactions (*ONLY*) include airline fares and hotel bills and, since neither were paid by me, there was *NO* need to contact the government or OFAC... or for that matter, anyone else. I didn't violate any required compliance. It didn't say I couldn't go... only that travel related transactions were monitored by OFAC."

"On page six in the Cigars and Cigarettes section of the pamphlet **Know Before You Go** is this, *'Not more than one hundred cigars... may be included in your exemption.'* The next sentence read, *'Products of Cuban tobacco may be included in your exemption if purchased in Cuba, see page 20.'* I looked at page 20 for disclaimers or exceptions. However, there was nothing there! I continued reading! I knew there had to be something... somewhere. Page 21 had nothing about what was on page six! Page 22 had more of nothing. On page 23, in large blocked print, was a section called Merchandise. It had a plethora of somewhat useless information in it. The 1ˢᵗ paragraph rehashed the same stuff I already read in my passport, *'The importation of goods from the following countries is **generally** prohibited... Cuba.'* I turned the page and continued reading. The 3ʳᵈ paragraph, 2ⁿᵈ sentence had, *'Spending money on travel-related transactions involving Cuba... is... closely controlled and monitored. It continued with, Because of... strict enforcement of prohibitions, anyone considering travel to any of the countries listed above should contact the Office of Foreign Assets Control.'* That was all there was about 'THE embargo!' No other word in any sentence in any paragraph in either book."

"Putting the two books together was the following. Were one not to spend money on travel-related transactions (airline fares and hotel bills) they were allowed or, in the minimum, NOT prohibited from traveling to Cuba. Since no money was going to be spent on those transactions, prohibitions and restrictions wouldn't be violated... and the Office of Foreign Assets Control ONLY monitored and controlled the spending of money. The public was ONLY advised (should), NOT ordered (must), to contract the government were they considering travel to Cuba... meaning travelers didn't require permission (per se) to go there. Once there, a limited number of cigars (100) as stated in the **Know Before You Go** pamphlet could be acquired and imported into America... provided they were *'imported directly as accompanied baggage.'*

"When I turned to the **Know Before You Go** pamphlet as my passport instructed, I found the **Know Before You Go** pamphlet stated what I was reading were the then *current* rules **and** Regulations. And I have to emphasize I was **NOT** confused by anything I read. However, to verify what I read, I showed both documents to more than numerous people, including lawyers, who thought the same thing I did... after reading it."

"I'd also like to emphasize that when I was at Customs, the issue about those books was raised... right then and there! For the government to say now I wouldn't or didn't declare anything is beyond reasonable... when taken in this context. I knew that in order to bring those cigars into the country they would have had to have been acquired in Cuba. The **Know Before You Go** book said that! Nowhere was it written that I had to say I went to Cuba before I was asked... if I went there. But when it was asked, I freely admitted to whoever asked that I went there."

The Court: **"Mr. Fabler, all this has already been stated and argued here. I could say many times. And that is what I have to decide based on the testimony."**

Mr. Fabler: "Yes... I know, Your Honor. But there is a point I'd like to make about 'THE embargo.' The Regulations came about through 'THE (Korean) embargo...' back in the 1950's. There were security and National Emergency issues then... what with the Cold War and all. But today, in the present political climate, the basis of 'THE embargo' has no basis in fact. None of the reasons for 'THE embargo' then ARE present today. My issue is if a law was predicated on certain conditions and those conditions don't exist... then the law shouldn't exist either. More to the point is why do U.S. citizens have to go to court to determine this? And it seems this is the only way the government provides the citizen to have a forum for an issue of this magnitude."

"When the government says they offered to return the cigars, out of the country, the fact is they never offered to give the cigars back until we had arrived at this juncture. By the time they finally made their offer, there was no incentive to NOT go the rest of the way. I felt they might be doing this to other people as well and the only way to deter this activity was to have the court make a decision based on the true facts... and not on a distorted misrepresentation of testimony."

"Regarding gifts, the government says a license is required. But they offer no avenue to obtain a license... even if one could be obtained. One can't get a license prior to getting a gift! That'd be impossible... because how would one know beforehand they're going to get a gift. And what benefit did my gift provide to the giver? It certainly didn't provide any benefit to a Cuban 'national' or otherwise."

"They argue I was confused... **ONLY** I wasn't confused. My point is... this is exactly how they've treated this issue the whole time. They say I've caused the issue because I was doing what I read. But besides everything telling me that, telling every American citizen that, those books are THE instructions regarding this issue... nothing stated anything about the Regulations. And if the Regulations control the issue, which they do, then the books should reflect that the Regulations control... which they don't. And those books shouldn't say things that are contrary to the Regulations... which they do. Your Honor, the books should've stated something about the Regulations and that those books only highlighted the Regulations. Which again... they didn't!

"Your Honor, about having a license. I believe I HAD a license! Having gone to Cuba as a Fully Hosted traveler **gave** me a license. That kind of travel **IS** approved by the Regulations as a way of travel to Cuba. And I've seen Supreme Court cases that cite the citizen's right to travel to Cuba WITHOUT government permission... to wit: <u>U.S. vs. Laub</u>, which legalizes travel to Cuba for U.S. citizens... as long as they follow Treasury Department regulations regarding the exchange of money. <u>Zemel vs. Rusk</u> resulted in NO geographic limitation for passports, except in time of war or other danger to the traveler. <u>Kent & Briehl vs. Dulles</u> held 'the right to travel is a part of the *liberty* of which the citizen **CANNOT be deprived without due process of law under the 5th Amendment.**' So, since Fully Hosted travel **IS** approved by the Regulations as a way of travel to Cuba and coupled with the just cited Supreme Court cases on the subject... I had THE LICENSE everyone is talking about here! Maybe, it wasn't written or specified, but it certainly was tacit **AND** approved!"

The Court: **"What are those case citings again?"**

Mr. Fabler: "<u>U.S. vs. Lamb</u>; <u>Zemel vs. Rusk</u>; and, <u>Kent & Briehl vs. Dulles</u>."

The Court: "Thank you, Mr. Fabler. I'll look them up. Now, continue.

Mr. Fabler:

"More important is the fact that **only some** people **are approved** by OFAC to have a license! As a natural born citizen, I'm NOT one of those who are granted a license. However, if I were a Cuban American, regardless of the reason for travel, then I'd get a license. And if I was designated a Designated Cuban 'national,' which I never was, then I could ALSO get a license. But since I'm not a Cuban American, I will NOT get a license... unless I'm in a certain group who has a reason for travel. That seems wholly unfair and un-American! That is, in that there is such discretion with regard to issuing the license... let alone the basis for which the government or OFAC or whoever holds me to a different standard than others who are granted permission to travel to Cuba and are granted a license to go there."

"Add to this the fact that the Regulations are subject to all those who ARE governed by the laws of the U.S. Government. Although Puerto Rico isn't a State, it is a Territory that is controlled by the laws of the U.S. Government. Therefore, every Puerto Rican 'national' is required to adhere to the Regulations as such. Yet, they can travel to Cuba, purchase Cuban products and openly sell them in Puerto Rico. All of which is done... and is done with, at least the tacit, approval of the U.S. Government! Walk into any bar, cigar shop or tourist store and Cuban cigars are openly sold. All places where members of the U.S. Customs service frequent frequently. However, those cigars are NOT confiscated nor are any persons prosecuted under the Regulations. And that, Your Honor, IS A violation of the Equal Protection section of the Due Process Clause in the 5th Amendment of the U.S. Constitution."

"Now, the government doesn't disclose **ANY** information about who they grant licenses to or how they grant those licenses. So, to bring an action based on a violation of Equal Protection of the law under the Due Process Clause of the 5th Amendment of the U.S. Constitution is almost rendered impossible because I can't obtain the necessary information to show I've been discriminated against... because of my nationality. And, Your Honor, that is why I'm here today... to have my day in court. Thank you!"

Ms. Beeche:

"Your Honor... I've listened to Mr. Fabler's comments and I'd just like to say that it seems that Mr. Fabler's argument is that he's pushing the issue of whether 'The (Cuban) embargo' is a good thing or a bad thing. But we're stuck with the Regulations AND 'THE (Cuban) embargo' IS IN effect. And, Your Honor, this really ISN'T the venue with which to argue such an issue."

The Court:

"Certainly, in this case what one may fairly ask, a citizen may fairly ask, regarding this case, is why in Heaven's name are we going to such an effort over less than a hundred dollars worth of cigars? And the answer, my answer, is because that is my duty as an Article III Judge... when there's a case of controversy before me. But, as a public policy question, I think reasonable minds can certainly ask those questions. And perhaps Mr. Fabler's desire, through this case, is to have those questions asked... so that there can be a debate about whether this, indeed, makes any sense at this late date. However, that's not in my pay grade to decide! But it's certainly as a citizen, it's an interesting issue, and one that people of good faith and who are reasonable can come to differing conclusions on it. And it well may be that a case of this nature where a citizen did his best, people might say does this make sense to put this kind of governmental resources into less than a hundred dollars worth of cigars? People could be forgiven for thinking that that does not make a whole lot of sense. But that's not for me to decide. And to the extent this case helps people consider that question, I think we *ALL* owe a great debt to Mr. Fabler. So thank you for bringing to us such an interesting case."

With his closing statement finished, Freeman Ruhle rose from his seat high above the contestants and witnesses who witnessed the contest, <u>U.S. v. 100 Cuban Cigars</u>. And just like that, when His Honor, the judge, left... the case was over! I'd had my day in court!

I said good-by to Editor Ed Ditor and watched him leave with everyone else. Marc Ken Tyme had disappeared a long time before... and, maybe, he never really came. He could've just been a figment of my imagination! Fillmor Cupps approached the desk my sharks and I stood behind with the Lady Grace. He congratulated us on fighting *the good fight...* win or lose!

All the government people began leaving, but the lady shark stopped when she passed me. She said she thought she might've known me... from another time in her life. However, I would've remembered. And I didn't. But I didn't remember Sandy... who I lived with for one year... either. So what did I know? I knew I didn't know her. Having nothing to talk about... she walked away. The D. Pete Animen ringer-shark exited the courthouse as when I first saw him walk into it... strutting his stuff like a flesh-eating fish in a sea of flesh-eating animals. When I last saw the man from OFAC, who was really a lad from glad, he was just happy to have retained any air of arrogance.

Out on the courthouse steps, the Lady Grace and I left with Fillmor Cupps. We went to celebrate the day with libation and a lighter side of fare. After all, she was a foodie! Both my sharks departed to other prearranged rounds. My case was over! They had other fish to fry! But, before we split, I asked the shark what he thought. He said he thought if any judge was going to rule in my favor it'd be Freeman Ruhle. Although, he also said he didn't like some things that were said when they were said... near the end of court. Then, he said that time would tell. And I knew... time would tell! It was then that Lady Grace told me I'd won... even if I lost! However, I knew a win was a win and a loss was a loss... and neither could be the other!

VISIT: www.ItsOnlyCigars.com

For Information On

'THE (Cuban) embargo'

Special Offer(s)

AND Other Related Stuff including

Book signing appearances

Cigar dinner events / parties

Where / how to acquire (*real*) Cuban stoogies legally

To Contact the Author

Send an e-mail to

HavanaDave@ItsOnlyCigars.com